2006 Edition
Tourism Market Trends

Africa

World Tourism Organization
Capitán Haya 42, 28020 Madrid, Spain
Tel: (+34) 915678100; Fax: (+34) 915713733
E-mail: omt@unwto.org
Web: www.unwto.org

Tourism Market Trends: Africa
ISBN-13: 978-92-844-1213-6

Published and printed by the World Tourism Organization, Madrid, Spain
First printing in July 2007

World Tourism Organization
Calle Capitán Haya, 42
28020 Madrid, Spain
Tel.: (+34) 915 678 100
Fax: (+34) 915 713 733
Website: www.unwto.org
Email: omt@unwto.org

Permission to photocopy UNWTO material in Spain must be obtained through:

CEDRO, Centro Español de Derechos Reprográficos
Calle Monte Esquinza, 14
28010 Madrid, Spain
Tel.: (+34) 91 308 63 30, Fax: (+34) 91 308 63 27
cedro@cedro.org; www.cedro.org

For authorization of the reproduction of UNWTO works outside of Spain, please contact one of CEDRO's partner organizations, with which bilateral agreements are in place (http://www.cedro.org/ingles_funcion_internacional.asp).

For all remaining countries as well as for other permissions, requests should be addressed directly to the World Tourism Organization. For applications see http://www.unwto.org/pub/rights.htm.

Foreword

This report has been prepared by the World Tourism Organization's (UNWTO's) Market Trends, Trade and Competitiveness Section. Chapters I and II, Highlights and Quantitative Analysis of Tourism Performance, were drafted by members of The Travel Business Partnership, led by UNWTO Consultant Nancy Cockerell. UNWTO's Regional Representation for Africa also made a valuable contribution, as did the organization's Panel of Experts from Africa, which monitors tourism trends and developments on a regular basis for the three times yearly *UNWTO World Tourism Barometer*.

Except where otherwise indicated, the data presented was gathered by the UNWTO Secretariat from the official institutions of the respective countries and territories. Quantitative data has been supplied by National Tourism Administrations (NTAs), National Tourism Organizations (NTOs), statistical offices, national banks and international organizations.

UNWTO wishes to express its sincere gratitude to all those who have participated in the elaboration of this report for their valuable cooperation, in particular to the organizations and individuals involved from the different countries and territories. It welcomes the active involvement of all countries, as well as their comments and suggestions on the design and contents of this series.

Explanation of symbols and conventions used

*	=	provisional figure or data
..	=	figure or data not (yet) available
0	=	rounded figure where the original figure is lower than 0.5 (-0 when rounding a negative figure)
0.0	=	rounded figure where the original figure is lower than 0.05 (-0.0 when rounding a negative figure)

|	=	change of series
(000)	=	thousand
mn	=	million (1,000,000)
bn	=	billion (1,000,000,000)

Due to rounding, some totals may not correspond exactly with the sum of the separate figures.

Table of Contents

The *Tourism Market Trends, 2006 Edition* series

Tourism Market Trends is one of UNWTO's regular series of reports, the objective of which is to present international tourism trends worldwide, as well as in each region, subregion and individual destination country. The full series, which was launched in 2001, comprises six volumes. The first, *World Overview & Tourism Topics*, provides an overview of global tourism trends, and the five regional volumes highlight international tourism trends in each of the UNWTO world regions – Africa, the Americas, Asia and the Pacific, Europe and the Middle East (including North Africa).

Some changes have been made to the structure of the *Tourism Market Trends* series. Each regional volume now includes the following:

- Section I, Highlights, provides a summary of key trends and developments in tourism in the region, stressing the main factors influencing trends in 2005.

- Section II, Quantitative Analysis of Tourism Performance, includes a more in-depth assessment of trends in the region and its subregions, in terms of international tourist arrivals and international tourism receipts, as well as a breakdown of inbound tourism by region of origin, transport mode and purpose of visit. Statistical trends in outbound tourism are also presented, including data on international tourism expenditure, volume of trips abroad and outbound flows by region of origin/destination.

- Section III, Statistical Trends by Destination Country, comprises detailed statistical results for the individual countries and/or territories of the region. For each country the following information is included (to the extent that data is available):

    - A summary table including the following data series:
        - International arrivals: different categories of inbound tourism;
        - Tourism accommodation: room capacity and number of nights (for inbound and domestic tourism);
        - Trips abroad (outbound tourism);
        - International tourism receipts and expenditure;
        - Various economic and general indicators.

    - Detailed tables on arrivals and nights broken down by country of origin/source market.

- Each of the six volumes concludes with an annex comprising detailed tables containing the latest yearly data on international tourist arrivals and international tourism receipts (in US dollars and in euros) for all countries worldwide for which data is available. Information is also provided on methodologies, concepts and definitions, as well as on sources of the data and other information.

Care should be taken in interpreting the data presented in these reports. In particular, the following should be noted:

- In accordance with the nature of the data provided by the countries and territories, the focus is on inbound tourism. Outbound tourism trends are largely derived from the same inbound-oriented data except for countries that monitor outbound departures.

- The main focus of the analysis, and corresponding tables, is on medium-term rather than on short-term trends and developments. For short-term trends, please refer to the *UNWTO World Tourism Barometer*, which is published three times a year (in January,

June and October). Each issue contains three regular sections: an overview of short-term tourism data from destination and generating countries and air transport; the results of the latest survey among the UNWTO Panel of Tourism Experts, providing an evaluation of and prospects for short-term tourism performance; and selected economic data relevant for tourism. (For further information, refer to the annex or to UNWTO's website at <www.unwto.org/facts/menu.html>).

- The reports generally reflect the data collected by the UNWTO Secretariat for the current edition. However, data is often still provisional and may be updated or revised by the reporting countries at a later stage without further notice. When making references to the data contained in the reports, it is therefore advisable to ensure that the statistics quoted are the most up to date available

- For the world and (sub)regional aggregates (totals, subtotals), estimates are included to make allowance for those countries and territories that do not yet have final full-year data, or which have estimated full-year results. The data presented for the individual countries, however, reflects what has been reported for each country and does not include estimates made by the UNWTO Secretariat.

- The UNWTO Secretariat is aware of the limitations of tourism data. Despite considerable progress made in recent years, statistics are rarely uniform since definitions and data collection methodologies tend to differ from one country to another. This means that the international comparability of statistical data still leaves a lot to be desired.

I

Highlights: Africa

I Highlights: Africa
Summary of Key Trends and Developments

I.1 Africa in the Context of World Tourism

Terrorism, natural disasters, health scares, oil price rises, exchange rate fluctuations and economic and political uncertainties – these were just some of the issues facing the tourism industry in 2005. Yet international tourist arrivals worldwide beat all expectations, reaching 802 million and, at the same time, achieving an all-time record. The estimated increase reflects a staggering 40 million additional arrivals – of which more than 16 million in Europe, 11 million in Asia and the Pacific, 7.5 million in the Americas, 3 million in Africa and 2 million in the Middle East.

The 2005 total of 802 million arrivals represents an increase of more than 5% worldwide – a consolidation of the bumper growth achieved in 2004 (+10%). Although world tourism growth was much more moderate in 2005, it was still more than one percentage point above the long-term average annual growth rate of 4%.

Results by region show that Europe recorded the weakest growth in percentage terms (+4%) although, as already stated, this translated into a higher volume of arrivals. Africa registered the strongest arrivals growth (+9%), ahead of Asia and the Pacific (+8%), the Middle East (+6%) and the Americas (+6%).

Worldwide, international tourism receipts totalled some US$ 676 billion in 2005, up US$ 47 billion in absolute terms. Most regions and subregions shared in the increase. Europe gained an additional US$ 20 billion, raising receipts to just US$ 349 billion – 52% of the world total. The Americas improved results by US$ 12 billion to US$ 145 billion – a 21% share – and Asia and the Pacific added US$ 11 billion, taking the regional total to US$ 134 billion, or a 20% share.

Estimates based on available data for the respective regions point to an increase of US$ 3 billion to US$ 22 billion for Africa and a rise of US$ 1 billion to US$ 26 billion for the Middle East, representing 3% and 4% of the world total respectively.

Inbound leaders

No country in Africa ranked among the world's top ten tourism destinations in 2005. In terms of reported arrivals, the leading destinations in the region are South Africa, Tunisia, Morocco, Algeria, Zimbabwe and Kenya, in order of importance. However, in terms of receipts, Morocco outranks Tunisia, Mauritius outranks Kenya, and Algeria and Zimbabwe fall far down the ranking.

Outbound leaders

South Africa was the only country in Africa to rank among the world's top 50 tourism source markets in 2005. Its citizens spent US$ 3.4 billion on tourism abroad. In second, third and fourth positions in the region, Nigerians spent US$ 1.1 billion, Sudanese US$ 0.7 billion and Moroccans US$ 0.6 billion.

I.2   Overall Performance

For the second year running, Africa was one of the fastest growing world regions in terms of international tourism in 2005. The available data is still patchy but, including estimates for those countries which have not yet reported their full-year figures, arrivals rose by 9% to 37 million and international tourism receipts rose by 10% (as expresed in local currencies, constant prices) to US$ 21.6 billion.

This healthy performance can be attributed to a number of factors. Most important, perhaps, was the continued progress towards the peaceful resolution of several conflicts, and the confidence engendered by progress made several years ago – it takes time before tourists return to the scenes of former conflicts, and before investors care to commit themselves. Nevertheless, conflicts, and threats of conflicts, in several areas of Africa continue to limit the potential for tourism in those regions.

Given a peaceful environment, however, worldwide prosperity is generating larger numbers of affluent and experienced tourists in search of more original and more exciting destinations. Africa itself is more prosperous – the continent's real GDP increased by around 5.5% a year in both 2004 and 2005, generating local and long-haul demand for business and leisure travel. And that growth in real GDP understates the increase in local purchasing power, because of the increases in the international prices of the commodities (including, increasingly, oil) on which so many African economies are based.

The strong euro continues to encourage Europeans to visit Africa. Many destinations report increased funding for tourism promotion, and better cooperation between the public and private sectors. Several are developing new products such as business tourism, cultural tourism, ecotourism and sports tourism, and are opening up new markets around the world. The number of African countries that have negotiated Approved Destination Status (ADS) agreements with China has grown and expectations are high for this market.

However, as usual there were significant variations between the different subregions within the continent. North Africa, Central and Southern Africa achieved the strongest growth in arrivals in 2005. Results in East Africa were very variable, while those in West Africa did not match the levels achieved in 2004. The tourism industries in West Africa and Central Africa remain much smaller than their counterparts in the other three regions.

International Tourist Arrivals

North Africa

The four countries of North Africa, benefiting from their proximity to prospering markets in Europe and the Middle East and from competitive exchange rates, produced a 9% increase in arrivals, after a 15% rise in 2004. The two principal destinations in the region, Tunisia and Morocco, reported increases of just 6-7%, but arrivals in Algeria were up 17% and those to the Sudan quadrupled from a small base. The 14 million arrivals in the subregion represented 37% of total arrivals in Africa.

Africa 2005:   International Tourist Arrivals (ITA): 37 million
International Tourism Receipts (ITR): US$ 22 billion

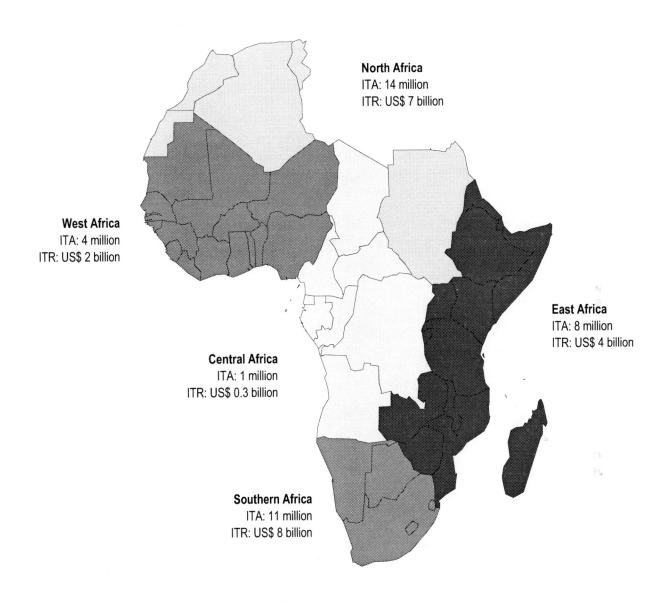

North Africa
ITA: 14 million
ITR: US$ 7 billion

West Africa
ITA: 4 million
ITR: US$ 2 billion

East Africa
ITA: 8 million
ITR: US$ 4 billion

Central Africa
ITA: 1 million
ITR: US$ 0.3 billion

Southern Africa
ITA: 11 million
ITR: US$ 8 billion

West Africa

West Africa makes a much smaller contribution to African tourism – its 4 million arrivals represent just 10% of the total. Information from several countries is lacking, but it seems that the subregion achieved a 4% increase in arrivals in 2005, after a 13% increase in 2004. Nigeria, by far the largest destination in terms of arrivals in the subregion shows a 5% growth.

Senegal, the next most important destination, produced increases in arrivals of 35% in 2004 and 15% in 2005. Arrivals in the Cape Verde, Gambia and Mali were all up by about a quarter, but those in Ghana were down by a quarter, after two good years. Sierra Leone also lost a little of the ground made up in 2003-2004.

Central Africa

Central Africa attracts an even smaller amount of international tourism, its 0.8 million arrivals in 2005 represented only 2% of the African total. Again based on partial data, it seems that arrivals rose by 14% in 2004 and 9% in 2005. Arrivals in a more peaceful Angola increased by 8% in 2005, consolidating an 82% increase in 2004. Those in the Democratic Republic of Congo ('Congo Kinshasa') doubled, but remain tiny, considering the size of the country.

East Africa

Overall, arrivals in East Africa increased by 6% in both 2004 and 2005, but this average disguises some large variations. Among the continental countries reliant on game parks for attracting long-haul tourists, Kenya, Zambia, Mozambique and Madagascar have notched up two successive years of very rapid growth, and if arrivals in Uganda fell by 9% in 2005, that was after a 68% increase in 2004 (arrivals remain far above their historical levels).

Arrivals in Zimbabwe fell by 18% in 2004 and 16% in 2005, but they remain within reach of their historical averages and are still the highest in East Africa, in spite of the political and economic difficulties of the country. Among the tourist resort islands of the Indian Ocean, arrivals in Mauritius and the Seychelles were both up about 6%, but those in Réunion slipped for the second year running.

Southern Africa

Southern Africa's performance largely reflects that of South Africa, which accounts for two thirds of all arrivals in the subregion. And South Africa is one of world tourism's recent success stories: arrivals were up 3% in 2004 and 13% in 2005. Arrivals in Botswana were up 10%; they have tripled since 1990.

Generating markets

Tourists to Africa come in equal shares from neighbouring countries and from outside the region. Exceptions include North Africa and the Atlantic and Indian Ocean islands where traffic from outside Africa is more relevant. Generating markets from outside Africa tend to be divided along the lines of linguistic and historical affinities. Thus tourists from France and Belgium predominate in French-speaking destinations such as Senegal, Côte d'Ivoire, Réunion, Madagascar and Djibouti, while the UK and other English-speaking countries are important non-African markets for South Africa, Kenya, Tanzania, Gambia and Sierra Leone, for business and the visiting friends and relations (VFR) market, as well as for leisure.

There are strong historical and business relations between East Africa and countries of the Middle East and India, and growing relations with Asia. Mauritius casts its net wider – it is popular in many European and Asian markets – but it is also becoming a major leisure and offshore business destination for the booming Indian market.

The South African market is becoming a major generating market for Southern and East African countries, many of which are heavily dependent on it as their main source of business and leisure visitors. The purchasing power of South African tourists is currently strong (the country has a high per capita income and a relatively large middle class, and the rand has strengthened dramatically since 2004).

International Tourism Receipts

International tourism receipts in Africa totalled US$ 22 billion in 2005 – just 3% of the world total. Compared with 2004, this represented an increase of 14% in US dollar terms or 10% in local currencies, current prices.

The strongest performance was recorded by West Africa, with a 21% increase (in sharp contrast to the modest 4% increase in arrivals). North and Central Africa also achieved double-digit increases, but in East Africa they were up just 2%. South Africa, which alone accounts for just over a third of Africa's tourism receipts, achieved a 9% increase.

I.3   Main Factors Influencing Tourism in 2005

Geopolitical situation

The world remains preoccupied with the unstable situation in Iraq, Palestine and other areas of the Middle East, and by the spillover into terrorist threats, visa restrictions and other security-related measures, not to mention a general unease about travelling in other areas. Although Africa is not immune to these effects, they have diluted Africa's image as a strife-ridden and dangerous destination.

The situation in many parts of Africa has also improved. Angola and Mozambique are now essentially at peace. In the Great Lakes region, peace negotiations were conducted under the auspices of the United Nations and the African Union in 2003-2004, and the situation in the area has continued to pick up. Advisories against travel to Kenya were relaxed in 2004. The situation in West Africa is also much improved. In Sudan, a peace agreement between the rebels in the south and the central government was signed in 2004, allowing an oil-related boom to get under way (the violence in Darfur is remote from the oil-bearing regions and the capital). Islamist rebellions in North Africa have faded. Generally speaking, conditions in most areas of the continent are calmer than they were a few years ago.

Nevertheless, the perception of the African continent as riven by warfare and violence continues to impede its further tourism development. The precarious situations in some West African countries are particularly damaging. The situation in Zimbabwe continues to be problematic. The ongoing instability in Somalia means that tourism development is currently impossible. And there is instability in a number of other countries in the region. The reputation of South Africa and some other countries for criminal violence does not help, either.

Economic situation

Nevertheless, in the context of the world economic boom and increased international commodities prices, Africa is prospering. Overall, African real GDP increased by 5% in 2005, much the same as in 2004. In general, macroeconomic management has improved, fiscal deficits eased, inflation has fallen back and exports have grown substantially. In many countries, debt relief and effective poverty reduction programmes are having useful effects. Given that tourist arrivals and international receipts are growing much faster than real GDP, tourism is clearly making an increasingly important contribution to the regional economies.

The economic prosperity had a positive impact on intraregional tourism, both for leisure and business. South Africa in particular is taking an active role in developing regional institutions and in promoting intraregional cultural and business relationships.

Exchange rates

2005 was characterized by a gradual (re)appreciation of the US dollar against major currencies from a low at the end of 2004 and by the new exchange rate regime for the Chinese renminbi. The euro slipped slightly from its highs in 2004, but its purchasing power remained stronger than in previous years, as did that of the South African rand. On balance, the major currencies were much more stable in 2005 than they were in 2003-2004, but the realignment of currencies in 2003-2004 continued to have an effect on the choice of destinations in 2005.

In detail, while the dollar only bought 75 euro cents in December 2004, in December 2005 this was up to 84 euro cents. However, as the downward trend of 2004 was reversed in 2005, the average rate for the full year showed no change compared with 2004 (US$ 1 = 0.80 euro). The American currency also rose slightly against the yen, but depreciated a little in real terms against currencies that were buoyed by international oil and commodity prices. The South African rand traded at an average of R6.36 = US$ 1 in 2005, 1.2% higher than in 2004.

Climatic events

The African continent continued to suffer from the usual climatic problems in 2005, such as droughts in Southern Africa and in the Horn of Africa, and floods in a number of countries. The December 2004 Indian Ocean seaquake and tsunami also affected several coastal and island countries in East Africa. But there is no evidence that climate had any impact on tourism performance.

II

Quantitative Analysis of Tourism Performance

II   Quantitative Analysis of Tourism Performance

II.1   Tourism Trends in the Region

II.1.1 Inbound Tourism

For the last 25 years, tourism trends in Africa have generally been positive. Between 1980 and 1990, the number of international tourist arrivals more than doubled, from 7.3 million to 15.2 million. The figure nearly doubled again over the following decade, when annual tourism growth in the region (6.3%) exceeded the world rate (4.6%) by nearly two percentage points. And during the difficult period of 2001-2003, Africa was the only UNWTO region to turn in consistently good results. From 1990 to 2005, Africa's share of the world total increased by just over one percentage point, from 3.5% to 4.7%.

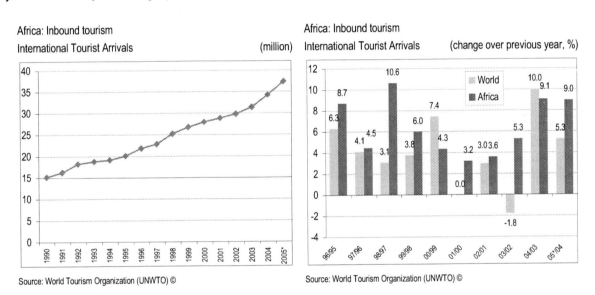

Africa: Inbound tourism
International Tourist Arrivals   (million)

Africa: Inbound tourism
International Tourist Arrivals   (change over previous year, %)

Source: World Tourism Organization (UNWTO) ©   Source: World Tourism Organization (UNWTO) ©

A quantitative analysis of tourism in Africa is hindered by the lack of statistical data for certain countries – hence the need to resort to estimates in some cases. In addition, the methods used to gather and process information can vary considerably depending on the destination. Some countries, for instance, only record the number of visitors at frontiers, or the number of overnight stays, distorting comparisons with countries that in most cases register tourist arrivals at frontiers.

International tourist arrivals

In 2005, Africa reported 37.3 million international tourist arrivals, an increase of 9% over 2004. This was in line with the increase achieved in 2004, making a distinct contrast with worldwide arrivals, which increased by 10% in 2004 but only 5% in 2005.

Southern Africa, North Africa and East Africa account for nearly 90% of arrivals in Africa, while West Africa and Central Africa for a mere 12%. In 2005, the fastest growth among the subregions was achieved by Southern Africa (+13%); in North Africa and Central Africa growth was close to the African average of 9%, but it lagged in East Africa (+6%) and West Africa (+4%).

World and regions: Inbound tourism
International Tourist Arrivals   (change 05*/04, %)

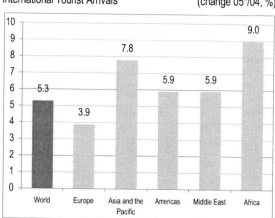

Source: World Tourism Organization (UNWTO) ©

Africa: Inbound tourism
International Tourist Arrivals   (share in world total, %)

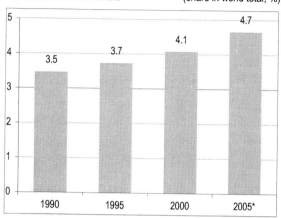

Source: World Tourism Organization (UNWTO) ©

Africa and subregions: Inbound tourism
International Tourist Arrivals, 2005*   (share, %)

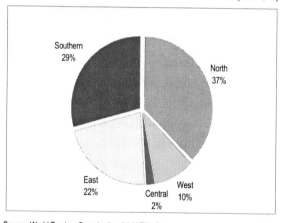

Source: World Tourism Organization (UNWTO) ©

Africa and subregions: Inbound tourism
International Tourist Arrivals   (change 05*/04, %)

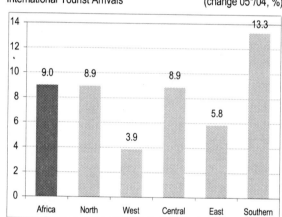

Source: World Tourism Organization (UNWTO) ©

International Tourist Arrivals by (Sub)region

	International Tourist Arrivals								Market share (%)		Growth rate (%)		Average annual growth (%)	
								(million)						
	1990	1995	2000	2001	2002	2003	2004	2005*	2000	2005*	04/03	05*/04	90-00	00-05*
World	438.4	538.5	684.7	684.4	704.7	692.2	761.4	801.6	100	100	10.0	5.3	4.6	3.2
Africa	*15.2*	*20.1*	*27.9*	*28.8*	*29.8*	*31.4*	*34.2*	*37.3*	*4.1*	*4.7*	*9.1*	*9.0*	*6.3*	*6.0*
North Africa	8.4	7.3	10.2	10.7	10.6	11.1	12.8	13.9	1.5	1.7	15.1	8.9	2.0	6.3
West Africa	1.4	1.9	2.4	2.6	2.7	3.1	3.5	3.6	0.4	0.4	12.7	3.9	6.1	8.1
Central Africa	0.4	0.4	0.7	0.6	0.6	0.6	0.7	0.8	0.1	0.1	14.4	8.9	6.2	3.5
East Africa	2.8	4.8	6.3	6.7	7.0	7.2	7.6	8.1	0.9	1.0	5.7	5.8	8.4	4.9
Southern Africa	2.2	5.8	8.2	8.2	9.0	9.4	9.7	11.0	1.2	1.4	3.0	13.3	13.9	5.9

Source: World Tourism Organization (UNWTO) ©   (Data as collected by UNWTO for TMT 2006 Edition)

International tourism receipts

In 2005, Africa earned US$ 21.6 billion in international tourism receipts, which represented a 3% share of the world total. The growth in receipts accelerated sharply from 2003-2005. In local currency terms and at constant prices, they increased by 24% in 2003, by 6% in 2004 and by 10% in 2005.

Among the different subregions, there were swings and roundabouts in 2004 and 2005: those that did well in one year generally did less well in the other. The exception was North Africa, which achieved increases in local currency terms of 13-15% in both years. Southern Africa (which alone accounts for nearly 40% of Africa's international tourism receipts) achieved a 9% increase in 2005, after a 4% decline in 2004 and an increase of no less than 75% in 2003. East Africa, which had achieved large increases in 2003 and 2004, saw receipts grow by only 2% in 2005. West Africa and Central Africa, which had sluggish results in 2004, achieved double-digit increases in 2005.

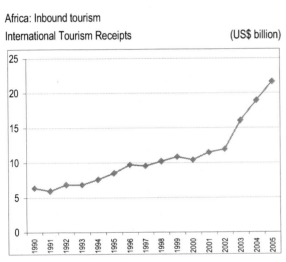

Africa: Inbound tourism
International Tourism Receipts (US$ billion)

Source: World Tourism Organization (UNWTO) ©

Africa: Inbound tourism
International Tourism Receipts (share in world total, %)

Source: World Tourism Organization (UNWTO) ©

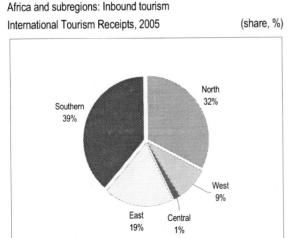

Africa and subregions: Inbound tourism
International Tourism Receipts, 2005 (share, %)

Source: World Tourism Organization (UNWTO) ©

Africa and subregions: Inbound tourism
Receipts per Arrival, 2005 (US$)

Source: World Tourism Organization (UNWTO) ©

It is worth noting that receipts per arrival are substantially higher in Southern Africa (US\$ 760 in 2005) than in the other four subregions (with an average of US\$ 580). The average for North Africa (also US\$ 505) reflects the attractive prices designed to compete in the sun & beach market. Average receipts per arrival for Africa as a whole (US\$ 580) are also substantially lower than for the world overall (US\$ 845).

International Tourism Receipts, Africa

	International Tourism Receipts							Change current prices (%)				Change constant prices (%)			
							(billion)								
	1990	1995	2000	2002	2003	2004	2005*	02/01	03/02	04/03	05*/04	02/01	03/02	04/03	05*/04
Local currencies								11.0	27.4	9.3	14.7	5.3	23.9	5.9	10.4
US\$	6.4	8.5	10.4	11.9	16.0	18.9	21.6	4.2	34.2	18.1	14.3	2.5	31.1	15.0	10.5
Euro	5.0	6.5	11.3	12.6	14.2	15.2	17.4	-1.3	12.2	7.4	14.3	-3.5	9.8	5.2	11.8

Source: World Tourism Organization (UNWTO) ©   (Data as collected in UNWTO database November 2006)

International Tourism Receipts by (Sub)region

	Change Local currencies, constant prices (%)					US\$ Receipts (billion)		per arrival	euro Receipts (billion)		per arrival	Market share (%)
	01/00	02/01	03/02	04/03	05*/04	2004	2005*	2005*	2004	2005*	2005*	2005*
World	-1.9	-0.5	-1.4	9.8	3.1	629.0	675.7	845	505.7	543.1	680	100
Africa	*17.1*	*5.3*	*23.9*	*5.9*	*10.4*	*18.9*	*21.6*	*580*	*15.2*	*17.4*	*465*	*3.2*
North Africa	21.3	-5.6	-2.3	13.4	15.0	6.1	7.0	505	4.9	5.6	405	1.0
West Africa	12.5	1.3	5.4	0.0	20.8	1.4	1.9	530	1.2	1.5	425	0.3
Central Africa	27.2	-2.2	14.1	-3.0	13.9	0.3	0.3	410	0.2	0.3	330	0.0
East Africa	14.5	0.7	8.0	18.2	2.2	3.8	4.1	505	3.1	3.3	405	0.6
Southern Africa	15.0	26.9	75.0	-4.0	8.8	7.3	8.3	760	5.9	6.7	610	1.2

Source: World Tourism Organization (UNWTO) ©   (Data as collected in UNWTO database November 2006)

World and regions: Inbound tourism
Receipts per Arrival, 2005   (US\$)

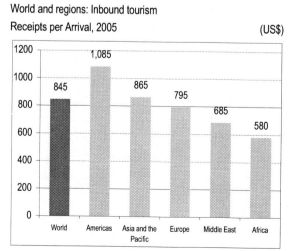

Source: World Tourism Organization (UNWTO) ©

World and regions: Inbound tourism   (change 05/04, %,
International Tourism Receipts   local currencies, constant prices)

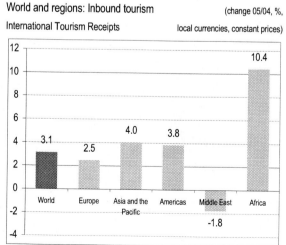

Source: World Tourism Organization (UNWTO) ©

World Tourism Organization ©

Inbound tourism by region of origin

In Africa as a whole, intraregional and interregional arrivals are roughly evenly balanced – bearing in mind that an unusually high proportion of arrivals are of unknown origin. Among the world's regions, only the Middle East has a similar balance; in all other regions, intraregional arrivals dominate strongly.

This average, however, disguises wide variations within the subregions. In North Africa, intraregional arrivals account for only 10% of the total while, in Southern Africa, they account for 73%.

Tourists from Europe account for 33% of arrivals in Africa. The Middle East, Americas and Asia and the Pacific each account for less than 5%. However, 13% of all arrivals are of unknown origin and must be distributed among the interregional and intraregional sources. (Some 28% of arrivals in North Africa are of unknown origin, largely because Algeria and Morocco record the extremely numerous arrivals of their own nationals residing abroad as 'nationals resident abroad', but not according to their countries of residence. It should also be noted that 26% of all arrivals in Central Africa are of unknown origin).

Africa: Inbound tourism by region of origin
International Tourist Arrivals, 2005*   (share, %)

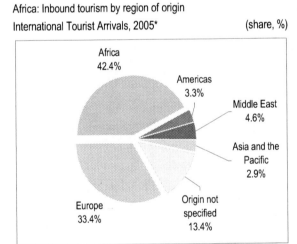

Source: World Tourism Organization (UNWTO) ©

Africa: Inbound tourism by region of origin
International Tourist Arrivals   (share, %)

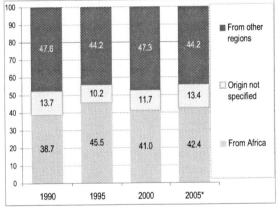

Source: World Tourism Organization (UNWTO) ©

Visitors from the Middle East go predominantly to North Africa (92%). Over half all visitors from Europe go to North Africa, and the remainder are relatively evenly distributed between East Africa, Southern Africa and West Africa. Smaller proportions of visitors from the Americas and Asia and the Pacific go to North Africa.

The strongest growth in 2005 was recorded by Asia and the Pacific (+15%). Arrivals from Europe and the Americas and from within Africa all increased by 10-11%, but those from the Middle East declined slightly. However, arrivals from the Middle East grew by far the fastest from 2000-2005 as a whole, by 13% a year.

World and regions: Inbound tourism by region of origin
International Tourist Arrivals, 2005*   (share, %)

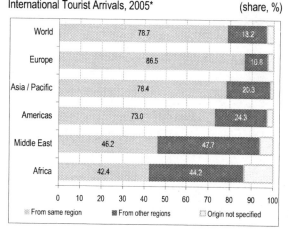

Source: World Tourism Organization (UNWTO) ©

World regions: Inbound tourism by region of origin
International Tourist Arrivals, 2005*   (million)

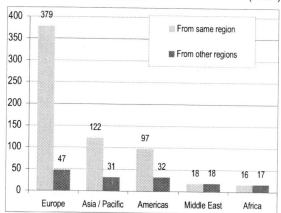

Source: World Tourism Organization (UNWTO) ©

Africa: Inbound tourism by region of origin
International Tourist Arrivals, 2005*   (million)

Source: World Tourism Organization (UNWTO) ©

Africa: Inbound tourism by region of origin
International Tourist Arrivals   (change 2005/2004, %)

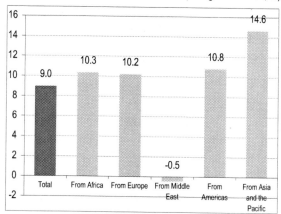

Source: World Tourism Organization (UNWTO) ©

Inbound Tourism by Region of Origin (including estimates for countries with missing data)

	International Tourist Arrivals (1000)					Market share (%)			Change (%)			Average annual growth (%)	
	1990	1995	2000	2004	2005*	1990	2000	2005*	03/02	04/03	05*/04	'95-'00	'00-'05*
Africa	**15,188**	**20,083**	**27,894**	**34,242**	**37,311**	**100**	**100**	**100**	**5.3**	**9.1**	**9.0**	**6.8**	**6.0**
From:													
Africa	5,872	9,142	11,442	14,340	15,823	38.7	41.0	42.4	5.3	4.9	10.3	4.6	6.7
Other regions	7,232	8,884	13,200	15,099	16,505	47.6	47.3	44.2	2.4	14.0	9.3	8.2	4.6
Americas	481	648	1,027	1,121	1,241	3.2	3.7	3.3	1.2	21.1	10.8	9.6	3.9
Asia and the Pacific	253	567	781	946	1,085	1.7	2.8	2.9	1.7	8.8	14.6	6.6	6.8
Europe	5,509	6,863	10,481	11,319	12,474	36.3	37.6	33.4	2.5	14.5	10.2	8.8	3.5
Middle East	989	806	910	1,713	1,705	6.5	3.3	4.6	2.9	9.1	-0.5	2.5	13.4
Origin not specified	2,085	2,057	3,252	4,803	4,984	13.7	11.7	13.4	14.9	7.4	3.8		

Source: World Tourism Organization (UNWTO) ©   (Data as collected by UNWTO for TMT 2006 Edition)

World Tourism Organization ©

Africa and subregions: Inbound tourism by region of origin

International Tourist Arrivals, 2005*

(share, %)

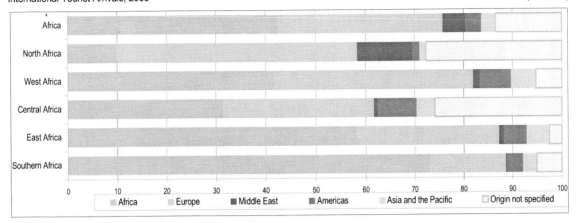

Source: World Tourism Organization (UNWTO) ©

Africa

Inbound Tourism by Region of Origin (including estimates for countries with missing data), 2005*

		Africa					
		Total	North	West	Central	East	Southern
		International Tourist Arrivals (000)					
Total		**37,311**	**13,911**	**3,585**	**792**	**8,059**	**10,964**
from:	Africa	15,823	1,357	1,499	250	4,690	8,027
	Other regions	16,505	8,722	1,899	339	3,165	2,381
	Europe	12,474	6,760	1,439	239	2,346	1,690
	Americas	1,241	204	228	63	376	370
	Middle East	1,705	1,560	51	6	71	17
	Asia and the Pacific	1,085	198	181	30	371	304
	Origin not specified	4,984	3,832	188	204	204	557
		% destination broken down by origin					
Total		**100**	**100**	**100**	**100**	**100**	**100**
from:	Africa	42.4	9.8	41.8	31.5	58.2	73.2
	Other regions	44.2	62.7	53.0	42.7	39.3	21.7
	Europe	33.4	48.6	40.1	30.2	29.1	15.4
	Americas	3.3	1.5	6.4	7.9	4.7	3.4
	Middle East	4.6	11.2	1.4	0.8	0.9	0.2
	Asia and the Pacific	2.9	1.4	5.1	3.8	4.6	2.8
	Origin not specified	13.4	27.5	5.2	25.8	2.5	5.1
		% origin broken down by destination					
Total		**100**	**37.3**	**9.6**	**2.1**	**21.6**	**29.4**
from:	Africa	100	8.6	9.5	1.6	29.6	50.7
	Other regions	100	52.8	11.5	2.1	19.2	14.4
	Europe	100	54.2	11.5	1.9	18.8	13.5
	Americas	100	16.4	18.4	5.1	30.3	29.8
	Middle East	100	91.5	3.0	0.4	4.2	1.0
	Asia and the Pacific	100	18.3	16.7	2.8	34.2	28.0
	Origin not specified	100	76.9	3.8	4.1	4.1	11.2

Source: World Tourism Organization (UNWTO) ©   (Data as collected by UNWTO for TMT 2006 Edition)

Inbound tourism by mode of transport

In 2005, slightly more international tourists travelled to African countries by air (48%) than by land (45%). Only 7% arrived by water.

Growth in arrivals by air, to 18 million in 2005, was especially fast between 1990 and 2000 (more than 7% per year on average), but slowed thereafter. However, they increased by 13% in 2004 and 10% in 2005. Although an inadequate supply of air transport to, from and within the region continues to hamper tourism, the situation has recently improved, owing in particular to policies liberalizing some of the region's air spaces. The number of land arrivals (17 million, mainly by road) grew by 5% a year in 1990-2000 and by 7% a year from 2000-2005, with a 10% increase in 2005. These increases reflect improvements in road infrastructure between destinations in the region. The portion of tourists arriving by water has increased by 2.5 percentage points – from 4.5% in 1990 to 7% in 2005.

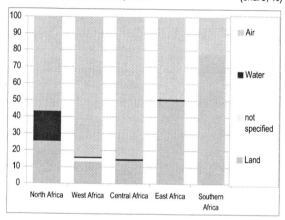

Africa: Inbound tourism by mode of transport
International Tourist Arrivals (share, %)

Africa and subregions: Inbound tourism by mode of transport
International Tourist Arrivals, 2005* (share, %)

Source: World Tourism Organization (UNWTO) ©

Source: World Tourism Organization (UNWTO) ©

Among the different subregions, air transport is by far the most important mode for tourist arrivals in West Africa and Central Africa (over 80% each). North Africa is also dependent on air traffic, but to a lesser degree (57%) – the subregion's geographic position allows it to attract 18% of its tourist arrivals by water. In Southern Africa, on the other hand, land transport is the preferred means of travel (78%). Only 22% arrived by air in 2005, underscoring the intraregional character of arrivals in this subregion. In East Africa, arrivals were divided more or less equally between air and land.

Africa

Arrivals by mode of transport (including estimates for countries with missing data)

| | International Tourist Arrivals | | | | | | Share | | | Change | | Average annual growth (%) | |
| | | | | | | (million) | | | (%) | | (%) | | |
	1990	1995	2000	2003	2004	2005*	1990	2000	2005*	04/03	05*/04	90-00	00-05*
Total	15.2	20.1	27.9	31.4	34.2	37.3	100	100	100	9.1	9.0	6.3	6.0
Air	6.9	9.4	14.0	14.4	16.3	17.9	45.2	50.1	48.0	13.4	10.1	7.4	5.1
Land	7.2	9.1	11.8	14.6	15.2	16.7	47.2	42.2	44.7	4.1	9.7	5.1	7.2
Water	0.7	1.3	2.1	2.3	2.7	2.6	4.5	7.4	7.1	15.4	-2.9	11.8	5.0
Not specified	0.5	0.2	0.1	0.1	0.1	0.1	3.1	0.2	0.2				

Source: World Tourism Organization (UNWTO) ©

(Data as collected by UNWTO for TMT 2006 Edition)

World Tourism Organization ©

Arrivals by mode of transport (including estimates for countries with missing data), 2005*

	Total	Air	Land	Water	Not specified
International Tourist Arrivals (million)					
Africa	37.3	17.9	16.7	2.6	0.1
North Africa	13.9	7.9	3.5	2.5	0.0
West Africa	3.6	3.0	0.5	0.0	0.1
Central Africa	0.8	0.7	0.1	0.0	0.0
East Africa	8.1	4.0	4.0	0.1	0.0
Southern Africa	11.0	2.4	8.5	0.0	0.0
%					
Africa	100	48.0	44.7	7.1	0.2
North Africa	100	56.7	25.4	17.9	0.0
West Africa	100	83.8	13.2	0.8	2.1
Central Africa	100	85.1	14.0	0.8	0.0
East Africa	100	49.1	49.7	1.2	0.0
Southern Africa	100	22.0	77.9	0.1	0.0

Source: World Tourism Organization (UNWTO) ©   (Data as collected by UNWTO for TMT 2006 Edition)

Inbound tourism by purpose of visit

Care must be taken in interpreting data on purpose of trip, since it is well known that travellers requiring visas for a particular destination often claim they are travelling for leisure rather than business as the visa requirements tend to be less strict. In addition, a significant share of trips involves more than one purpose. As a result of these different factors, the respective shares might be distorted.

About 54% of arrivals in 2005 were tourists visiting Africa for leisure, recreation and holidays. About 27%, or more than a quarter of the arrivals, were visiting friends and relations (VFR), or travelling to the destination for reasons of health, religion or other private reasons, and 15% were on business.

Although the numbers of arrivals for leisure and business more or less kept pace with each other from 1990-2005, arrivals for leisure outpaced those for business in 2004 and 2005: they rose by 8% and 10% in the two years, compared with 6% and 2% increases for business travellers. Arrivals in the 'VFR, health, religion, other' category have outpaced both leisure and business travellers since 2000, rising by 14% in 2004 and 10% in 2005.

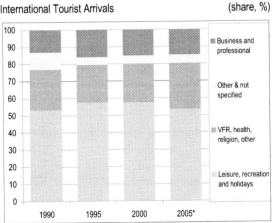

Africa: Inbound tourism by purpose of visit
International Tourist Arrivals   (share, %)

Source: World Tourism Organization (UNWTO) ©

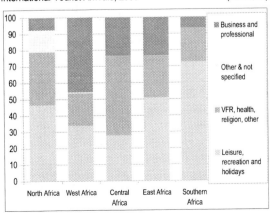

Africa and subregions: Inbound tourism by purpose of visit
International Tourist Arrivals, 2005*   (share, %)

Source: World Tourism Organization (UNWTO) ©

In 2005, nearly three-quarters (73%) of all tourists visiting Southern Africa did so for the purpose of 'leisure, recreation and holidays'. This was also the major purpose for visits to East Africa (51%) and North Africa (47%). In West Africa, 46% of all tourist visits are motivated by business or professional reasons, which is about twice the share of tourists (23%) visiting East Africa and Central Africa for these purposes. VFR, religion, health, and other reasons account for a significant share of visits to all regions, and higher shares for Central Africa (49%) and North Africa (32%). This is explained by the large numbers of nationals from these regions residing in European countries.

Africa

Arrivals by purpose of visit (including estimates for countries with missing data)

| | International Tourist Arrivals | | | | | | Share | | | Change | | Average annual growth (%) | |
| | | | | | | (million) | | | (%) | | (%) | | |
	1990	1995	2000	2003	2004	2005*	1990	2000	2005*	04/03	05*/04	90-00	00-05*
Total	15.2	20.1	27.9	31.4	34.2	37.3	100	100	100	9.1	9.0	6.3	6.0
Leisure, recreation and holidays	8.1	11.6	16.1	16.8	18.2	20.0	53.3	57.7	53.6	8.3	10.0	7.1	4.5
Business and professional	2.0	3.2	4.2	5.0	5.4	5.5	13.0	15.1	14.7	6.2	2.0	7.9	5.3
VFR, health, religion, other	3.6	4.4	6.3	7.9	9.0	10.0	23.6	22.5	26.7	14.0	10.2	5.8	9.7
Not specified	1.5	0.9	1.3	1.6	1.7	1.9	10.1	4.7	5.0				

Source: World Tourism Organization (UNWTO) ©   (Data as collected by UNWTO for TMT 2006 Edition)

Arrivals by purpose of visit (including estimates for countries with missing data), 2005*

	Total	Leisure, recreation and holidays	Business and professional	VFR, health, religion, other	Not specified
	International Tourist Arrivals (million)				
Africa	37.3	20.0	5.5	10.0	1.9
North Africa	13.9	6.5	1.1	4.5	1.9
West Africa	3.6	1.2	1.6	0.7	0.0
Central Africa	0.8	0.2	0.2	0.4	0.0
East Africa	8.1	4.1	1.9	2.1	0.0
Southern Africa	11.0	8.0	0.7	2.3	0.0
	%				
Africa	100	53.6	14.7	26.7	5.0
North Africa	100	46.7	7.6	32.4	13.3
West Africa	100	33.9	45.7	20.0	0.5
Central Africa	100	27.8	23.3	49.0	0.0
East Africa	100	50.9	23.4	25.6	0.0
Southern Africa	100	72.7	6.4	20.9	0.0

Source: World Tourism Organization (UNWTO) ©   (Data as collected by UNWTO for TMT 2006 Edition)

II.1.2 Outbound Tourism

Outbound tourism by destination (sub)region

In 2005, Africa generated 21 million international tourist arrivals, 8% more than in 2004. As a generating market, the region grew by an average of 5% a year from 1990-2005. However, those 21 million arrivals represented just less than 3% of the world total.

Nearly three quarters of all international tourist arrivals generated by African source countries in 2005 were received within the region (15.8 million). Southern Africa received the greatest share of these visits (38%). The social changes observed in the southern subregion have provided a catalyst for tourism, as evidenced by average annual increases of 11% between 1990 and 2005. North Africa is again receiving larger numbers of tourists from Africa, after an average annual decline of 11% between 1990 and 2000: arrivals increased by 8.5% in 2005, and by 11% a year in 2000-2005.

World and regions: Outbound tourism by region of destination
International Tourist Arrivals, 2005*   (share, %)

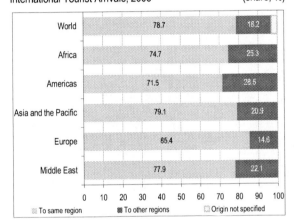

Source: World Tourism Organization (UNWTO) ©

World regions: Outbound tourism by region of destination
International Tourist Arrivals, 2005*   (million)

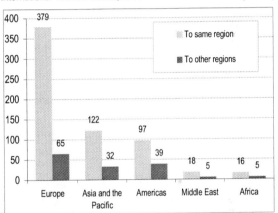

Source: World Tourism Organization (UNWTO) ©

Africa: Outbound tourism by region of destination
International Tourist Arrivals, 2005*   (share, %)

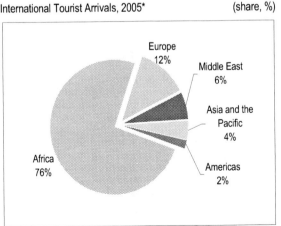

Source: World Tourism Organization (UNWTO) ©

Africa: Outbound tourism by region of destination
International Tourist Arrivals   (share, %)

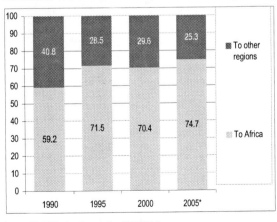

Source: World Tourism Organization (UNWTO) ©

In terms of interregional traffic, Europe is the leading destination, accounting for 12.5% of total arrivals out of Africa in destinations worldwide and 49% of interregional arrivals out of Africa. Europe's share (and particularly Western Europe's share) has declined dramatically since 1990 (from 29% to 12.5%). The numbers of travellers to Asia and the Pacific and the

Americas have increased, particularly as commercial and cultural links to countries like China and Brazil have grown. (Note the 22% average annual increase in arrivals from Africa in North-East Asia in 2000-2005, and the 13% increase in arrivals in 'other Americas' – i.e. Latin America and the Caribbean – in the same period.)

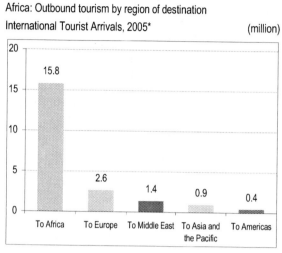

Africa: Outbound tourism by region of destination
International Tourist Arrivals, 2005*   (million)

Source: World Tourism Organization (UNWTO) ©

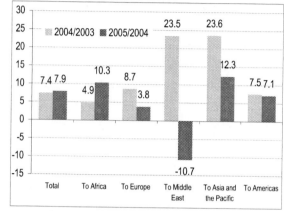

Africa: Outbound tourism by region of destination
International Tourist Arrivals   (change, %)

Source: World Tourism Organization (UNWTO) ©

Africa

Outbound Tourism by (sub)region of destination (including estimates for countries with missing data)

	International Tourist Arrivals (1000)					Market share (%)			Growth rate (%)		Average annual growth (%)	
	1990	1995	2000	2004	2005*	1990	2000	2005*	04/03	05*/04	90-00	00-05*
Total	**9,921**	**12,778**	**16,263**	**19,641**	**21,190**	**100**	**100**	**100**	**7.4**	**7.9**	**5.1**	**5.4**
To:												
Africa	*5,872*	*9,142*	*11,442*	*14,340*	*15,823*	*59.2*	*70.4*	*74.7*	*4.9*	*10.3*	*6.9*	*6.7*
North Africa	2,539	1,200	816	1,250	1,357	25.6	5.0	6.4	14.3	8.5	-10.7	10.7
West Africa	518	883	1,000	1,429	1,499	5.2	6.1	7.1	12.9	4.9	6.8	8.4
Central Africa	95	104	260	218	250	1.0	1.6	1.2	2.6	14.5	10.6	-0.8
East Africa	1,151	2,456	3,224	4,462	4,690	11.6	19.8	22.1	2.4	5.1	10.8	7.8
Southern Africa	1,569	4,498	6,143	6,981	8,027	15.8	37.8	37.9	3.5	15.0	14.6	5.5
Interregional	*4,049*	*3,636*	*4,821*	*5,301*	*5,367*	*40.8*	*29.6*	*25.3*	*14.7*	*1.2*	*1.8*	*2.2*
Europe	**2,903**	**2,318**	**2,667**	**2,545**	**2,642**	**29.3**	**16.4**	**12.5**	**8.7**	**3.8**	**-0.8**	**-0.2**
Northern Europe	543	557	657	701	725	5.5	4.0	3.4	12.3	3.3	1.9	2.0
Western Europe	1,992	1,410	1,521	1,329	1,335	20.1	9.4	6.3	0.0	0.4	-2.7	-2.6
Central/Eastern Europe	55	64	82	96	96	0.6	0.5	0.5	17.9	0.1	4.0	3.3
Southern Europe	313	286	408	419	487	3.2	2.5	2.3	36.2	16.1	2.7	3.6
Middle East	**665**	**574**	**1,099**	**1,522**	**1,359**	**6.7**	**6.8**	**6.4**	**23.5**	**-10.7**	**5.2**	**4.3**
Asia and the Pacific	**260**	**479**	**639**	**845**	**949**	**2.6**	**3.9**	**4.5**	**23.6**	**12.3**	**9.4**	**8.2**
North-East Asia	83	124	150	301	402	0.8	0.9	1.9	47.2	33.7	6.1	21.8
South-East Asia	89	195	280	324	303	0.9	1.7	1.4	14.3	-6.3	12.1	1.6
Oceania	20	54	93	82	86	0.2	0.6	0.4	-0.1	4.4	16.6	-1.5
South Asia	68	106	117	139	158	0.7	0.7	0.7	21.2	13.8	5.6	6.2
Americas	**220**	**265**	**416**	**389**	**417**	**2.2**	**2.6**	**2.0**	**7.5**	**7.1**	**6.6**	**0.1**
North America	187	235	360	298	314	1.9	2.2	1.5	3.5	5.4	6.8	-2.7
Other Americas	33	30	56	91	103	0.3	0.3	0.5	23.2	13.0	5.3	13.0

Source: World Tourism Organization (UNWTO) ©   (Data as collected by UNWTO for TMT 2006 Edition)

World Tourism Organization ©

International tourism expenditure

International tourism expenditure (by African residents travelling on same-day as well as overnight trips) rose by 13% in 2005, to US$ 10.8 billion. However, it represented less than 2% of the world total – an even smaller share than Africa's share of arrivals worldwide. Spending per capita was just US$ 13, compared with an average of US$ 105 for the world's population overall.

Nevertheless, spending by Africans has been rising fast. Southern Africa – the region's leading generator of international tourism expenditure, accounting for 35% of the total – contributed an increase of 6% in 2005, only half its 2004 rate. North Africa, with a 19% share, increased its spending by 17% in 2004 and by 41% in 2005. This can in large part be explained by the increase in hydrocarbons revenues (particularly in Sudan, which is joining the world's major oil producers). East Africa and (from a much smaller base) Central Africa also contributed large increases in 2004-2005. However, spending generated by West Africa declined by 21% in 2004 (principally due to large declines out of Nigeria and Sierra) and rose just 3% in 2005. However, it should be noted that the 2005 figures for West Africa and Central Africa are still very much preliminary estimates, since data is not available for many countries.

World and regions: Outbound tourism
International Tourism Expenditure, 2005*   (share, %)

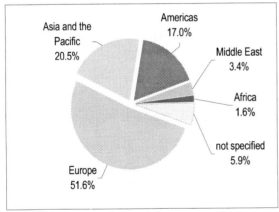

Source: World Tourism Organization (UNWTO) ©

World and regions: Outbound tourism
International Tourism Expenditure, 2005*   (US$ per capita)

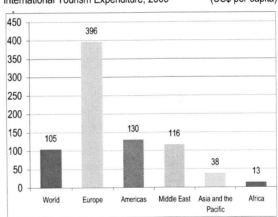

Source: World Tourism Organization (UNWTO) ©

Africa: Outbound tourism
International Tourism Expenditure, 2005*   (US$ billion)

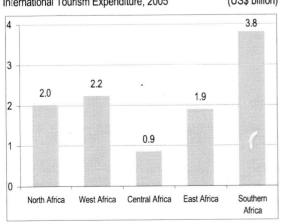

Source: World Tourism Organization (UNWTO) ©

Africa: Outbound tourism
International Tourism Expenditure, 2005*   (US$ per capita)

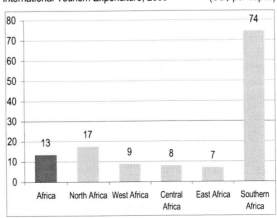

Source: World Tourism Organization (UNWTO) ©

International Tourism Expenditure by Generating Country

	International Tourism Expenditure (US$, million)						Market share in the region (%)			Change (%)		Population (million)	per capita[1]
	1990	1995	2000	2003	2004	2005*	1990	2000	2005*	04/03	05*/04	2005	US$
Africa	*4,195*	*6,031*	*6,538*	*9,303*	*9,583*	*10,803*	*100*	*100*	*100*	*3.0*	*12.7*	*808*	*13*
North Africa	**563**	**784**	**937**	**1,221**	**1,431**	**2,012**	**13.4**	**14.3**	**18.6**	**17.2**	**40.6**	**116**	**17**
Algeria	149	188	193	255	341	370	3.6	2.9	3.4	33.7	8.5	32.5	11
Morocco	184	302	426	548	575	614	4.4	6.5	5.7	4.9	6.9	32.7	19
Sudan	51	43	55	119	176	667	1.2	0.8	6.2	47.9	279.2	40.2	17
Tunisia	179	251	263	299	339	360	4.3	4.0	3.3	13.2	6.2	10.1	36
West Africa	**1,142**	**1,478**	**1,166**	**2,750**	**2,171**	**2,235**	**27.2**	**17.8**	**20.7**	**-21.1**	**3.0**	**255**	**9**
Benin	15	35	12	21	29	..	0.4	0.2		38.1		7.6	4
Burkina Faso	32	..	20	36	19	..	0.8	0.3		-47.1		13.5	1
Cape Verde	5	16	36	72	78	67	0.1	0.6	0.6	7.2	-13.6	0.4	161
Côte d'Ivoire	169	190	189	387	382	346	4.0	2.9	3.2	-1.3	-9.4	17.3	20
Gambia	8	14	..	4	4	5	0.2		0.0	0.0	25.0	1.6	3
Ghana	13	21	100	138	186	303	0.3	1.5	2.8	34.8	62.9	21.9	14
Guinea	30	21	9	26	25	..	0.7	0.1		-3.8		9.5	3
Guinea-Bissau	..	4	..	13	13	..				0.0		1.4	9
Mali	62	49	40	48	66	77	1.5	0.6	0.7	37.5	16.7	11.4	7
Mauritania	23	23	..	..	..	..	0.5					3.1	
Niger	44	13	26	22	22	32	1.0	0.4	0.3	0.0	45.5	12.2	3
Nigeria	576	907	591	1,793	1,156	1,109	13.7	9.0	10.3	-35.5	-4.1	128.8	9
Senegal	105	72	47	55	57	..	2.5	0.7		3.6		11.7	5
Sierra Leone	4	50	32	37	30	32	0.1	0.5	0.3	-18.9	6.7	5.9	5
Togo	40	19	2	7	8	..	1.0	0.0		14.3		5.4	2
Central Africa	**714**	**449**	**596**	**662**	**771**	**851**	**17.0**	**9.1**	**7.9**	**16.4**	**10.4**	**109**	**8**
Angola	38	75	136	12	39	74	0.9	2.1	0.7	220.7	90.7	11.8	6
Cameroon	279	105	205	212	..	..	6.7	3.1				17.0	13
Cent.Afr.Rep.	51	43	33	31	32	..	1.2	0.5		3.2		4.2	8
Chad	70	38	56	..	..	..	1.7	0.9				9.7	7
Congo	113	52	50	78	103	103	2.7	0.8	1.0	32.1	0.0	3.6	29
Dem.R.Congo	16	..	..	..	..	..	0.4					60.8	
Equatorial Guinea	8	67	19	..	..	..	0.2	0.3				0.5	
Gabon	137	60	84	194	214	..	3.3	1.3		10.3		1.4	157
Sao Tome Prn	2	..	1	..	..	..	0.0	0.0				0.2	3
East Africa	**476**	**1,178**	**1,396**	**1,451**	**1,622**	**1,898**	**11.4**	**21.4**	**17.6**	**11.8**	**17.0**	**277**	**7**
Burundi	17	25	14	15	24	60	0.4	0.2	0.6	60.0	150.0	7.8	8
Comoros	6	7	..	..	..	..	0.1					0.7	
Djibouti	..	4	..	3	3	3			0.0	-3.0	3.2	0.5	6
Ethiopia	11	25	74	50	58	77	0.3	1.1	0.7	16.0	32.3	73.1	1
Kenya	38	145	132	127	107	124	0.9	2.0	1.1	-15.4	15.2	33.8	4
Madagascar	40	59	116	37	35	25	1.0	1.8	0.2	-5.4	-28.6	18.0	1
Malawi	16	39	50	48	50	50	0.4	0.8	0.5	4.3	-0.1	12.7	4
Mauritius	94	159	182	216	255	275	2.2	2.8	2.5	17.9	8.0	1.2	223
Mozambique	..	..	108	140	134	176		1.6	1.6	-4.0	31.2	19.4	9
Rwanda	23	10	22	27	31	37	0.5	0.3	0.3	13.8	19.4	8.4	4
Seychelles	34	28	24	36	34	39	0.8	0.4	0.4	-7.6	15.3	0.1	476
Tanzania	23	360	337	353	445	554	0.5	5.2	5.1	26.1	24.4	36.8	15
Uganda	8	80	..	..	133	133	0.2		1.2		0.0	27.3	5
Zambia	54	..	44	77	89	94	1.3	0.7	0.9	15.6	5.6	11.3	8
Zimbabwe	66	106	..	..	..	..	1.6					12.2	
Southern Africa	**1,300**	**2,142**	**2,443**	**3,218**	**3,589**	**3,807**	**31.0**	**37.4**	**35.2**	**11.5**	**6.1**	**51**	**74**
Botswana	56	145	198	230	276	282	1.3	3.0	2.6	20.2	2.3	1.6	172
Lesotho	12	13	9	26	30	27	0.3	0.1	0.2	15.4	-10.0	2.0	13
Namibia	63	90	86	73	122	108	1.5	1.3	1.0	66.4	-11.8	2.0	53
South Africa	1,134	1,851	2,086	2,846	3,144	3,375	27.0	31.9	31.2	10.5	7.3	44.3	76
Swaziland	35	43	64	43	16	15	0.8	1.0	0.1	-62.8	-6.3	1.1	13

Source: World Tourism Organization (UNWTO) ©

(Data as collected by UNWTO for TMT 2006 Edition)

[1] Last year with data available

In terms of expenditure per capita, residents in Southern Africa spend by far more than those in the other subregions: in fact, their spending, at US$ 74 per head in 2005, is not very far short of the world average of US$ 105. Several African countries sustain per capita spending levels approaching those in the less affluent OECD countries, including the Seychelles (US$ 476), Mauritius (US$ 223), Botswana (US$ 172), the Cape Verde Islands (US$ 161) and Gabon (US$ 157). Elsewhere in Africa, however, spending on outbound travel remains very low, rarely exceeding US$ 20 per person per year.

Trips abroad

Data on outbound tourist travel is not available for many generating countries, as the gaps in the following table shows, and it is often difficult to determine whether the figures indicated refer to tourists (ovenight visitors) or to visitors in general. For this reason, it is also not feasible to present regional and subregional aggregates. Furthermore, it is important to note that the number of trips is not equal to the number of arrivals, as a single trip can produce arrivals in various destinations.

According to the available data, in absolute terms, South Africa remains the largest source market in Africa, with 3.8 million trips abroad in 2002 (the latest year for which statistics are available). Morocco and Tunisia follow with 2.2 million trips each in 2005. Algeria reported 1.5 million trips for the same year and Swaziland 1.1 million, but no other country in Africa reports more than 400,000 trips.

Outbound Tourism, trips abroad (trips can either refer to overnight visits only, or also include same-day visits)

						(1000)	per 100 popu-	Change (%)		Average (%)	
	1990	1995	2000	2003	2004	2005*	lation[1]	04/03	05*/04	'90-'00	'00-'05*
Africa											
North Africa											
Algeria	3,828	1,090	1,006	1,254	1,417	1,513	5	13.0	6.8	-12.5	8.5
Morocco	1,202	1,317	1,508	1,612	1,603	2,247	7	-0.6	40.2	2.3	8.3
Sudan	..	195	..	..	..	..					
Tunisia	1,727	1,778	1,632	2,274	2,312	2,241	22	1.7	-3.1	-0.6	6.5
West Africa											
Côte d'Ivoire	2	..	..	..	..	..					
Gambia	..	..	..	..	..	387	24				
Niger	18	10	..	..	..	..					
Sierra Leone	..	..	13	13	28	63	1	115.4	125.0		37.1
Central Africa											
Angola	..	3	..	..	..	..					
Cent.Afr.Rep.	..	..	..	6	7	..	0	16.7			
Chad	24	..	27	..	..	..				1.2	
Gabon	161	..	168	236	..	..	18			0.4	
East Africa											
Burundi	24	36	28	..	..	..				1.6	
Ethiopia	89	120	..	..	..	..					
Kenya	210	..	..	..	..	..					
Madagascar	34	39	..	..	67	41	0		-38.8		
Mauritius	89	107	163	161	180	183	15	11.8	1.7	6.2	2.3
Reunion	190	238	322	333	385	395	51	15.6	2.6	5.4	4.2
Seychelles	18	31	36	50	48	52	64	-4.0	8.3	7.2	7.6
Tanzania	301	157	..	..	..	..					
Uganda	..	..	153	189	231	189	1	22.2	-18.2		4.3
Zimbabwe	..	256	..	..	..	..					
Southern Africa											
Botswana	192	..	..	..	..	..					
South Africa	616	2,520	3,834	..	..	..				20.1	
Swaziland	..	..	..	..	..	1,082	95				

Source: World Tourism Organization (UNWTO) ©   (Data as collected by UNWTO for TMT 2006 Edition)

[1] values correspond to most recent year with data available

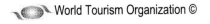

II.2   Tourism Trends by Subregion

II.2.1   North Africa

International tourist arrivals

The North African subregion consists of just four countries – Morocco and Tunisia, which are well-established sun & beach destinations for European and Middle Eastern tourists; Algeria, which has ambitions along the same lines; and Sudan. Arrivals in the subregion as a whole have been rising steadily since the mid-1990s, and they rose by a further 15% in 2004 and 9% in 2005, to 13.9 million (37% of the African total).

Morocco and Tunisia achieved growth of 6-7% in arrivals in 2005, building on their strong increases of 15-17% in 2004. In the case of Morocco, this is attributable to the positive returns generated by enhanced promotions and marketing, as well as by the increased public and private sector investments in tourism infrastructure, hotels, attractions and other facilities.

The pattern in Algeria was the reverse, with increases of 6% in 2004 and 17% in 2005. All three countries benefited from the high value of the euro, which sustained their price competitiveness. Morocco and Tunisia reported large increases in arrivals from most of their major European markets in 2005.

Conditions were also favourable for investments: all three countries are politically more stable and peaceful than they were in the 1990s, and all three are benefiting from the high international prices of oil and gas, which are generating funds for investment in infrastructure and in tourism facilities. These same conditions are also encouraging inbound and outbound business travel.

But the outstanding story in 2005 was the fourfold increase in arrivals in Sudan – albeit from a very small base (they reached 246,000 in 2005). Following the peace negotiated with the rebels in the south in 2004, investments in the oilfields have been stepped up and a very ambitious construction programme has got underway in the capital, financed by the promise of those oil revenues. However, the political situation in the Sudan remains fragile, not least because of the terrible events in the Darfur region.

International Tourist Arrivals by Country of Destination

	Series	International Tourist Arrivals (1000)						Market share in the region (%)			Change (%)		Average annual growth (%)	
		1990	1995	2000	2003	2004	2005*	1990	2000	2005*	04/03	05*/04	90-00	00-05*
North Africa		8,398	7,271	10,240	11,094	12,769	13,911	55.3	36.7	37.3	15.1	8.9	2.0	6.3
Algeria	VF	1,137	520	866	1,166	1,234	1,443	7.5	3.1	3.9	5.8	17.0	-2.7	10.8
Morocco	TF	4,024	2,602	4,278	4,761	5,477	5,843	26.5	15.3	15.7	15.0	6.7	0.6	6.4
Sudan	TF	33	29	38	52	61	246	0.2	0.1	0.7	15.8	305.8	1.4	45.3
Tunisia	TF	3,204	4,120	5,058	5,114	5,998	6,378	21.1	18.1	17.1	17.3	6.3	4.7	4.7

Source: World Tourism Organization (UNWTO) ©   (Data as collected by UNWTO for TMT 2006 Edition)

World Tourism Organization ©

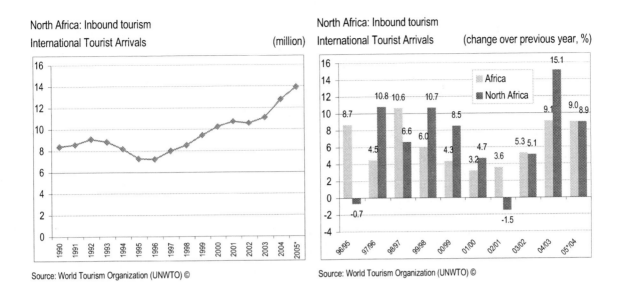

North Africa: Inbound tourism
International Tourist Arrivals   (million)

Source: World Tourism Organization (UNWTO) ©

North Africa: Inbound tourism
International Tourist Arrivals   (change over previous year, %)

Source: World Tourism Organization (UNWTO) ©

It should be pointed out that, in 2005, 69% of arrivals in Algeria and 48% of those in Morocco were by nationals resident abroad. Tunisia measures arrivals by nationality, but its own nationals are not included in the total arrivals count. Nearly 45% of arrivals in Sudan in 2005 came from Asia – presumably mainly from China, which is heavily committed to the investments in the country.

International tourism receipts

International tourism receipts in North African destinations reached US$ 7.0 billion in 2005, ranking North Africa second in terms of receipts of all African subregions after Southern Africa. This represented a growth of 15% expressed in local currencies at constant prices.

Morocco, with US$ 4.6 billion in 2005, accounts for 66% of North African tourism receipts, and Tunisia, with US$ 2.1 billion, for 30%. That leaves just 4% of the total for Algeria and Sudan.

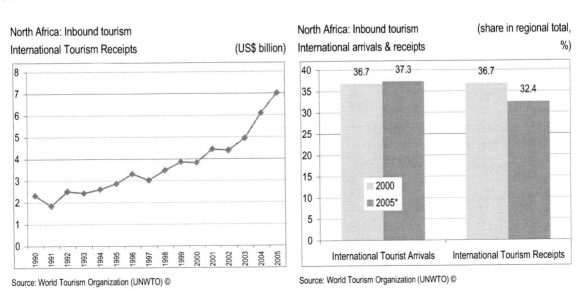

North Africa: Inbound tourism
International Tourism Receipts   (US$ billion)

Source: World Tourism Organization (UNWTO) ©

North Africa: Inbound tourism   (share in regional total,
International arrivals & receipts   %)

Source: World Tourism Organization (UNWTO) ©

Receipts per tourist arrival in North Africa averaged US$ 505 in 2005, but this disguises wide variations: US$ 790 for Morocco (with its more sophisticated tourism offer, attracting higher yield tourists), US$ 335 for Tunisia, US$ 365 for Sudan and just US$ 130 for Algeria (with its high proportion of VFR visitors).

International Tourism Receipts by Country of Destination

	International Tourism Receipts (US$, million)						Market share in the region (%)			Change (%)		Receipts per arrival[1]	Receipts per capita[1]
	1990	1995	2000	2003	2004	2005*	1990	2000	2005*	04/03	05*/04		US$
North Africa	**2,333**	**2,867**	**3,822**	**4,938**	**6,093**	**7,018**	**36.4**	**36.7**	**32.4**	**23.4**	**15.2**	**505**	**61**
Algeria	105	33	96	112	179	184	1.6	0.9	0.9	59.4	3.1	130	6
Morocco	1,259	1,296	2,039	3,225	3,924	4,621	19.7	19.6	21.4	21.6	17.8	790	141
Sudan	21	8	5	18	21	89	0.3	0.0	0.4	16.7	324.4	365	2
Tunisia	948	1,530	1,682	1,582	1,970	2,124	14.8	16.2	9.8	24.5	7.8	335	211

Source: World Tourism Organization (UNWTO) ©   (Data as collected by UNWTO for TMT 2006 Edition)

[1] Last year with data available

II.2.2 West Africa

International tourist arrivals

The countries of West Africa recorded 3.6 million international tourist arrivals in 2005, 4% more than in 2004. This was a fairly modest performance, but the subregion's tourism industry has nevertheless been growing fairly rapidly over the longer term – arrivals grew by an average of 7% a year from 1990-2005.

The most important destination in the subregion is Nigeria, with just over 1 million arrivals in 2005, but this is small related to the size of the country's population (it is the most populous country in the whole of Africa). Other countries along the Atlantic seaboard have more developed tourism industries, many of them geared to attracting tourists from Europe and North America. They include Côte d'Ivoire, Gambia and Senegal. The most tourism intensive destination is the Cape Verde Islands. In 2005 Senegal added 5,000 rooms to its tourist capacity (making a total of 15,842 rooms) and Cape Verde added 1,250 rooms (making a total of 4,406).

West Africa: Inbound tourism
International Tourist Arrivals   (million)

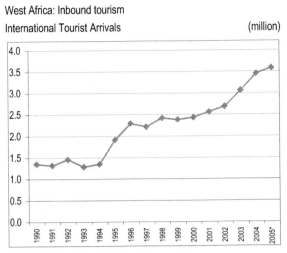

Source: World Tourism Organization (UNWTO) ©

West Africa: Inbound tourism
International Tourist Arrivals   (change over previous year, %)

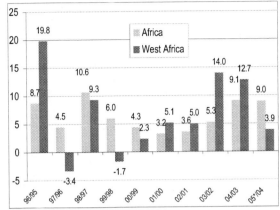

Source: World Tourism Organization (UNWTO) ©

In terms of arrivals, the best performances in 2005 came from Mali (+27%, but from a small base), the Cape Verde Islands (+26%), Gambia (+23%), Senegal (+15%, after a 35% rise in 2004) and Burkina Faso (+10%, after +36% in 2004). From 2000-2005 Sierra Leone's arrivals have grown the fastest, by 20% a year, but they slipped by 8% in 2005. Arrivals in Ghana dropped by a quarter in 2005.

International Tourist Arrivals by Country of Destination

	Series	International Tourist Arrivals (1000)						Market share in the region (%)			Change (%)		Average annual growth (%)	
		1990	1995	2000	2003	2004	2005*	1990	2000	2005*	04/03	05*/04	90-00	00-05*
West Africa		**1,352**	**1,913**	**2,434**	**3,062**	**3,452**	**3,585**	**8.9**	**8.7**	**9.6**	**12.7**	**3.9**	**6.1**	**8.1**
Benin	TF	110	138	96	175	174	176	0.7	0.3	0.5	-0.9	1.4	-1.4	12.9
Burkina Faso	THS	74	124	126	163	222	245	0.5	0.5	0.7	36.2	10.1	5.5	14.2
Cape Verde	TF	24	28	115	150	157	198	0.2	0.4	0.5	4.7	26.0	17.0	11.5
Côte d'Ivoire	TF	196	188	..	180	..	..	1.3						
Gambia	TF	100	45	77	89	90	111	0.7	0.3	0.3	1.1	23.2	-2.5	7.5
Ghana	TF	146	286	399	531	584	429	1.0	1.4	1.1	10.0	-26.6	10.6	1.4
Guinea	TF	..	..	33	44	45	45		0.1	0.1	1.5	1.6		6.6
Mali	TF	44	42	86	110	113	143	0.3	0.3	0.4	2.1	26.8	7.0	10.6
Mauritania	TF	..	..	30	..	..	..		0.1					
Niger	TF	21	35	50	55	57	63	0.1	0.2	0.2	3.6	11.3	9.1	4.9
Nigeria	TF	190	656	813	924	962	1,010	1.3	2.9	2.7	4.1	5.0	15.6	4.4
Senegal	THS/TF	246	280	389	495	667	769	1.6	1.4	2.1	34.7	15.3	4.7	14.6
Sierra Leone	TF	98	38	16	38	44	40	0.6	0.1	0.1	14.3	-8.1	-16.6	20.1
Togo	THS	103	53	60	61	83	81	0.7	0.2	0.2	36.5	-2.3	-5.3	6.1

Source: World Tourism Organization (UNWTO) ©   (Data as collected by UNWTO for TMT 2006 Edition)

International tourism receipts

Estimates based on the data available indicate that West African destinations earned US$ 1.9 billion from international tourism in 2005, 21% more than in 2004 in local currencies and at constant prices, or 31% more in US dollar terms.

According to the available data, Ghana took the lion's share – US$ 796 million, or 42% of the West African total. This represented a 71% increase on 2004 – in sharp contrast to the 27% decline in reported arrivals.

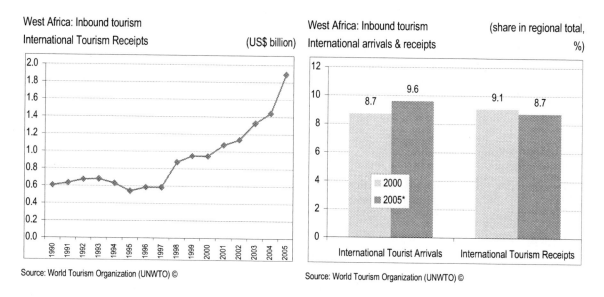

West Africa: Inbound tourism
International Tourism Receipts (US$ billion)

Source: World Tourism Organization (UNWTO) ©

West Africa: Inbound tourism
International arrivals & receipts (share in regional total, %)

Source: World Tourism Organization (UNWTO) ©

West Africa's receipts per international tourist arrival averaged US$ 530. The highest reported figures were US$ 1,855 for Ghana, US$ 1,600 for Sierra Leone and US$ 1,035 for Mali. These were also among the highest reported for African countries generally.

International Tourism Receipts by Country of Destination

	International Tourism Receipts (US$, million)						Market share in the region (%)			Change (%)		Receipts per arrival[1]	Receipts per capita[1]
	1990	1995	2000	2003	2004	2005*	1990	2000	2005*	04/03	05*/04		US$
West Africa	605	541	944	1,329	1,442	1,891	9.5	9.1	8.7	8.5	31.1	530	7
Benin	55	85	77	106	119	..	0.9	0.7		12.3		685	16
Burkina Faso	11	..	19	29	45	..	0.2	0.2		55.3		205	3
Cape Verde	6	10	41	87	99	127	0.1	0.4	0.6	13.9	28.5	645	305
Côte d'Ivoire	51	89	49	69	82	83	0.8	0.5	0.4	18.8	1.2	385	5
Gambia	26	28	48	51	58	62	0.4	0.5	0.3	12.5	8.2	560	39
Ghana	81	11	335	414	466	796	1.3	3.2	3.7	12.6	70.8	1,855	36
Guinea	30	1	12	31	30	..	0.5	0.1		-3.2		670	3
Guinea-Bissau	..	..	..	2	1	..				-50.0			1
Mali	47	25	40	128	140	148	0.7	0.4	0.7	9.4	5.7	1,035	13
Mauritania	9	11	..	..	..	..	0.1						
Niger	17	7	23	28	31	34	0.3	0.2	0.2	10.7	9.7	535	3
Nigeria	25	17	101	49	21	18	0.4	1.0	0.1	-57.6	-14.2	20	0
Senegal	167	168	144	209	212	..	2.6	1.4		1.4		320	19
Sierra Leone	19	57	11	60	58	64	0.3	0.1	0.3	-3.3	10.3	1,600	11
Togo	58	13	8	15	19	..	0.9	0.1		26.7		230	4

Source: World Tourism Organization (UNWTO) ©

(Data as collected by UNWTO for TMT 2006 Edition)

[1] Last year with data available

World Tourism Organization ©

II.2.3 Central Africa

International tourist arrivals

International tourist arrivals in the nine countries of Central Africa are estimated to have increased in 2005 by 9% to 0.8 million – just 2% of the African total. Several destinations have been embroiled in geopolitical conflicts, impeding the full development of their tourism potential. Nevertheless, the 9% increase in arrivals, following a 14% rise in 2004, was stronger than the annual growth from 1990-2000 (6.2% a year), and from 2000-2005 (3.5% a year).

Only three countries reported more than 100,000 arrivals in 2005: Angola (with 210,000), Cameroon (176,000) and Gabon (222,000 in 2003). The tourism industries in the other countries are generally very small. Given the size of the Democratic Republic of Congo, which also has a population of 61 million, its 61,000 arrivals in 2005 were extremely modest.

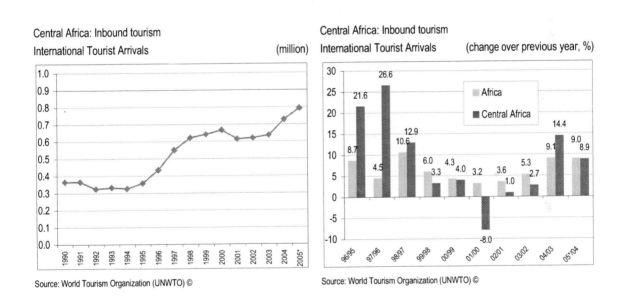

Central Africa: Inbound tourism
International Tourist Arrivals (million)

Central Africa: Inbound tourism
International Tourist Arrivals (change over previous year, %)

Source: World Tourism Organization (UNWTO) ©

Source: World Tourism Organization (UNWTO) ©

International Tourist Arrivals by Country of Destination

	Series	International Tourist Arrivals (1000)						Market share in the region (%)			Change (%)		Average annual growth (%)	
		1990	1995	2000	2003	2004	2005*	1990	2000	2005*	04/03	05*/04	90-00	00-05*
Central Africa		365	357	666	636	728	792	2.4	2.4	2.1	14.4	8.9	6.2	3.5
Angola	TF	67	9	51	107	194	210	0.4	0.2	0.6	82.3	8.0	-2.7	32.7
Cameroon	THS	89	100	277	..	190	176	0.6	1.0	0.5		-7.1	12.0	-8.6
Cent.Afr.Rep.	TF	..	26	11	6	8	12		0.0	0.0	43.4	47.1		1.4
Chad	THS	9	19	43	21	26	29	0.1	0.2	0.1	23.5	13.3	16.9	-7.3
Congo	THS	33	37	19	..	..	..	0.2	0.1				-5.4	
Dem.R.Congo	TF	55	35	103	35	30	61	0.4	0.4	0.2	-14.6	103.3	6.5	-9.9
Gabon	TF	109	125	155	222	..	..	0.7	0.6				3.6	
Sao Tome Prn	TF	3	6	7	14	11	11	0.0	0.0	0.0	-21.6	-1.9	9.0	8.1

Source: World Tourism Organization (UNWTO) ©   (Data as collected by UNWTO for TMT 2006 Edition)

With a more peaceful and increasingly wealthy environment (given its oil and minerals resources), Angola's tourism industry is finally growing. Arrivals were up 82% in 2004 and 8% in 2005. However, Cameroon's arrivals in 2005 were down 7% on 2004.

International tourism receipts

Only three of the nine countries in Central Africa have reported international tourism receipts for 2005. UNWTO estimates that the total for the subregion increased by 13% in local currencies at constant prices, or by 18% in US dollar terms, to US$ 323 million – just 1.5% of the African total.

Angola reported increases in international tourism receipts of 34% (in US dollar terms) in both 2004 and 2005.

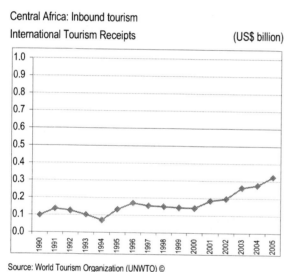

Central Africa: Inbound tourism
International Tourism Receipts (US$ billion)

Source: World Tourism Organization (UNWTO) ©

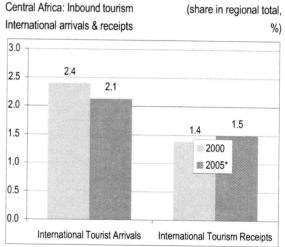

Central Africa: Inbound tourism (share in regional total, %)
International arrivals & receipts

Source: World Tourism Organization (UNWTO) ©

International Tourism Receipts by Country of Destination

	International Tourism Receipts (US$, million)						Market share in the region (%)			Change (%)		Receipts per arrival[1]	Receipts per capita[1]
	1990	1995	2000	2003	2004	2005*	1990	2000	2005*	04/03	05*/04		US$
Central Africa	98	133	143	261	274	323	1.5	1.4	1.5	5.0	18.0	410	3
Angola	13	10	18	49	66	88	0.2	0.2	0.4	34.3	34.0	420	7
Cameroon	53	36	57	114	..	..	0.8	0.5					7
Cent.Afr.Rep.	3	4	5	4	4	..	0.0	0.0		0.0		490	1
Chad	8	43	14	..	..	..	0.1	0.1					
Congo	8	14	12	29	22	34	0.1	0.1	0.2	-24.1	54.5		9
Dem.R.Congo	7	..	..	1	1	..	0.1			2.3		30	0
Equatorial Guinea	1	1	5	..	..	..	0.0	0.0					
Gabon	3	18	20	15	10	..	0.0	0.2		-33.3		70	7
Sao Tome Prn	2	..	10	11	13	14	0.0	0.1	0.1	20.8	6.3	1,295	73

Source: World Tourism Organization (UNWTO) ©

(Data as collected by UNWTO for TMT 2006 Edition)

[1] Last year with data available

II.2.4 East Africa

International tourist arrivals

East Africa recorded a total of 8.1 million international tourist arrivals in 2005. The annual increase in arrivals was very steady from 1990-2005, at +7.2% a year – with growth not even pausing in 2001-2002. Arrivals increased by 6% in both 2004 and 2005. This was below the average for Africa as a whole, mainly because of the continuing decline in arrivals in the subregion's leading destination, Zimbabwe. Although the calculation is not entirely valid, because some of Zimbabwe's potential tourists were diverted to neighbouring countries, it is interesting to note that, excluding Zimbabwe, arrivals in East Africa rose 16% in 2004 and 13% in 2005.

East Africa is the continent's third largest tourism receiving subregion, after North Africa and Southern Africa. It accounted for 22% of the region's arrivals in 2005.

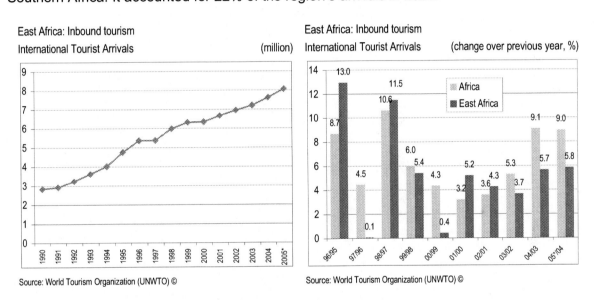

East Africa: Inbound tourism
International Tourist Arrivals   (million)

East Africa: Inbound tourism
International Tourist Arrivals   (change over previous year, %)

Source: World Tourism Organization (UNWTO) ©

Source: World Tourism Organization (UNWTO) ©

Among the continental countries reliant on their natural attractions and game parks for long-haul tourism, Kenya, Zambia, Mozambique and Madagascar have notched up two successive years of very rapid growth – generally well over 20% a year. And Kenya is regarded as the star performer in the region, thanks mainly to increased infrastructure development and enhanced cooperation between the public and private sectors. Although arrivals in Uganda fell by 9% in 2005, this was after a 68% increase in 2004 (arrivals remain far above their historical levels). Arrivals in Tanzania have been growing more moderately (by 2.5% in 2004 and 4.2% in 2005).

Arrivals in Zimbabwe fell by 18% in 2004 and 16% in 2005, but they remain within reach of their historical averages and are still nominally the highest in East Africa, in spite of the country's political and economic difficulties (nominally because the statistical series for arrivals in Zimbabwe refer to 'international visitors at frontiers' – i.e. both tourists and same-day visitors – which inflates the number of arrivals relative to destinations that record only tourists at frontiers).

Among the tourist resort islands of the Indian Ocean, Mauritius and the Seychelles both recorded an increase in arrivals of about 6% in 2005, but arrivals in Réunion slipped by 5%.

Réunion (which depends on France for 80% of its arrivals) has not seen any significant growth in numbers since 2000. Mauritius has liberalized its air transport regime and is accepting more charter flights. It is focusing on developing its potential as a leisure, shopping and MICE destination for the booming Indian market. Seychelles is focusing on its status as an upmarket, environmentally friendly destination, but is aware of a shortage of hotel capacity.

Finally, there are several countries in East Africa whose political unrest make tourism more difficult. They include, in the Horn of Africa, Somalia, Eritrea and Ethiopia, and by association Djibouti, and in the Great Lakes region Rwanda and Burundi. But Ethiopia shows signs of being able to break out of this group – arrivals rose by 24% in 2005 to 227,000.

International Tourist Arrivals by Country of Destination

	Series	International Tourist Arrivals (1000)						Market share in the region (%)			Change (%)		Average annual growth (%)	
		1990	1995	2000	2003	2004	2005*	1990	2000	2005*	04/03	05*/04	90-00	00-05*
East Africa		2,842	4,752	6,338	7,206	7,614	8,059	18.7	22.7	21.6	5.7	5.8	8.4	4.9
Burundi	TF	109	34	29	74	133	148	0.7	0.1	0.4	79.8	11.4	-12.4	38.6
Comoros	TF	8	23	24	14	18	20	0.1	0.1	0.1	23.7	11.1	11.6	-4.0
Djibouti	TF	33	21	20	23	26	30	0.2	0.1	0.1	13.4	14.8	-4.8	8.5
Eritrea	VF	..	315	70	80	87	83		0.3	0.2	9.1	-4.6		3.5
Ethiopia	TF	79	103	136	180	184	227	0.5	0.5	0.6	2.3	23.5	5.6	10.8
Kenya	TF	814	896	899	927	1,193	1,536	5.4	3.2	4.1	28.7	28.8	1.0	11.3
Madagascar	TF	53	75	160	139	229	277	0.3	0.6	0.7	64.6	21.3	11.7	11.6
Malawi	TF	130	192	228	424	427	438	0.9	0.8	1.2	0.8	2.4	5.8	13.9
Mauritius	TF	292	422	656	702	719	761	1.9	2.4	2.0	2.4	5.9	8.4	3.0
Mozambique	TF	..	..	..	441	470	578			1.5	6.6	23.0		
Reunion	TF	200	304	430	432	430	409	1.3	1.5	1.1	-0.5	-4.9	8.0	-1.0
Rwanda	TF	..	..	104	..	..	..		0.4					
Seychelles	TF	104	121	130	122	121	129	0.7	0.5	0.3	-1.0	6.5	2.3	-0.2
Tanzania	TF	..	285	459	552	566	590		1.6	1.6	2.5	4.2		5.1
Uganda	TF	69	160	193	305	512	468	0.5	0.7	1.3	68.2	-8.7	10.8	19.4
Zambia	TF	141	163	457	413	515	669	0.9	1.6	1.8	24.8	29.9	12.5	7.9
Zimbabwe	VF	636	1,416	1,967	2,256	1,854	1,559	4.2	7.1	4.2	-17.8	-15.9	12.0	-4.5

Source: World Tourism Organization (UNWTO) ©   (Data as collected by UNWTO for TMT 2006 Edition)

East Africa seems to be having some success in diversifying its source markets. Individual countries are reporting large increases in arrivals from some countries in Asia and the Pacific, Eastern Europe and South America. Several countries also reported a recovery in arrivals from the USA and Canada.

International tourism receipts

In 2005, East Africa recorded US$ 4.1 billion in international tourism receipts – 19% of the total for Africa. Compared with 2004, receipts grew by 2% in local currencies at constant prices, and rose by 7% in US dollar terms (after a 24% increase in 2004). Again, the figures are distorted by Zimbabwe's totals, not least because of its unrealistic exchange rates – but not as much might be imagined, because of the low reported receipts per arrival. The government believes the industry is under-reporting its earnings, but the industry holds that high-yielding long-haul arrivals have collapsed, and that the remaining tourists are mainly low-spending cross-border visitors.

Mauritius remained the highest earner in 2005, taking in US$ 871 million – nearly a quarter of total East African receipts. This was an increase of 2% over 2004. Several countries reported very substantial increases in receipts in US dollar terms. In 2004 these included Ethiopia (+53%), Kenya (+40%), Uganda (+39%) and Madagascar (+27%). In 2005 they included Uganda (+49%), Mozambique (+36%) and Kenya (+19%). Rwanda and Burundi also reported very large increases for both years, but from very low bases.

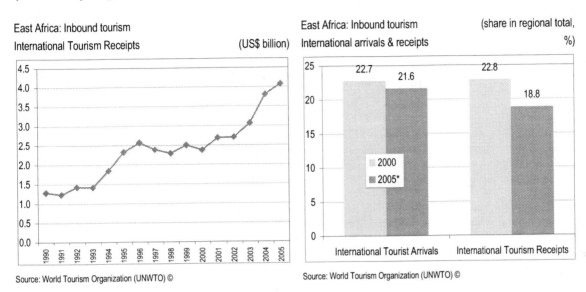

East Africa: Inbound tourism
International Tourism Receipts (US$ billion)

Source: World Tourism Organization (UNWTO) ©

East Africa: Inbound tourism
International arrivals & receipts (share in regional total, %)

Source: World Tourism Organization (UNWTO) ©

Receipts per arrival in East Africa for 2005 are estimated at US$ 505. The Seychelles, with its high-end tourism supply, took first place, earning nearly three times more per arrival than the subregional average – US$ 1,495. Other destinations with high receipts per arrival were Tanzania (US$ 1,395), Mauritius (US$ 1,145) and Réunion (US$ 1,080).

International Tourism Receipts by Country of Destination

	International Tourism Receipts (US$, million)						Market share in the region (%)			Change (%)		Receipts per arrival[1]	Receipts per capita[1]
	1990	1995	2000	2003	2004	2005*	1990	2000	2005*	04/03	05*/04		US$
East Africa	**1,285**	**2,323**	**2,377**	**3,065**	**3,802**	**4,074**	**20.1**	**22.8**	**18.8**	**24.0**	**7.2**	**505**	**15**
Burundi	4	1	1	1	1	2	0.1	0.0	0.0	71.4	25.0	10	0
Comoros	2	22	15	11	13	14	0.0	0.1	0.1	16.8	12.8	720	21
Djibouti	..	4	..	7	7	7			0.0	-1.8	4.3	235	15
Eritrea	..	58	36	74	73	66		0.3	0.3	-1.4	-9.6	790	14
Ethiopia	25	16	57	114	174	168	0.4	0.5	0.8	52.6	-3.3	740	2
Kenya	443	486	283	347	486	579	6.9	2.7	2.7	39.8	19.2	375	17
Madagascar	40	58	121	44	56	62	0.6	1.2	0.3	27.3	10.7	225	3
Malawi	16	17	25	23	24	24	0.2	0.2	0.1	2.9	-0.1	55	2
Mauritius	244	430	542	696	853	871	3.8	5.2	4.0	22.5	2.2	1,145	708
Mozambique	..	..	74	98	95	130		0.7	0.6	-2.4	36.0	225	7
Reunion	..	283	296	413	448	442		2.8	2.0	8.5	-1.3	1,080	569
Rwanda	10	2	4	26	44	49	0.2	0.0	0.2	69.1	11.4		6
Seychelles	126	129	139	171	172	192	2.0	1.3	0.9	0.3	11.9	1,495	2,366
Tanzania	65	502	377	647	746	824	1.0	3.6	3.8	15.4	10.4	1,395	22
Uganda	10	78	165	184	256	381	0.2	1.6	1.8	39.1	48.8	815	14
Zambia	41	47	111	149	161	164	0.6	1.1	0.8	8.1	1.9	245	15
Zimbabwe	60	145	125	61	194	99	0.9	1.2	0.5	217.5	-48.9	65	8

Source: World Tourism Organization (UNWTO) ©

(Data as collected by UNWTO for TMT 2006 Edition)

[1] Last year with data available

II.2.5 Southern Africa

International tourist arrivals

Southern Africa – a subregion which is dominated, in statistical terms, by South Africa – is second only to North Africa in number of arrivals. These increased by 3% in 2004 and 13% in 2005 to 11 million – i.e. considerably more slowly than the African average in 2004, but considerably faster in 2005. These 11 million arrivals represent 29% of total arrivals in African countries. The regional share of African arrivals increased dramatically between 1990 and 2000 (from 15% to 29%), but has since stabilized.

South Africa's 7.4 million arrivals represent two thirds of the subregional total, and it saw an increase of 10% in arrivals in 2005, after a modest 3% increase in 2004. Botswana, whose 1.7 million arrivals are very large in relation to a population of only 2 million, also saw a 10% increase in 2005, but in this case after a more robust 8% increase in 2004. Namibia's arrivals seem to have been growing more modestly since 2000, and Lesotho's have stagnated. Swaziland, however, reported an extraordinary 83% increase in arrivals at hotels and similar establishments in 2005 – these have increased by an average of 24.5% a year since 2000.

Southern Africa: Inbound tourism
International Tourist Arrivals   (million)

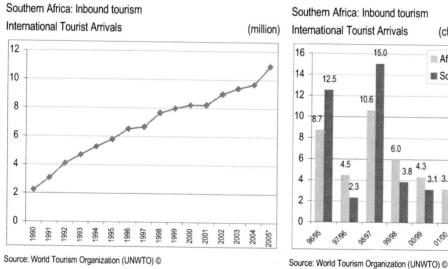

Source: World Tourism Organization (UNWTO) ©

Southern Africa: Inbound tourism
International Tourist Arrivals   (change over previous year, %)

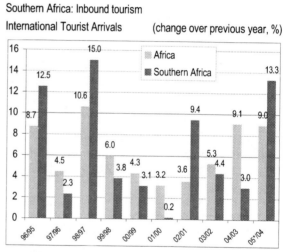

Source: World Tourism Organization (UNWTO) ©

International Tourist Arrivals by Country of Destination

	Series	International Tourist Arrivals (1000)						Market share in the region (%)			Change (%)		Average annual growth (%)	
		1990	1995	2000	2003	2004	2005*	1990	2000	2005*	04/03	05*/04	90-00	00-05*
Southern Africa		2,231	5,790	8,215	9,396	9,679	10,964	14.7	29.5	29.4	3.0	13.3	13.9	5.9
Botswana	TF	543	521	1,104	1,406	1,523	1,675	3.6	4.0	4.5	8.3	10.0	7.4	8.7
Lesotho	VF	242	209	302	329	304	304	1.6	1.1	0.8	-7.8	0.0	2.2	0.1
Namibia	TF	..	272	656	695	..	778		2.4	2.1				3.5
South Africa	TF	..	4,488	5,872	6,505	6,678	7,369		21.1	19.7	2.7	10.3		4.6
Swaziland	THS	263	300	281	461	459	839	1.7	1.0	2.2	-0.4	82.8	0.7	24.5

Source: World Tourism Organization (UNWTO) ©

(Data as collected by UNWTO for TMT 2006 Edition)

World Tourism Organization ©

South Africa continues to be the most visited destination on the African continent. However, the growth in arrivals has moderated since 2000 with a less than 5% growth a year in 2000-2005. Visitors from countries in Africa represented 73% of its total arrivals in 2005. However, there were substantial increases in arrivals from markets further afield, including the USA, Canada, India, Japan, Spain, Brazil and the Republic of Korea.

International tourism receipts

International tourism receipts in Southern Africa exceeded US$ 8.3 billion in 2005 – 39% of the African total. Southern Africa therefore ranks second to North Africa in terms of tourist arrivals, but first in terms of receipts. Southern Africa's receipts grew by 9% in local currencies at constant prices, or by 14% in US dollar terms.

The lion's share went to South Africa, with US$ 7.3 billion, followed by Botswana (US$ 562 million) and Namibia (US$ 348 million) some way behind the leader. South Africa enjoys by far the highest earnings among all African destinations. Its receipts increased by 14% in 2004 and by 17% in 2005. After large increases in 2004, Namibia's receipts fell back, while Botswana's stabilized.

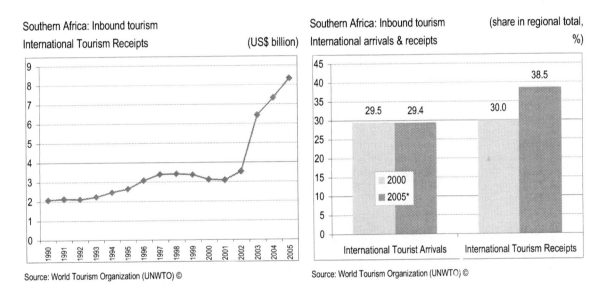

Southern Africa: Inbound tourism
International Tourism Receipts (US$ billion)

Southern Africa: Inbound tourism
International arrivals & receipts (share in regional total, %)

Source: World Tourism Organization (UNWTO) ©

Source: World Tourism Organization (UNWTO) ©

Southern Africa recorded an average US$ 760 in receipts per arrival in 2005, with South Africa earning the most per arrival (US$ 995). Namibia's count was US$ 445 and Botswana US$ 335.

International Tourism Receipts by Country of Destination

	International Tourism Receipts (US$, million)						Market share in the region (%)			Change (%)		Receipts per arrival[1]	Receipts per capita[1]
	1990	1995	2000	2003	2004	2005*	1990	2000	2005*	04/03	05*/04		US$
Southern Africa	**2,081**	**2,640**	**3,118**	**6,439**	**7,323**	**8,336**	**32.5**	**30.0**	**38.5**	**13.7**	**13.8**	**760**	**163**
Botswana	117	162	222	457	549	562	1.8	2.1	2.6	20.2	2.3	335	343
Lesotho	17	27	24	28	34	30	0.3	0.2	0.1	21.4	-11.8	100	15
Namibia	85	278	160	330	403	348	1.3	1.5	1.6	22.1	-13.8	445	171
South Africa	1,832	2,125	2,675	5,523	6,282	7,327	28.6	25.7	33.9	13.7	16.6	995	165
Swaziland	30	48	37	101	54	69	0.5	0.4	0.3	-46.5	27.8	80	61

Source: World Tourism Organization (UNWTO) ©   (Data as collected by UNWTO for TMT 2006 Edition)

[1] Last year with data available

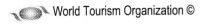

II.3 Tourism Trends in Mediterranean Destinations

International tourist arrivals in Mediterranean-bordering destinations – the world's leading tourism destination region – increased by 3% in 2004, accelerating further in 2005 to 260 million (+5%). This important region, comprising 25 countries, attracts almost one third of total international tourist arrivals worldwide. Over the past decade, emerging destinations in the East Mediterranean and North Africa have gained share – last year's solid performance is attributable in no small part to Turkey, for example – but the mature destinations of France, Spain and Italy still dominate arrivals, accounting together for slightly less than two thirds of the Mediterranean's total arrivals count.

Mediterranean tourism results 2005

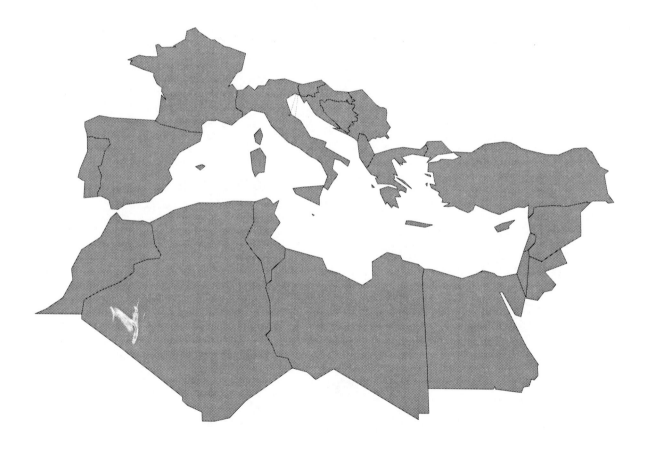

- *International Tourist Arrivals:*   *260 million*
- *International Tourism Receipts:*   *165 billion euros / US$ 205 billion*

World Tourism Organization ©

International Tourist Arrivals

The top five destinations in the Mediterranean, in terms of arrivals in 2005, were unchanged from the previous year – France, Spain, Italy, Turkey and Greece, in order of arrivals volume. Of the top three, Italy recorded a 2% decline and France managed only a 1% rise. But Spain achieved 7% growth, largely as a result of the boom in demand for low-cost airline (LCC) flights to the destination. The availability of LCCs has stimulated demand for short city breaks, contributing to a healthy diversification of Spain's market mix. It has also helped the country reduce its dependence on mass-market, low- yield "Sun & Beach" tourism.

Turkey was one of the region's best performers in terms of arrivals growth, up 21% on 2004's level. And, following a disappointing 2004, when the country's capital Athens hosted the summer Olympic Games, Greece recorded an arrivals increase of 7%, highlighting the fact that many would-be visitors stayed away during the actual Games. Like Greece, Portugal – in sixth position in the Mediterranean ranking – had also failed to maximize the expected growth potential of a major event in 2004, the Euro Footbal Cup.

In 2005, there were strong performances from Israel (+26%), Syria (+11%), Croatia, and Morocco (both +7%), as well as from a number of smaller destinations such as Serbia & Montenegro and Bosnia & Herzegovina. Lebanon was the only country to record a double-digit decline (-11%), this was due to the civil unrest and violence that started with the assassination of Lebanon's Prime Minister, Rafiq Hariri, on 14 February 2005. By contrast, slight decreases were only observed in two destinations: Italy (-1.5%) and Portugal (-0.3%).

Cyprus staged a recovery (+5%) following a disappointing 2004, thanks to concerted efforts to improve standards and ensure greater value for money. But both government and the industry believe the destination has suffered from two important factors: having to impose visa restrictions on growth markets such as Russia (following its entry into membership of the EU), and the lack of LCCs serving the destination. Israel had a second consecutive year of very healthy growth (+26%), hopefully reflecting a major step on the path to full recovery. But it is still early days, especially given the overall uncertainties in the region

European destinations in the Mediterranean region have generally benefited from LCCs and most say they cannot afford not to have them, because it makes them look much less attractive to potential holidaymakers. Some North African destinations, notably Morocco, are looking to attract LCCs to boost inbound tourism demand. But other Mediterranean destinations, like Malta, fear that the LCCs may use them simply as a hub, diverting tourists who might have stayed in the country to destinations further afield.

Following its outbreak in Turkey and apparent spread to the Aegean coast, there are understandably concerns about the spread of avian flu within bird populations, and the risk that the H5N1 virus might mutate, resulting in a possible human flu pandemic. While all evidence so far suggests that the new cases provide no indication that the virus can spread easily from human to human, UNWTO member countries have been developing contingency plans, under the leadership of the UNWTO Secretariat and the World Health Organization, to ensure they are ready for all eventualities.

Mediterranean: Inbound tourism
International Tourist Arrivals   (million)

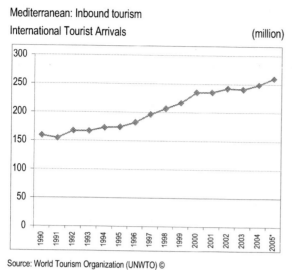

Source: World Tourism Organization (UNWTO) ©

Mediterranean: Inbound tourism
International Tourist Arrivals   (change over previous year, %)

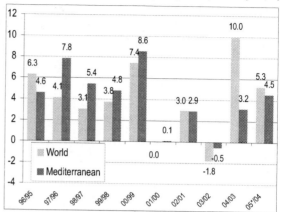

Source: World Tourism Organization (UNWTO) ©

International Tourist Arrivals by Country of Destination

	Series	International Tourist Arrivals (1000)						Market share in the region (%)			Change (%)		Average annual growth (%)	
		1990	1995	2000	2003	2004	2005*	1990	2000	2005*	04/03	05*/04	90-00	00-05*
Mediterranean		158,879	173,933	235,356	241,132	248,755	259,996	100	100	100	3.2	4.5	4.0	2.0
Portugal	TF	8,020	9,511	12,097	11,707	10,639	10,612	5.0	5.1	4.1	-9.1	-0.3	4.2	-2.6
Spain	TF	34,085	34,920	47,898	50,854	52,430	55,916	21.5	20.4	21.5	3.1	6.6	3.5	3.1
France	TF	52,497	60,033	77,190	75,048	75,121	75,910	33.0	32.8	29.2	0.1	1.1	3.9	-0.3
Monaco	THS	245	233	300	235	250	286	0.2	0.1	0.1	6.6	14.2	2.0	-1.0
Italy	TF	26,679	31,052	41,181	39,604	37,071	36,513	16.8	17.5	14.0	-6.4	-1.5	4.4	-2.4
Malta	TF	872	1,116	1,216	1,118	1,156	1,171	0.5	0.5	0.5	3.4	1.3	3.4	-0.8
Yugoslav SFR	TF	7,880	..	..	..	..	..	5.0						
Slovenia	TC	..	732	1,090	1,373	1,499	1,555		0.5	0.6	9.2	3.7		7.4
Croatia	TCE	..	1,485	5,831	7,409	7,912	8,467		2.5	3.3	6.8	7.0		7.7
Bosnia & Herzg	TCE	..	..	171	165	190	217		0.1	0.1	15.0	14.2		4.9
Serbia & Montenegro	TCE	..	228	239	481	580	725		0.1	0.3	20.5	25.0		24.8
Albania	THS	30	40	32	41	42	46	0.0	0.0	0.0	2.4	9.5	0.6	7.5
Greece	TF	8,873	10,130	13,096	13,969	13,313	14,276	5.6	5.6	5.5	-4.7	7.2	4.0	1.7
Turkey	TF	4,799	7,083	9,586	13,341	16,826	20,273	3.0	4.1	7.8	26.1	20.5	7.2	16.2
Cyprus	TF	1,561	2,100	2,686	2,303	2,349	2,470	1.0	1.1	1.0	2.0	5.2	5.6	-1.7
Syrian Arab Republic	TCE/TF	562	815	1,685	2,085	3,033	3,368	0.4	0.7	1.3	45.5	11.0	11.6	14.9
Lebanon	TF	..	450	742	1,016	1,278	1,140		0.3	0.4	25.9	-10.9		9.0
Israel	TF	1,063	2,215	2,417	1,063	1,506	1,903	0.7	1.0	0.7	41.6	26.4	8.6	-4.7
Palestine	THS	..	..	310	37	56	88		0.1	0.0	51.4	57.1		-22.3
Jordan	TF	572	1,075	1,580	2,353	2,853	2,987	0.4	0.7	1.1	21.2	4.7	10.7	13.6
Egypt	TF	2,411	2,871	5,116	5,746	7,795	8,244	1.5	2.2	3.2	35.7	5.8	7.8	10.0
Libyan Arab Jamahiriya	TF	96	56	174	142	149	..	0.1	0.1		4.9		6.1	
Tunisia	TF	3,204	4,120	5,058	5,114	5,998	6,378	2.0	2.1	2.5	17.3	6.3	4.7	4.7
Algeria	VF	1,137	520	866	1,166	1,234	1,443	0.7	0.4	0.6	5.8	17.0	-2.7	10.8
Morocco	TF	4,024	2,602	4,278	4,761	5,477	5,843	2.5	1.8	2.2	15.0	6.7	0.6	6.4

Source: World Tourism Organization (UNWTO) ©

(Data as collected by UNWTO for TMT 2006 Edition)

World Tourism Organization ©

International tourism receipts

International tourism receipts also showed good growth, increasing by 5.5% in both euro and US dollar terms, at current prices but only by 1.8% in local currencies, constant prices. Among the three leading destinations, Spain and France recorded an increase in receipts, but Italy's slipped slightly. However, the strongest growth was seen in countries in the Eastern Mediterranean and North Africa, including Albania, Cyprus, Israel, Libya, Morocco and Syria.

The euro is the official currency of five of the major tourism destinations in the Mediterranean – Spain (with receipts of 39 billion euros), France (34 billion euros), Italy (28 billion euros), Greece (11 billion euros) and Portugal (6 billion euros), accounting together for 72% of international tourism receipts generated in the region. The appreciation of the euro against the US dollar in 2004 (and therefore against many currencies in the Middle East and North Africa, which are either pegged to the US dollar or loosely associated with it) did not continue in 2005, but the high exchange rate of the euro sustained the price competitiveness of the Middle Eastern and North African destinations vis-à-vis their eurozone competitors.

International Tourism Receipts, Mediterranean

	International Tourism Receipts							Change current prices (%)				Change constant prices (%)			
							(billion)								
	1990	1995	2000	2002	2003	2004	2005*	02/01	03/02	04/03	05*/04	02/01	03/02	04/03	05*/04
Local currencies								1.2	3.6	5.9	4.7	-1.0	1.4	3.0	1.8
US$	76.2	114.9	138.0	143.2	169.7	194.6	205.3	5.1	18.5	14.7	5.5	3.5	15.9	11.7	2.0
Euro	59.8	87.9	149.4	151.4	150.0	156.4	165.0	-0.4	-0.9	4.3	5.5	-2.7	-3.0	2.1	3.2

Source: World Tourism Organization (UNWTO) ©   (Data as collected in UNWTO database November 2006)

Receipts per tourist arrival in the Mediterranean region averaged 635 euros in 2005, slightly below the European average of 640 euros and some 8% below the world average of 680 euros. However, this figure should only be used as a rough indicator since international tourism receipts not only account for expenditure by overnight visitors, but also for that of same-day visitors. The effect of the latter is in particular significant for many of the European destinations where cross-border traffic over land is substantial.

Mediterranean: Inbound tourism
International Tourism Receipts   (euro billion)

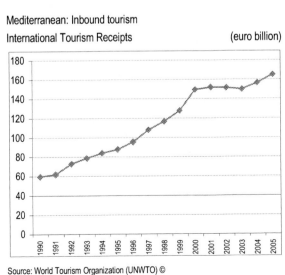

Source: World Tourism Organization (UNWTO) ©

Mediterranean: Inbound tourism
Receipts per Arrival, 2005   (euro)

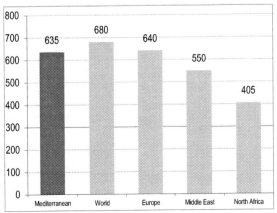

Source: World Tourism Organization (UNWTO) ©

Mediterranean: Inbound tourism
International Tourist Arrivals   (share in world total, %)

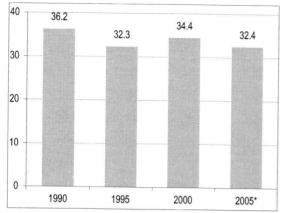

Source: World Tourism Organization (UNWTO) ©

Mediterranean: Inbound tourism
International Tourism Receipts   (share in world total, %)

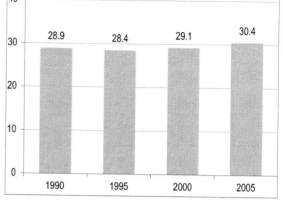

Source: World Tourism Organization (UNWTO) ©

International Tourism Receipts by Country of Destination

	International Tourism Receipts (euro, million)						Market share in the region (%)			Change (%)		Receipts per arrival[1]	Receipts per capita[1]
	1990	1995	2000	2003	2004	2005*	1990	2000	2005*	04/03	05*/04		euro
Mediterranean	59,799	87,855	149,446	150,004	156,439	165,040	100	100	100	4.3	5.5	635	349
Portugal	2,792	3,693	5,677	5,849	6,195	6,199	4.7	3.8	3.8	5.9	0.1	585	587
Spain	14,515	19,306	32,446	35,047	36,376	38,558	24.3	21.7	23.4	3.8	6.0	690	956
France	15,850	21,056	33,301	32,349	32,833	33,981	26.5	22.3	20.6	1.5	3.5	450	560
Italy	12,924	21,965	29,767	27,623	28,665	28,453	21.6	19.9	17.2	3.8	-0.7	780	490
Malta	389	500	639	638	622	610	0.7	0.4	0.4	-2.5	-1.9	520	1,530
Yugoslav SFR	2,178	..	..	..	..	..	3.6						
Slovenia	..	827	1,045	1,184	1,310	1,447		0.7	0.9	10.6	10.5	930	720
Croatia	..	1,031	3,012	5,573	5,506	5,999		2.0	3.6	-1.2	9.0	710	1,334
Bosnia & Herzg	..	..	252	332	388	413		0.2	0.3	16.8	6.4	1,900	93
Serbia & Montenegro	..	32	32	178	..	..		0.0				370	16
Albania	3	50	421	461	585	692	0.0	0.3	0.4	26.7	18.3	15,035	194
Greece	2,032	3,161	9,981	9,495	10,348	11,037	3.4	6.7	6.7	9.0	6.7	775	1,035
Turkey	2,533	3,790	8,268	11,672	12,773	14,590	4.2	5.5	8.8	9.4	14.2	720	209
Cyprus	988	1,375	2,102	1,848	1,811	1,874	1.7	1.4	1.1	-2.0	3.5	760	2,402
Syrian Arab Republic	251	962	1,171	683	1,447	1,748	0.4	0.8	1.1	111.8	20.8	520	95
Lebanon	..	..	..	5,635	4,350	4,366			2.6	-22.8	0.4	3,830	1,141
Israel	1,097	2,288	4,426	1,821	1,914	2,293	1.8	3.0	1.4	5.1	19.8	1,205	365
Palestine	..	195	306	95	45	..		0.2		-52.4		805	12
Jordan	402	505	783	939	1,069	1,158	0.7	0.5	0.7	13.9	8.3	390	201
Egypt	864	2,052	4,704	4,052	4,924	5,506	1.4	3.1	3.3	21.5	11.8	670	71
Libyan Arab Jamahiriya	5	2	81	181	175	201	0.0	0.1	0.1	-3.3	14.7	1,175	35
Tunisia	744	1,170	1,821	1,399	1,584	1,707	1.2	1.2	1.0	13.2	7.8	270	169
Algeria	82	25	104	99	144	148	0.1	0.1	0.1	44.9	3.1	100	5
Morocco	989	991	2,208	2,851	3,154	3,714	1.7	1.5	2.3	10.6	17.8	635	114

Source: World Tourism Organization (UNWTO) ©

(Data as collected by UNWTO for TMT 2006 Edition)

World Tourism Organization ©

51

III

Statistical Trends by Destination Country

III.1   North Africa

III.1.1   Algeria   North Africa

Promotional: www.algérie-tourisme.dz
Institutional/corporate: www.tourisme.dz

Profile

Algeria

Capital	Algiers
Year of entry in UNWTO	1976
Area (1000 km²)	2,382
Population (2005, million)	32.5
Gross Domestic Product (GDP) (2005, US$ million)	102,026
GDP per capita (2005, US$)	3,086

Africa
North Africa

GDP growth (real, %)
'-> 2004: 5.2;   2005: 5.3;   2006*: 4.9;   2007*: 5.0

	2003	2004	2005*	2004/2003	2005*/2004
International Arrivals					
Visitors (1000)	1,166	1,234	1,443	5.8	17.0
- per 100 of inhabitants	4	4	4		
Tourism accommodation					
Number of bed-places	77,473	82,034	83,895	5.9	2.3
Nights spent in hotels and similar establishments (1000)	4,319	4,543	4,705	5.2	3.6
by non-residents (inbound tourism)	371	394	483	6.2	22.6
by residents (domestic tourism)	3,948	4,149	4,222	5.1	1.8
Outbound Tourism					
Trips abroad (1000)	1,254	1,417	1,513	13.0	6.8
- per 100 of inhabitants	4	4	5		
Receipts and Expenditure for International Tourism					
International Tourism Receipts (US$ million)	112	179	184	59.4	3.1
- per Visitor Arrival (US$)	96	145	128	50.7	-11.9
- per capita (US$)	4	6	6		
International Tourism Expenditure (US$ million)	255	341	370	33.7	8.5
- per trip (US$)	203	241	245	18.3	1.6
- per capita (US$)	8	11	11		
Δ International Tourism Balance (US$ million)	-143	-162	-186		

Source: World Tourism Organization (UNWTO)   (Data as collected by UNWTO for TMT 2006 Edition)

See annex for methodological notes and reference of external sources used.

International Tourism by Origin

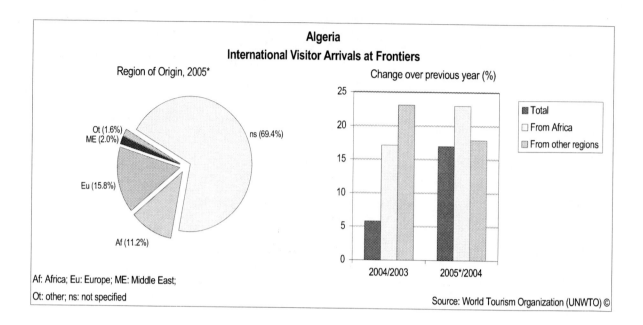

Af: Africa; Eu: Europe; ME: Middle East;
Ot: other; ns: not specified

Source: World Tourism Organization (UNWTO) ©

World Tourism Organization ©

Algeria
International Visitor Arrivals at Frontiers (by nationality)

	1995	2000	2003	2004	2005*	Market share (%) 2000	Market share (%) 2005*	Growth rate (%) 04/03	Growth rate (%) 05*/04	Average per year (%) 2000-2005*
Total	**519,576**	**865,984**	**1,166,287**	**1,233,719**	**1,443,090**	**100**	**100**	**5.8**	**17.0**	**10.8**
From Africa	*42,878*	*55,508*	*111,941*	*131,066*	*161,182*	*6.4*	*11.2*	*17.1*	*23.0*	*23.8*
Tunisia	24,207	32,481	86,025	103,593	128,765	3.8	8.9	20.4	24.3	31.7
Mali	5,874	8,857	14,453	11,520	12,817	1.0	0.9	-20.3	11.3	7.7
Morocco	4,797	3,805	4,186	5,424	9,984	0.4	0.7	29.6	84.1	21.3
Mauritania	1,967	1,489	1,596	1,914	3,028	0.2	0.2	19.9	58.2	15.3
Niger	1,507	1,751	1,343	2,025	1,262	0.2	0.1	50.8	-37.7	-6.3
Other Africa	4,526	7,125	4,338	6,590	5,326	0.8	0.4	51.9	-19.2	-5.7
From other regions	*54,772*	*120,030*	*192,973*	*237,496*	*280,024*	*13.9*	*19.4*	*23.1*	*17.9*	*18.5*
France	26,349	64,839	106,042	138,473	153,398	7.5	10.6	30.6	10.8	18.8
Spain	1,621	7,048	8,600	11,030	14,007	0.8	1.0	28.3	27.0	14.7
Italy	2,791	7,158	10,571	10,642	13,676	0.8	0.9	0.7	28.5	13.8
Libyan Arab Jamahiriya	7,698	4,851	9,391	10,007	11,803	0.6	0.8	6.6	17.9	19.5
Germany	1,398	4,784	7,049	7,306	9,392	0.6	0.7	3.6	28.6	14.4
United Kingdom	935	2,313	4,549	6,956	8,126	0.3	0.6	52.9	16.8	28.6
Turkey	663	2,081	3,741	6,013	7,548	0.2	0.5	60.7	25.5	29.4
Belgium	508	2,163	3,801	4,769	5,393	0.2	0.4	25.5	13.1	20.0
United States	1,286	1,312	2,098	3,321	3,549	0.2	0.2	58.3	6.9	22.0
Canada	416	1,435	2,255	2,655	3,305	0.2	0.2	17.7	24.5	18.2
Switzerland	353	1,753	2,558	2,345	2,905	0.2	0.2	-8.3	23.9	10.6
Japan	78	815	1,236	1,435	1,721	0.1	0.1	16.1	19.9	16.1
Portugal	122	427	1,049	920	1,571	0.0	0.1	-12.3	70.8	29.8
Netherlands	117	844	1,525	1,496	1,536	0.1	0.1	-1.9	2.7	12.7
Sweden	223	639	945	984	1,275	0.1	0.1	4.1	29.6	14.8
Austria	114	688	959	665	900	0.1	0.1	-30.7	35.3	5.5
Norway	35	176	291	464	776	0.0	0.1	59.5	67.2	34.5
Greece	237	279	395	384	518	0.0	0.0	-2.8	34.9	13.2
Denmark	93	250	458	592	513	0.0	0.0	29.3	-13.3	15.5
Australia	35	180	281	333	420	0.0	0.0	18.5	26.1	18.5
Finland	26	94	239	202	245	0.0	0.0	-15.5	21.3	21.1
Brazil	82	56	83	144	233	0.0	0.0	73.5	61.8	33.0
Mexico	22	74	85	150	227	0.0	0.0	76.5	51.3	25.1
Argentina	60	93	118	111	200	0.0	0.0	-5.9	80.2	16.5
Luxembourg	27	58	73	94	89	0.0	0.0	28.8	-5.3	8.9
Other interregional	9,483	15,620	24,581	26,005	36,698	1.8	2.5	5.8	41.1	18.6
Nationals residing abroad	*421,926*	*690,446*	*861,373*	*865,157*	*1,001,884*	*79.7*	*69.4*	*0.4*	*15.8*	*7.7*

Source: World Tourism Organization (UNWTO) ©   (Data as collected by UNWTO for TMT 2006 Edition)

III.1.2   Morocco   North Africa

Promotional: www.tourism-in-morocco.com ; www.tourisme-marocain.com
Institutional/corporate: www.tourisme.gov.ma
Research and data: www.tourisme.gov.ma

Profile

Morocco

Capital	Rabat
Year of entry in UNWTO	1975
Area (1000 km²)	447
Population (2005, million)	32.7
Gross Domestic Product (GDP) (2005, US$ million)	51,621
GDP per capita (2005, US$)	1,713
GDP growth (real, %)	

Africa
North Africa

'-> 2004: 4.2;   2005: 1.7;   2006*: 7.3;   2007*: 3.3

	2003	2004	2005*	2004/2003	2005*/2004
International Arrivals					
Visitors (1000)	5,021	5,732	6,077	14.2	6.0
Tourists (overnight visitors) (1000)	4,761	5,477	5,843	15.0	6.7
- per 100 of inhabitants	15	17	18		
Cruise passengers (1000)	260	256	233	-1.5	-9.0
Tourism accommodation					
Number of rooms	52,918	57,431	59,864	8.5	4.2
Nights spent in hotels and similar establishments (1000)	11,173	13,165	15,215	17.8	15.6
by non-residents (inbound tourism)	8,515	10,307	12,259	21.0	18.9
by residents (domestic tourism)	2,658	2,858	2,956	7.5	3.4
Outbound Tourism					
Trips abroad (1000)	1,612	1,603	2,247	-0.6	40.2
- per 100 of inhabitants	5	5	7		
Receipts and Expenditure for International Tourism					
International Tourism Receipts (US$ million)	3,225	3,924	4,621	21.6	17.8
- per Tourist Arrival (US$)	677	716	791	5.8	10.4
- per Visitor Arrival (US$)	642	684	760	6.6	11.1
- per capita (US$)	102	122	141		
International Fare Receipts (US$ million)	581	618	816	6.4	32.0
International Tourism Expenditure (US$ million)	548	575	614	4.9	6.9
- per trip (US$)	340	359	273	5.5	-23.8
- per capita (US$)	17	18	19		
International Fare Expenditure (US$ million)	297	338	387	13.8	14.5
Δ International Tourism Balance (US$ million)	2,677	3,349	4,007		
Δ International Fare Balance (US$ million)	284	280	429		

Source: World Tourism Organization (UNWTO)   (Data as collected by UNWTO for TMT 2006 Edition)

See annex for methodological notes and reference of external sources used.

World Tourism Organization ©

International Tourism by Origin

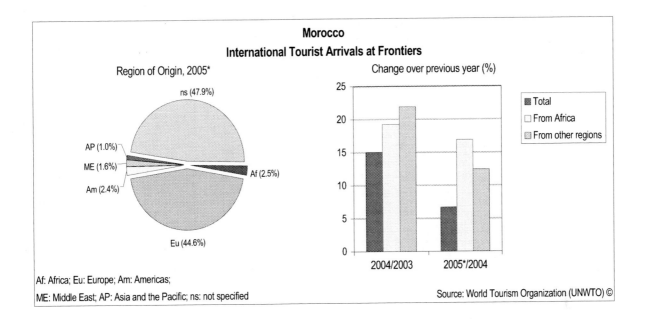

Morocco
International Tourist Arrivals at Frontiers

Region of Origin, 2005*

Change over previous year (%)

- Total
- From Africa
- From other regions

Af: Africa; Eu: Europe; Am: Americas;

ME: Middle East; AP: Asia and the Pacific; ns: not specified

Source: World Tourism Organization (UNWTO) ©

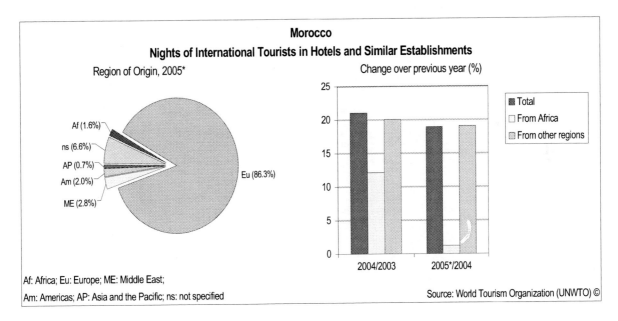

Morocco
Nights of International Tourists in Hotels and Similar Establishments

Region of Origin, 2005*

Change over previous year (%)

- Total
- From Africa
- From other regions

Af: Africa; Eu: Europe; ME: Middle East;

Am: Americas; AP: Asia and the Pacific; ns: not specified

Source: World Tourism Organization (UNWTO) ©

Morocco

International Tourist Arrivals at Frontiers (by nationality)

	1995	2000	2003	2004	2005*	Market share (%) 2000	Market share (%) 2005*	Growth rate (%) 04/03	Growth rate (%) 05*/04	Average per year (%) 2000-2005*
Total	2,601,641	4,278,120	4,761,271	5,476,712	5,843,360	100	100	15.0	6.7	6.4
From Africa	66,258	88,689	103,194	123,070	143,855	2.1	2.5	19.3	16.9	10.2
Algeria	13,178	20,251	23,095	29,744	37,298	0.5	0.6	28.8	25.4	13.0
Tunisia	27,689	26,495	24,645	23,904	25,709	0.6	0.4	-3.0	7.6	-0.6
Senegal	5,355	7,775	10,674	16,208	20,922	0.2	0.4	51.8	29.1	21.9
Mauritania	4,326	5,886	15,913	18,895	20,889	0.1	0.4	18.7	10.6	28.8
Guinea	2,755	5,926	8,907	11,218	10,175	0.1	0.2	25.9	-9.3	11.4
Côte d'Ivoire	1,568	1,969	3,314	4,121	5,982	0.0	0.1	24.4	45.2	24.9
Mali	3,893	6,145	4,507	4,679	5,603	0.1	0.1	3.8	19.7	-1.8
South Africa	1,586	3,072	1,950	2,233	3,093	0.1	0.1	14.5	38.5	0.1
Congo	107	1,350	1,346	1,747	2,288	0.0	0.0	29.8	31.0	11.1
Niger	799	1,887	1,366	1,496	2,161	0.0	0.0	9.5	44.5	2.7
Gabon	1,302	1,203	1,016	1,266	1,955	0.0	0.0	24.6	54.4	10.2
Other intraregional	3,700	6,730	6,461	7,559	7,780	0.2	0.1	17.0	2.9	2.9
From other regions	1,455,696	2,230,277	2,113,727	2,577,109	2,897,930	52.1	49.6	21.9	12.4	5.4
France	421,890	813,865	916,147	1,167,088	1,337,204	19.0	22.9	27.4	14.6	10.4
Spain	199,133	232,245	231,156	317,119	367,811	5.4	6.3	37.2	16.0	9.6
United Kingdom	128,913	137,247	134,059	150,398	193,565	3.2	3.3	12.2	28.7	7.1
Germany	161,748	211,039	129,391	141,210	144,200	4.9	2.5	9.1	2.1	-7.3
Belgium	44,102	79,918	80,062	105,821	125,890	1.9	2.2	32.2	19.0	9.5
Italy	101,212	142,426	100,001	112,807	120,955	3.3	2.1	12.8	7.2	-3.2
United States	80,168	121,068	64,445	76,889	82,980	2.8	1.4	19.3	7.9	-7.3
Netherlands	44,615	59,436	66,486	73,190	80,090	1.4	1.4	10.1	9.4	6.1
Switzerland	25,586	44,556	42,173	41,758	46,508	1.0	0.8	-1.0	11.4	0.9
Portugal	16,472	31,302	36,389	38,951	36,980	0.7	0.6	7.0	-5.1	3.4
Canada	24,725	34,320	27,606	31,321	36,825	0.8	0.6	13.5	17.6	1.4
Saudi Arabia	26,957	31,749	28,921	31,478	36,406	0.7	0.6	8.8	15.7	2.8
Sweden	12,000	29,725	24,094	26,723	26,638	0.7	0.5	10.9	-0.3	-2.2
Japan	17,206	23,643	13,982	15,723	17,044	0.6	0.3	12.5	8.4	-6.3
Austria	12,489	23,297	12,798	13,561	14,634	0.5	0.3	6.0	7.9	-8.9
Ireland	6,803	10,943	15,166	18,112	13,202	0.3	0.2	19.4	-27.1	3.8
Australia	4,505	11,636	10,047	12,544	12,327	0.3	0.2	24.9	-1.7	1.2
Turkey	3,031	4,616	8,012	7,900	12,161	0.1	0.2	-1.4	53.9	21.4
Denmark	7,669	14,619	15,593	15,143	12,115	0.3	0.2	-2.9	-20.0	-3.7
Egypt	4,290	9,427	9,648	9,890	11,553	0.2	0.2	2.5	16.8	4.2
Poland	5,535	8,628	5,457	8,913	10,632	0.2	0.2	63.3	19.3	4.3
Norway	6,258	21,826	17,651	13,988	10,585	0.5	0.2	-20.8	-24.3	-13.5
Libyan Arab Jamahiriya	11,369	11,357	9,572	9,426	9,653	0.3	0.2	-1.5	2.4	-3.2
Finland	19,084	11,765	9,661	10,012	9,290	0.3	0.2	3.6	-7.2	-4.6
Russian Federation	4,915	8,089	8,039	11,318	8,670	0.2	0.1	40.8	-23.4	1.4
Other interregional	65,021	101,535	97,171	115,826	120,012	2.4	2.1	19.2	3.6	3.4
Nationals residing abroad	1,077,522	1,952,615	2,537,396	2,769,132	2,787,825	45.6	47.7	9.1	0.7	7.4
Other World/Not specified	2,165	6,539	6,954	7,401	13,750	0.2	0.2	6.4	85.8	16.0

Source: World Tourism Organization (UNWTO) ©

(Data as collected by UNWTO for TMT 2006 Edition)

Morocco

Nights of International Tourists in Hotels and Similar Establishments (by nationality)

	1995	2000	2003	2004	2005*	Market share (%) 2000	Market share (%) 2005*	Growth rate (%) 04/03	Growth rate (%) 05*/04	Average per year (%) 2000-2005*
Total	**8,501,511**	**13,251,700**	**8,515,293**	**10,307,268**	**12,259,489**	**100**	**100**	**21.0**	**18.9**	**-1.5**
From Africa	*309,432*	*261,058*	*172,589*	*193,527*	*195,873*	*2.0*	*1.6*	*12.1*	*1.2*	*-5.6*
All Africa	309,432	..	..	..	..					
Algeria	..	37,243	33,478	54,997	59,556	0.3	0.5	64.3	8.3	9.8
Tunisia	..	50,623	38,882	38,582	42,085	0.4	0.3	-0.8	9.1	-3.6
Mauritania	..	88,713	21,929	17,159	9,327	0.7	0.1	-21.8	-45.6	-36.3
Other Africa	..	84,479	78,300	82,789	84,905	0.6	0.7	5.7	2.6	0.1
From other regions	*7,719,360*	*12,344,211*	*7,875,443*	*9,456,135*	*11,259,660*	*93.2*	*91.8*	*20.1*	*19.1*	*-1.8*
France	2,189,394	5,400,395	4,329,870	5,240,184	6,231,344	40.8	50.8	21.0	18.9	2.9
Germany	2,262,641	2,048,457	761,604	823,916	904,777	15.5	7.4	8.2	9.8	-15.1
United Kingdom	742,220	679,591	450,654	567,385	860,904	5.1	7.0	25.9	51.7	4.8
Spain	376,179	728,886	354,495	559,481	699,362	5.5	5.7	57.8	25.0	-0.8
Belgium	250,295	514,864	356,957	498,876	624,088	3.9	5.1	39.8	25.1	3.9
Italy	641,043	867,381	439,014	519,290	568,695	6.5	4.6	18.3	9.5	-8.1
Scandinavia	248,536	..	..	..	..					
All Middle East	240,145	..	..	..	..					
United States	260,216	390,824	133,333	153,725	184,634	2.9	1.5	15.3	20.1	-13.9
Netherlands	132,655	194,897	136,800	140,202	181,167	1.5	1.5	2.5	29.2	-1.5
Saudi Arabia	..	175,708	131,269	155,768	158,516	1.3	1.3	18.7	1.8	-2.0
Switzerland	162,631	213,793	129,539	131,133	145,623	1.6	1.2	1.2	11.0	-7.4
Sweden	..	240,368	112,706	125,153	117,957	1.8	1.0	11.0	-5.7	-13.3
Portugal	61,247	121,641	91,840	70,718	88,862	0.9	0.7	-23.0	25.7	-6.1
Japan	75,052	130,139	61,275	70,596	84,436	1.0	0.7	15.2	19.6	-8.3
Canada	77,106	101,731	43,293	46,609	57,927	0.8	0.5	7.7	24.3	-10.7
Finland	..	67,994	49,967	45,914	43,747	0.5	0.4	-8.1	-4.7	-8.4
Austria	..	72,425	40,432	48,790	41,161	0.5	0.3	20.7	-15.6	-10.7
Denmark	..	68,370	34,278	36,137	39,044	0.5	0.3	5.4	8.0	-10.6
Egypt	..	29,027	27,528	26,041	31,850	0.2	0.3	-5.4	22.3	1.9
Norway	..	120,124	38,340	27,961	21,080	0.9	0.2	-27.1	-24.6	-29.4
Untd Arab Emirates	..	10,609	15,945	16,213	16,761	0.1	0.1	1.7	3.4	9.6
Libyan Arab Jamahiriya	..	37,447	17,284	14,765	16,494	0.3	0.1	-14.6	11.7	-15.1
Commonwealth Indep. States	..	19,191	26,839	32,766	15,829	0.1	0.1	22.1	-51.7	-3.8
Syrian Arab Republic	..	9,323	8,556	10,446	13,012	0.1	0.1	22.1	24.6	6.9
Other interregional	..	101,026	83,625	94,066	112,390	0.8	0.9	12.5	19.5	2.2
Nationals residing abroad	*..*	*30,374*	*25,195*	*23,956*	*34,030*	*0.2*	*0.3*	*-4.9*	*42.1*	*2.3*
Other World/Not specified	*472,719*	*616,057*	*442,066*	*633,650*	*769,926*	*4.6*	*6.3*	*43.3*	*21.5*	*4.6*

Source: World Tourism Organization (UNWTO) ©   (Data as collected by UNWTO for TMT 2006 Edition)

III.1.3   Sudan   North Africa

Profile

Sudan

Capital	Khartoum
Year of entry in UNWTO	1975
Area (1000 km²)	2,506
Population (2005, million)	40.2
Gross Domestic Product (GDP) (2005, US$ million)	27,542
GDP per capita (2005, US$)	820

Africa
North Africa

GDP growth (real, %)
› 2004: 5.2;   2005: 7.9;   2006*: 12.1;   2007*: 11.3

	2003	2004	2005*	2004/2003	2005*/2004
International Arrivals					
Tourists (overnight visitors) (1000)	52	61	246	15.8	305.8
- per 100 of inhabitants	0	0	1		
Tourism accommodation					
Number of rooms	..	4,200	4,200		
Receipts and Expenditure for International Tourism					
International Tourism Receipts (US$ million)	18	21	89	16.7	324.4
- per Tourist Arrival (US$)	344	347	363	0.7	4.6
- per capita (US$)	0	1	2		
International Tourism Expenditure (US$ million)	119	176	667	47.9	279.2
- per capita (US$)	3	4	17		
Δ International Tourism Balance (US$ million)	-101	-155	-578		

Source: World Tourism Organization (UNWTO)   (Data as collected by UNWTO for TMT 2006 Edition)
See annex for methodological notes and reference of external sources used.

International Tourism by Origin

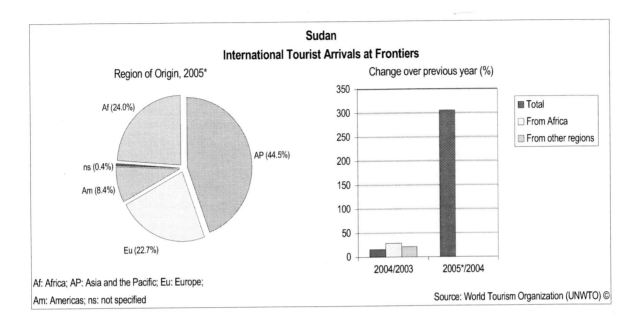

Sudan
International Tourist Arrivals at Frontiers

Region of Origin, 2005*

Af (24.0%)
ns (0.4%)
Am (8.4%)
AP (44.5%)
Eu (22.7%)

Change over previous year (%)

- Total
- From Africa
- From other regions

Af: Africa; AP: Asia and the Pacific; Eu: Europe;
Am: Americas; ns: not specified

Source: World Tourism Organization (UNWTO) ©

Sudan

International Tourist Arrivals at Frontiers (by nationality)

	1995	2000	2003	2004	2005*	Market share (%) 2000	Market share (%) 2005*	Growth rate (%) 04/03	Growth rate (%) 05*/04	Average per year (%) 2000-2005*
Total	63,040	38,000	52,291	60,577	245,798	100	100	15.8	305.8	45.3
From Africa	5,715	5,000	7,000	9,000	58,991	13.2	24.0	28.6	555.5	63.8
All Africa	..	5,000	7,000	9,000	58,991	13.2	24.0	28.6	555.5	63.8
Ethiopia	3,215	..	..	..	..					
Other Africa	2,500	..	..	..	..					
From other regions	51,725	33,000	28,000	34,000	185,927	86.8	75.6	21.4	446.8	41.3
All Asia	..	7,000	14,000	17,000	109,380	18.4	44.5	21.4	543.4	73.3
All Europe	..	9,000	14,000	17,000	55,796	23.7	22.7	21.4	228.2	44.0
All Americas	..	4,000	..	..	20,751	10.5	8.4			39.0
All Middle East	..	9,000	..	..	..	23.7				
All South Asia	..	4,000	..	..	..	10.5				
China	3,534	..	..	..	..					
Egypt	3,283	..	..	..	..					
Canada	3,237	..	..	..	..					
United States	3,125	..	..	..	..					
France	2,235	..	..	..	..					
Japan	2,158	..	..	..	..					
Greece	2,155	..	..	..	..					
All South America	2,110	..	..	..	..					
Yemen	1,795	..	..	..	..					
India	1,725	..	..	..	..					
Saudi Arabia	1,520	..	..	..	..					
Germany	1,322	..	..	..	..					
Pakistan	1,295	..	..	..	..					
Switzerland	1,235	..	..	..	..					
Lebanon	1,230	..	..	..	..					
Australia	1,225	..	..	..	..					
Netherlands	1,153	..	..	..	..					
Bulgaria	1,095	..	..	..	..					
Italy	1,092	..	..	..	..					
United Kingdom	1,022	..	..	..	..					
Other interregional	14,179	..	..	..	..					
Other World/Not specified	5,600	..	17,291	17,577	880		0.4	1.7	-95.0	

Source: World Tourism Organization (UNWTO) ©

(Data as collected by UNWTO for TMT 2006 Edition)

III.1.4   Tunisia   North Africa

Promotional: www.tourismtunisia.com

Profile

Tunisia

Capital	Tunis
Year of entry in UNWTO	1975
Area (1000 km²)	164
Population (2005, million)	10.1
Gross Domestic Product (GDP) (2005, US$ million)	28,674
GDP per capita (2005, US$)	2,829

Africa
North Africa

GDP growth (real, %)
'-> 2004: 6.0;   2005: 4.2;   2006*: 5.8;   2007*: 6.0

	2003	2004	2005*	2004/2003	2005*/2004
International Arrivals					
Visitors (1000)	5,492	6,419	6,975	16.9	8.7
Tourists (overnight visitors) (1000)	5,114	5,998	6,378	17.3	6.3
- per 100 of inhabitants	52	60	63		
Cruise passengers (1000)	378	421	597	11.4	41.8
Tourism accommodation					
Number of rooms	111,009	113,076	114,919	1.9	1.6
Nights spent in hotels and similar establishments (1000)	28,110	33,487	36,310	19.1	8.4
by non-residents (inbound tourism)	25,301	30,665	33,587	21.2	9.5
by residents (domestic tourism)	2,809	2,822	2,723	0.5	-3.5
Outbound Tourism					
Trips abroad (1000)	2,274	2,312	2,241	1.7	-3.1
- per 100 of inhabitants	23	23	22		
Receipts and Expenditure for International Tourism					
International Tourism Receipts (US$ million)	1,582	1,970	2,063	24.5	4.7
- per Tourist Arrival (US$)	309	329	323	6.2	-1.5
- per Visitor Arrival (US$)	288	307	296	6.5	-3.6
- per capita (US$)	160	198	205		
International Fare Receipts (US$ million)	352	462	658	31.3	42.4
International Tourism Expenditure (US$ million)	300	340	385	13.2	13.1
- per trip (US$)	132	147	172	11.4	16.7
- per capita (US$)	30	34	38		
International Fare Expenditure (US$ million)	56	87	78	55.9	-10.3
Δ International Tourism Balance (US$ million)	1,282	1,630	1,679		
Δ International Fare Balance (US$ million)	296	375	580		

Source: World Tourism Organization (UNWTO)   (Data as collected by UNWTO for TMT 2006 Edition)

See annex for methodological notes and reference of external sources used.

International Tourism by Origin

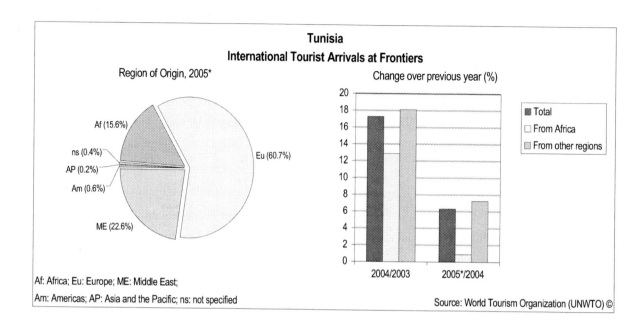

Tunisia
International Tourist Arrivals at Frontiers

Region of Origin, 2005*

Af (15.6%)
ns (0.4%)
AP (0.2%)
Am (0.6%)
Eu (60.7%)
ME (22.6%)

Change over previous year (%)

- Total
- From Africa
- From other regions

2004/2003   2005*/2004

Af: Africa; Eu: Europe; ME: Middle East;
Am: Americas; AP: Asia and the Pacific; ns: not specified

Source: World Tourism Organization (UNWTO) ©

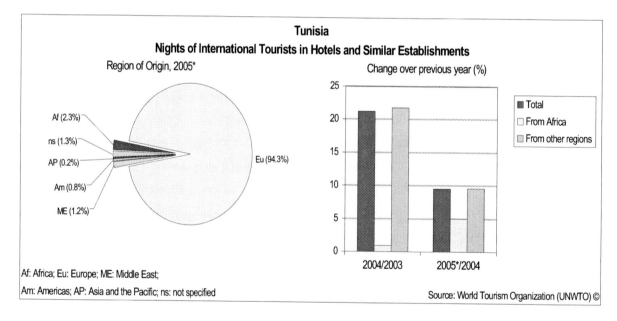

Tunisia
Nights of International Tourists in Hotels and Similar Establishments

Region of Origin, 2005*

Af (2.3%)
ns (1.3%)
AP (0.2%)
Am (0.8%)
ME (1.2%)
Eu (94.3%)

Change over previous year (%)

- Total
- From Africa
- From other regions

2004/2003   2005*/2004

Af: Africa; Eu: Europe; ME: Middle East;
Am: Americas; AP: Asia and the Pacific; ns: not specified

Source: World Tourism Organization (UNWTO) ©

World Tourism Organization ©

Tunisia
International Tourist Arrivals at Frontiers (by nationality)

	1995	2000	2003	2004	2005*	Market share (%) 2000	Market share (%) 2005*	Growth rate (%) 04/03	Growth rate (%) 05*/04	Average per year (%) 2000-2005*
Total	**4,119,847**	**5,057,513**	**5,114,304**	**5,997,929**	**6,378,435**	**100**	**100**	**17.3**	**6.3**	**4.8**
From Africa	*1,034,479*	*666,199*	*872,251*	*984,538*	*993,378*	*13.2*	*15.6*	*12.9*	*0.9*	*8.3*
Algeria	988,608	611,620	811,463	914,064	930,715	12.1	14.6	12.6	1.8	8.8
Morocco	26,689	37,689	35,003	35,897	29,912	0.7	0.5	2.6	-16.7	-4.5
Mauritania	6,367	5,558	6,962	8,111	7,871	0.1	0.1	16.5	-3.0	7.2
Sudan	..	387	691	774	1,038	0.0	0.0	12.0	34.1	21.8
Other Africa	12,815	10,945	18,132	25,692	23,842	0.2	0.4	41.7	-7.2	16.8
From other regions	*3,046,434*	*4,367,956*	*4,228,791*	*4,994,935*	*5,358,334*	*86.4*	*84.0*	*18.1*	*7.3*	*4.2*
Libyan Arab Jamahiriya	618,746	685,208	1,325,660	1,435,785	1,404,007	13.5	22.0	8.3	-2.2	15.4
France	465,103	997,882	833,989	1,020,810	1,170,100	19.7	18.3	22.4	14.6	3.2
Germany	837,116	1,011,298	488,481	569,475	571,934	20.0	9.0	16.6	0.4	-10.8
Italy	245,933	393,891	379,773	448,292	472,768	7.8	7.4	18.0	5.5	3.7
United Kingdom	239,567	299,376	223,189	300,784	327,542	5.9	5.1	34.8	8.9	1.8
Belgium	74,198	139,846	132,596	140,790	155,082	2.8	2.4	6.2	10.2	2.1
Spain	33,289	102,828	78,223	114,871	146,404	2.0	2.3	46.9	27.5	7.3
Czech Rep	32,749	54,762	90,038	128,404	145,881	1.1	2.3	42.6	13.6	21.6
Poland	19,772	49,837	54,443	75,133	122,627	1.0	1.9	38.0	63.2	19.7
Russian Federation	12,967	20,979	73,376	99,406	96,175	0.4	1.5	35.5	-3.3	35.6
Switzerland	74,539	118,449	85,765	99,117	92,766	2.3	1.5	15.6	-6.4	-4.8
Austria	65,036	110,160	70,065	84,383	86,412	2.2	1.4	20.4	2.4	-4.7
Netherlands	70,507	67,587	44,490	53,683	66,096	1.3	1.0	20.7	23.1	-0.4
Scandinavia	59,663	..	..	..	..					
Hungary	19,687	33,445	55,532	52,895	58,546	0.7	0.9	-4.7	10.7	11.8
Slovakia	6,970	18,412	21,898	34,733	39,966	0.4	0.6	58.6	15.1	16.8
Portugal	13,601	17,668	28,197	35,795	38,901	0.3	0.6	26.9	8.7	17.1
Denmark	..	19,574	10,487	17,266	36,982	0.4	0.6	64.6	114.2	13.6
Sweden	..	24,651	23,286	34,328	36,428	0.5	0.6	47.4	6.1	8.1
Ireland	13,275	32,945	22,713	20,736	21,163	0.7	0.3	-8.7	2.1	-8.5
Finland	..	18,257	11,009	13,942	19,902	0.4	0.3	26.6	42.7	1.7
Yugoslav SFR	4,676	6,986	14,419	15,325	19,795	0.1	0.3	6.3	29.2	23.2
Norway	..	13,312	25,599	15,273	18,711	0.3	0.3	-40.3	22.5	7.0
Canada	13,318	14,902	11,913	15,803	17,039	0.3	0.3	32.7	7.8	2.7
United States	11,499	16,373	10,279	13,205	15,737	0.3	0.2	28.5	19.2	-0.8
Other interregional	114,223	99,328	113,371	154,701	177,370	2.0	2.8	36.5	14.7	12.3
Other World/Not specified	*38,934*	*23,358*	*13,262*	*18,456*	*26,723*	*0.5*	*0.4*	*39.2*	*44.8*	*2.7*

Source: World Tourism Organization (UNWTO) ©   (Data as collected by UNWTO for TMT 2006 Edition)

Tunisia

Nights of International Tourists in Hotels and Similar Establishments (by nationality)

	1995	2000	2003	2004	2005*	Market share (%) 2000	Market share (%) 2005*	Growth rate (%) 04/03	Growth rate (%) 05*/04	Average per year (%) 2000-2005*
Total	23,514,405	33,168,301	25,301,322	30,664,500	33,587,183	100	100	21.2	9.5	0.3
From Africa	682,609	563,431	726,309	732,914	769,590	1.7	2.3	0.9	5.0	6.4
Algeria	592,398	437,757	581,137	564,544	630,719	1.3	1.9	-2.9	11.7	7.6
Morocco	50,952	59,135	52,119	54,045	44,500	0.2	0.1	3.7	-17.7	-5.5
Other Africa	39,259	66,539	93,053	114,325	94,371	0.2	0.3	22.9	-17.5	7.2
From other regions	22,656,274	32,288,498	24,265,994	29,545,312	32,378,575	97.3	96.4	21.8	9.6	0.1
France	3,546,073	7,205,700	5,671,187	6,835,348	7,798,901	21.7	23.2	20.5	14.1	1.6
Germany	10,282,862	11,284,300	5,498,718	6,535,380	6,641,427	34.0	19.8	18.9	1.6	-10.1
Italy	1,860,574	2,922,107	2,711,719	3,251,102	3,393,580	8.8	10.1	19.9	4.4	3.0
United Kingdom	2,303,954	3,036,300	2,289,934	2,963,841	3,234,237	9.2	9.6	29.4	9.1	1.3
Belgium	654,794	1,306,600	1,267,594	1,395,542	1,492,812	3.9	4.4	10.1	7.0	2.7
Czech Rep	322,677	503,709	984,417	1,288,584	1,432,338	1.5	4.3	30.9	11.2	23.2
Russian Federation	88,409	190,827	859,273	1,181,314	1,210,330	0.6	3.6	37.5	2.5	44.7
Spain	232,448	753,359	626,072	863,780	1,139,270	2.3	3.4	38.0	31.9	8.6
Poland	136,937	481,044	524,725	748,308	1,135,783	1.5	3.4	42.6	51.8	18.7
Switzerland	700,424	1,062,200	649,799	739,582	605,240	3.2	1.8	13.8	-18.2	-10.6
Scandinavia	478,839	617,800	..	..	..	1.9				
Austria	480,437	819,600	465,220	544,331	515,557	2.5	1.5	17.0	-5.3	-8.9
Netherlands	640,413	540,700	329,628	364,455	443,862	1.6	1.3	10.6	21.8	-3.9
Hungary	110,641	194,788	357,055	388,071	375,856	0.6	1.1	8.7	-3.1	14.0
Sweden	..	..	193,718	258,070	301,314		0.9	33.2	16.8	
Slovakia	18,609	88,847	133,816	217,774	295,534	0.3	0.9	62.7	35.7	27.2
Denmark	..	..	78,565	123,591	284,395		0.8	57.3	130.1	
Libyan Arab Jamahiriya	179,511	234,700	256,658	247,209	242,810	0.7	0.7	-3.7	-1.8	0.7
Canada	88,961	157,126	132,463	195,352	200,195	0.5	0.6	47.5	2.5	5.0
Finland	..	..	114,222	142,074	184,770		0.6	24.4	30.1	
Luxembourg	64,696	103,785	113,472	155,952	179,088	0.3	0.5	37.4	14.8	11.5
Yugoslav SFR	18,048	47,199	92,011	129,266	151,120	0.1	0.4	40.5	16.9	26.2
Norway	..	..	237,582	122,271	133,971		0.4	-48.5	9.6	
Portugal	75,955	85,200	88,140	143,148	116,162	0.3	0.3	62.4	-18.9	6.4
Malta	10,094	24,838	51,515	61,872	95,060	0.1	0.3	20.1	53.6	30.8
Other interregional	360,918	627,769	538,491	649,095	774,963	1.9	2.3	20.5	19.4	4.3
Nationals residing abroad	..	..	7,036	12,328	17,239		0.1	75.2	39.8	
Other World/Not specified	175,522	316,372	301,983	373,946	421,779	1.0	1.3	23.8	12.8	5.9

Source: World Tourism Organization (UNWTO) ©

(Data as collected by UNWTO for TMT 2006 Edition)

III.2   West Africa

III.2.1   Benin   West Africa

Promotional: www.benintourisme.com
Institutional/corporate: www.benintourisme.com ; www.penjari.net
Research and data: www.benintourisme.com

Profile

Benin

Capital	Porto-Novo
Year of entry in UNWTO	1975
Area (1000 km²)	113
Population (2005, million)	7.6
Gross Domestic Product (GDP) (2005, US$ million)	4,406
GDP per capita (2005, US$)	592

Africa
West Africa

GDP growth (real, %)
'-> 2004: 3.1;   2005: 2.9;   2006*: 4.5;   2007*: 5.1

	2003	2004	2005*	2004/2003	2005*/2004
International Arrivals					
Visitors (1000)	850	845	960	-0.6	13.6
Tourists (overnight visitors) (1000)	175	174	176	-0.9	1.4
- per 100 of inhabitants	2	2	2		
Tourism accommodation					
Nights spent in collective establishments (1000)					
by non-residents (inbound tourism)	219	215	348	-1.8	61.9
Receipts and Expenditure for International Tourism					
International Tourism Receipts (US$ million)	106	119	..	12.3	
- per Tourist Arrival (US$)	606	686	..	13.2	
- per Visitor Arrival (US$)	125	141	..	12.9	
- per capita (US$)	15	16	..		
International Fare Receipts (US$ million)	2	3	..	52.6	
International Tourism Expenditure (US$ million)	21	29	..	38.1	
- per capita (US$)	3	4	..		
International Fare Expenditure (US$ million)	32	30	..	-6.3	
Δ International Tourism Balance (US$ million)	85	90	..		
Δ International Fare Balance (US$ million)	-30	-27	..		

Source: World Tourism Organization (UNWTO)   (Data as collected by UNWTO for TMT 2006 Edition)
See annex for methodological notes and reference of external sources used.

International Tourism by Origin

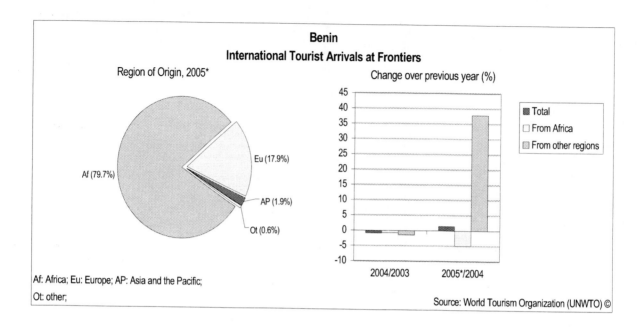

Benin
International Tourist Arrivals at Frontiers

Region of Origin, 2005*

Af (79.7%)
Eu (17.9%)
AP (1.9%)
Ot (0.6%)

Af: Africa; Eu: Europe; AP: Asia and the Pacific;
Ot: other;

Change over previous year (%)

- Total
- From Africa
- From other regions

Source: World Tourism Organization (UNWTO) ©

Benin

Nights of International Tourists in All Accommodation Establishments (by residence)

| | 1995 | 2000 | 2002 | 2003 | 2004 | Market share (%) | | Growth rate (%) | | Average per year (%) |
						2000	2004	03/02	04/03	2000-2004
Total	313,799	199,626	..	..	..	100				
From Africa	207,499	121,067	..	..	..	60.6				
All Africa	207,499	121,067	..	..	..	60.6				
From other regions	106,300	78,559	..	..	..	39.4				
All Europe	90,800	66,851	..	..	..	33.5				
All Americas	10,800	9,464	..	..	..	4.7				
All Asia	4,700	2,244	..	..	..	1.1				

Source: World Tourism Organization (UNWTO) ©   (Data as collected by UNWTO for TMT 2006 Edition)

Benin
International Tourist Arrivals at Frontiers (by residence)

	1995	2000	2003	2004	2005*	Market share (%) 2000	2005*	Growth rate (%) 04/03	05*/04	Average per year (%) 2000-2005*
Total	..	**96,146**	**175,000**	**173,500**	**176,000**	**100**	**100**	**-0.9**	**1.4**	**12.9**
From Africa	..	*50,140*	*148,646*	*147,536*	*140,185*	*52.1*	*79.7*	*-0.7*	*-5.0*	*22.8*
Congo	..	2,036	37,781	36,376	35,320	2.1	20.1	-3.7	-2.9	76.9
Nigeria	..	15,277	19,800	20,200	20,500	15.9	11.6	2.0	1.5	6.1
Cameroon	..	2,255	9,814	10,599	11,500	2.3	6.5	8.0	8.5	38.5
Côte d'Ivoire	..	7,814	12,000	10,705	10,900	8.1	6.2	-10.8	1.8	6.9
Togo	..	4,696	10,400	11,200	10,590	4.9	6.0	7.7	-5.4	17.7
Angola	..	115	8,592	9,613	10,540	0.1	6.0	11.9	9.6	146.8
Ghana	..	1,349	7,311	7,511	6,600	1.4	3.8	2.7	-12.1	37.4
Niger	..	4,320	6,810	5,900	5,300	4.5	3.0	-13.4	-10.2	4.2
Burkina Faso	..	2,857	2,200	3,750	3,900	3.0	2.2	70.5	4.0	6.4
Burundi	..	253	2,100	2,157	2,749	0.3	1.6	2.7	27.4	61.1
Madagascar	..	74	1,800	1,102	2,172	0.1	1.2	-38.8	97.1	96.6
Chad	..	374	1,870	2,110	1,950	0.4	1.1	12.8	-7.6	39.1
Tunisia	..	149	1,724	1,918	1,885	0.2	1.1	11.3	-1.7	66.1
Gabon	..	1,013	6,830	5,878	1,600	1.1	0.9	-13.9	-72.8	9.6
Senegal	..	1,926	3,800	1,100	1,339	2.0	0.8	-71.1	21.7	-7.0
Guinea	..	1,028	730	1,810	1,320	1.1	0.8	147.9	-27.1	5.1
Mozambique	..	15	650	548	1,236	0.0	0.7	-15.7	125.5	141.6
Dem.R.Congo	..	158	1,125	1,221	996	0.2	0.6	8.5	-18.4	44.5
Rwanda	..	106	884	987	991	0.1	0.6	11.7	0.4	56.4
Comoros	..	2	938	898	978	0.0	0.6	-4.3	8.9	245.0
Mali	..	2,314	1,300	1,210	900	2.4	0.5	-6.9	-25.6	-17.2
Cent.Afr.Rep.	..	218	2,000	1,877	880	0.2	0.5	-6.2	-53.1	32.2
Gambia	..	42	799	633	850	0.0	0.5	-20.8	34.3	82.5
Malawi	..	11	2,100	2,330	700	0.0	0.4	11.0	-70.0	129.5
Other intraregional	..	1,738	5,288	5,903	4,489	1.8	2.6	11.6	-24.0	20.9
From other regions	..	*46,006*	*26,348*	*25,964*	*35,795*	*47.9*	*20.3*	*-1.5*	*37.9*	*-4.9*
France	..	19,388	11,000	14,210	16,147	20.2	9.2	29.2	13.6	-3.6
Belgium	..	5,250	3,500	3,125	4,630	5.5	2.6	-10.7	48.2	-2.5
Austria	..	8,262	4,000	3,000	2,500	8.6	1.4	-25.0	-16.7	-21.3
Germany	..	1,797	2,500	1,520	1,900	1.9	1.1	-39.2	25.0	1.1
Switzerland	..	800	1,040	1,315	1,800	0.8	1.0	26.4	36.9	17.6
Netherlands	..	821	1,100	220	1,360	0.9	0.8	-80.0	518.2	10.6
India	..	185	110	99	1,300	0.2	0.7	-10.0	1213.1	47.7
Iran	..	29	8	7	810	0.0	0.5	-12.5	11471.4	94.6
Pakistan	..	77	17	19	656	0.1	0.4	11.8	3352.6	53.5
Italy	..	688	380	415	500	0.7	0.3	9.2	20.5	-6.2
Portugal	..	..	458	322	364		0.2	-29.7	13.0	
Denmark	..	556	450	477	350	0.6	0.2	6.0	-26.6	-8.8
Sweden	..	995	97	147	257	1.0	0.1	51.5	74.8	-23.7
Canada	..	1,197	110	127	220	1.2	0.1	15.5	73.2	-28.7
China	..	189	100	124	209	0.2	0.1	24.0	68.5	2.0
Spain	..	352	275	277	199	0.4	0.1	0.7	-28.2	-10.8
Libyan Arab Jamahiriya	..	388	51	25	189	0.4	0.1	-51.0	656.0	-13.4
Other interregional	..	5,032	1,152	535	2,404	5.2	1.4	-53.6	349.3	-13.7
Other World/Not specified	..	..	*6*	..	*20*		*0.0*			

Source: World Tourism Organization (UNWTO) ©   (Data as collected by UNWTO for TMT 2006 Edition)

World Tourism Organization ©

III.2.2   Burkina Faso   West Africa

Promotional: www.ontb.bf
Institutional/corporate: www.culture.gov.bf

Profile

Burkina Faso

Africa
West Africa

Capital	Ouagadougou
Year of entry in UNWTO	1975
Area (1000 km²)	274
Population (2005, million)	13.5
Gross Domestic Product (GDP) (2005, US$ million)	5,635
GDP per capita (2005, US$)	430
GDP growth (real, %)	
'-> 2004: 4.0; 2005: 7.1; 2006*: 5.6; 2007*: 5.8	

	2003	2004	2005*	2004/2003	2005*/2004
International Arrivals					
Tourists (overnight visitors) (1000)	163	222	245	36.2	10.1
- per 100 of inhabitants	1	2	2		
Tourism accommodation					
Nights spent in hotels and similar establishments (1000)	673	767	962	14.0	25.4
by non-residents (inbound tourism)	554	632	789	14.1	24.8
by residents (domestic tourism)	119	135	173	13.4	28.1
Receipts and Expenditure for International Tourism					
International Tourism Receipts (US$ million)	29	45	..	55.3	
- per Tourist Arrival (US$)	179	204	..	14.0	
- per capita (US$)	2	3	..		
International Fare Receipts (US$ million)	12	8	..	-32.0	
International Tourism Expenditure (US$ million)	36	19	..	-47.1	
- per capita (US$)	3	1	..		
International Fare Expenditure (US$ million)	19	22	..	14.0	
Δ International Tourism Balance (US$ million)	-7	27	..		
Δ International Fare Balance (US$ million)	-7	-14	..		

Source: World Tourism Organization (UNWTO)   (Data as collected by UNWTO for TMT 2006 Edition)
See annex for methodological notes and reference of external sources used.

International Tourism by Origin

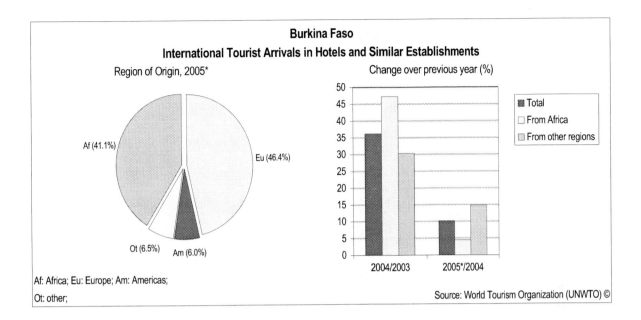

Burkina Faso
International Tourist Arrivals in Hotels and Similar Establishments

Region of Origin, 2005*

Change over previous year (%)

Af: Africa; Eu: Europe; Am: Americas;
Ot: other;

Source: World Tourism Organization (UNWTO) ©

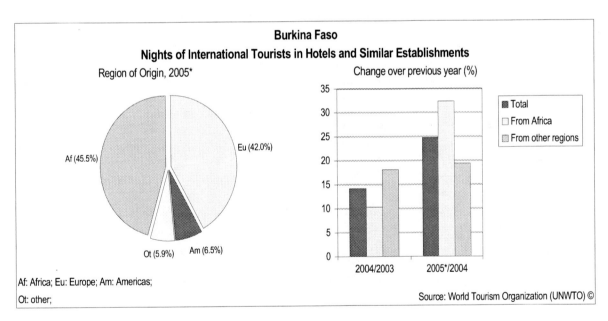

Burkina Faso
Nights of International Tourists in Hotels and Similar Establishments

Region of Origin, 2005*

Change over previous year (%)

Af: Africa; Eu: Europe; Am: Americas;
Ot: other;

Source: World Tourism Organization (UNWTO) ©

Burkina Faso
International Tourist Arrivals in Hotels and Similar Establishments (by nationality)

	1995	2000	2003	2004	2005*	Market share (%) 2000	Market share (%) 2005*	Growth rate (%) 04/03	Growth rate (%) 05*/04	Average per year (%) 2000-2005*
Total	124,270	125,699	163,123	222,201	244,728	100	100	36.2	10.1	14.3
From Africa	51,617	47,208	65,459	96,385	100,674	37.6	41.1	47.2	4.4	16.4
Côte d'Ivoire	13,631	7,567	9,229	14,924	14,454	6.0	5.9	61.7	-3.1	13.8
Mali	7,718	5,297	7,785	12,411	12,018	4.2	4.9	59.4	-3.2	17.8
Niger	4,730	4,728	7,016	11,455	10,836	3.8	4.4	63.3	-5.4	18.0
Senegal	4,919	4,171	5,950	9,882	9,792	3.3	4.0	66.1	-0.9	18.6
Benin	2,895	3,660	6,443	8,765	9,186	2.9	3.8	36.0	4.8	20.2
Togo	4,103	3,938	5,394	6,961	7,974	3.1	3.3	29.1	14.6	15.2
Ghana	1,661	2,300	3,831	5,456	4,914	1.8	2.0	42.4	-9.9	16.4
Guinea	1,627	1,678	2,759	4,528	3,534	1.3	1.4	64.1	-22.0	16.1
Nigeria	1,460	2,137	2,328	4,097	3,366	1.7	1.4	76.0	-17.8	9.5
Mauritania	1,079	983	1,652	1,834	1,854	0.8	0.8	11.0	1.1	13.5
Other Africa	7,794	10,749	13,072	16,072	22,746	8.6	9.3	22.9	41.5	16.2
From other regions	61,990	74,709	91,486	119,265	137,022	59.4	56.0	30.4	14.9	12.9
France	28,409	38,103	47,663	62,510	77,220	30.3	31.6	31.1	23.5	15.2
United States	3,653	3,906	6,030	6,872	7,290	3.1	3.0	14.0	6.1	13.3
Belgium	2,536	6,614	4,984	6,482	6,438	5.3	2.6	30.1	-0.7	-0.5
Canada	2,816	2,696	3,000	4,548	6,048	2.1	2.5	51.6	33.0	17.5
Italy	2,187	2,485	3,215	3,727	5,244	2.0	2.1	15.9	40.7	16.1
Germany	4,418	3,131	4,683	5,523	5,190	2.5	2.1	17.9	-6.0	10.6
Switzerland	2,539	2,090	4,025	5,192	3,828	1.7	1.6	29.0	-26.3	12.9
United Kingdom	2,031	1,729	2,475	3,618	3,288	1.4	1.3	46.2	-9.1	13.7
Netherlands	2,991	2,460	2,734	2,932	3,198	2.0	1.3	7.2	9.1	5.4
Lebanon	608	652	1,447	1,982	2,220	0.5	0.9	37.0	12.0	27.8
China	421	1,249	910	1,473	1,830	1.0	0.7	61.9	24.2	7.9
Other Americas	905	937	995	1,571	1,386	0.7	0.6	57.9	-11.8	8.1
Other Asia	1,512	2,291	2,361	3,077	4,752	1.8	1.9	30.3	54.4	15.7
Other Europe	6,964	6,366	6,964	9,758	9,090	5.1	3.7	40.1	-6.8	7.4
Nationals residing abroad	10,663	3,782	6,178	6,551	7,032	3.0	2.9	6.0	7.3	13.2

Source: World Tourism Organization (UNWTO) ©

(Data as collected by UNWTO for TMT 2006 Edition)

Burkina Faso
Nights of International Tourists in Hotels and Similar Establishments (by nationality)

	1995	2000	2003	2004	2005*	Market share (%) 2000	Market share (%) 2005*	Growth rate (%) 04/03	Growth rate (%) 05*/04	Average per year (%) 2000-2005*
Total	**287,957**	**394,379**	**553,740**	**632,340**	**788,910**	**100**	**100**	**14.2**	**24.8**	**14.9**
From Africa	*119,489*	*151,933*	*246,060*	*271,508*	*359,310*	*38.5*	*45.5*	*10.3*	*32.3*	*18.8*
Côte d'Ivoire	31,623	22,789	34,000	33,995	58,296	5.8	7.4	0.0	71.5	20.7
Mali	17,904	15,732	26,306	29,370	38,628	4.0	4.9	11.6	31.5	19.7
Niger	10,974	14,311	22,938	27,829	37,512	3.6	4.8	21.3	34.8	21.3
Senegal	11,410	13,460	24,281	27,095	36,132	3.4	4.6	11.6	33.4	21.8
Togo	9,568	11,590	17,994	20,884	27,252	2.9	3.5	16.1	30.5	18.6
Benin	6,416	11,846	22,905	23,368	..	3.0		2.0		
Ghana	3,853	7,587	11,696	12,129	..	1.9		3.7		
Guinea	3,773	5,825	8,564	9,423	..	1.5		10.0		
Nigeria	3,386	6,421	8,058	8,180	..	1.6		1.5		
Mauritania	2,502	3,143	4,453	5,446	..	0.8		22.3		
Other Africa	18,080	39,229	64,865	73,789	161,490	9.9	20.5	13.8	118.9	32.7
From other regions	*143,732*	*230,150*	*290,817*	*343,520*	*410,184*	*58.4*	*52.0*	*18.1*	*19.4*	*12.3*
France	65,907	114,552	141,156	170,956	216,708	29.0	27.5	21.1	26.8	13.6
United States	8,468	13,818	27,314	21,357	27,762	3.5	3.5	-21.8	30.0	15.0
Belgium	5,883	18,307	18,148	21,238	22,212	4.6	2.8	17.0	4.6	3.9
Canada	6,530	10,028	12,466	21,525	19,762	2.5	2.5	72.7	-8.2	14.5
Germany	10,248	8,107	13,813	13,973	16,908	2.1	2.1	1.2	21.0	15.8
Italy	5,074	7,489	10,188	13,640	14,118	1.9	1.8	33.9	3.5	13.5
United Kingdom	4,709	5,706	8,295	12,928	..	1.4		55.9		
Netherlands	6,885	7,481	8,415	9,451	..	1.9		12.3		
Switzerland	5,889	6,313	9,911	9,116	..	1.6		-8.0		
China	973	3,503	4,490	5,636	7,434	0.9	0.9	25.5	31.9	16.2
Lebanon	1,409	2,035	4,392	5,330	5,184	0.5	0.7	21.4	-2.7	20.6
Other Americas	2,098	2,831	3,335	4,640	4,028	0.7	0.5	39.1	-13.2	7.3
Other Asia	3,505	7,178	8,263	9,183	14,796	1.8	1.9	11.1	61.1	15.6
Other Europe	16,154	22,802	20,631	24,547	61,272	5.8	7.8	19.0	149.6	21.9
Nationals residing abroad	*24,736*	*12,296*	*16,863*	*17,312*	*19,416*	*3.1*	*2.5*	*2.7*	*12.2*	*9.6*

Source: World Tourism Organization (UNWTO) ©   (Data as collected by UNWTO for TMT 2006 Edition)

III.2.3   Cape Verde   West Africa

Profile

Cape Verde

Capital	Praia
Year of entry in UNWTO	2001
Area (100 km²)	40
Population (2005, 1000)	418
Gross Domestic Product (GDP) (2005, US$ million)	983
GDP per capita (2005, US$)	2,066

Africa
West Africa

GDP growth (real, %)
'-> 2004: 4.4;   2005: 5.8;   2006*: 5.5;   2007*: 6.0

	2003	2004	2005*	2004/2003	2005*/2004
International Arrivals					
Tourists (overnight visitors) (1000)	150	157	198	4.7	26.0
- per 100 of inhabitants	36	38	47		
Tourism accommodation					
Number of rooms	3,146	3,150	4,406	0.1	39.9
Nights spent in hotels and similar establishments (1000)	903	865	935	-4.2	8.1
by non-residents (inbound tourism)	820	787	850	-4.0	8.0
by residents (domestic tourism)	83	78	85	-6.0	9.0
Receipts and Expenditure for International Tourism					
International Tourism Receipts (US$ million)	87	98	123	13.5	24.7
- per Tourist Arrival (US$)	577	626	619	8.5	-1.0
- per capita (US$)	210	237	293		
International Fare Receipts (US$ million)	52	54	55	3.8	1.9
International Tourism Expenditure (US$ million)	72	78	67	7.2	-13.6
- per capita (US$)	176	187	161		
International Fare Expenditure (US$ million)	18	13	15	-27.8	15.4
Δ International Tourism Balance (US$ million)	14	21	55		
Δ International Fare Balance (US$ million)	34	41	40		

Source: World Tourism Organization (UNWTO)   (Data as collected by UNWTO for TMT 2006 Edition)

See annex for methodological notes and reference of external sources used.

World Tourism Organization ©

International Tourism by Origin

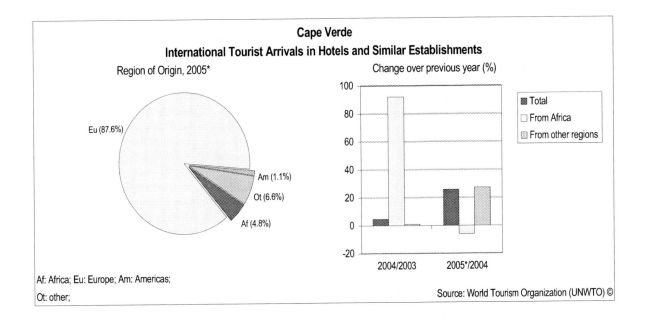

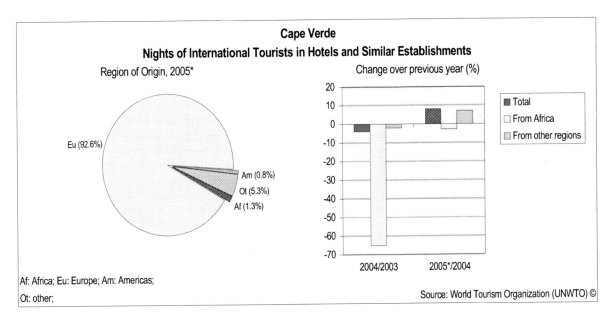

Cape Verde
International Tourist Arrivals in Hotels and Similar Establishments (by residence)

	1995	2000	2003	2004	2005*	Market share (%)		Growth rate (%)		Average per year (%)
						2000	2005*	04/03	05*/04	2000-2005*
Total	..	115,015	150,048	157,052	197,844	100	100	4.7	26.0	11.5
From Africa	..	4,469	5,225	10,034	9,432	3.9	4.8	92.0	-6.0	16.1
South Africa	..	4,469	5,225	10,034	9,432	3.9	4.8	92.0	-6.0	16.1
From other regions	..	102,590	136,489	137,776	175,420	89.2	88.7	0.9	27.3	11.3
Italy	..	28,514	54,278	55,200	69,728	24.8	35.2	1.7	26.3	19.6
Portugal	..	32,182	28,548	38,129	50,240	28.0	25.4	33.6	31.8	9.3
Germany	..	17,631	18,095	14,433	21,121	15.3	10.7	-20.2	46.3	3.7
France	..	10,223	12,847	11,160	14,284	8.9	7.2	-13.1	28.0	6.9
Spain	..	4,704	7,679	10,281	7,626	4.1	3.9	33.9	-25.8	10.1
Belgium	..	2,828	9,702	4,159	5,121	2.5	2.6	-57.1	23.1	12.6
United Kingdom	..	665	1,140	824	2,284	0.6	1.2	-27.7	177.2	28.0
United States	..	2,035	1,740	1,472	2,102	1.8	1.1	-15.4	42.8	0.6
Switzerland	..	2,326	1,638	1,415	1,976	2.0	1.0	-13.6	39.6	-3.2
Austria	..	1,482	822	703	938	1.3	0.5	-14.5	33.4	-8.7
Other World/Not specified	..	7,956	8,334	9,242	12,992	6.9	6.6	10.9	40.6	10.3

Source: World Tourism Organization (UNWTO) ©   (Data as collected by UNWTO for TMT 2006 Edition)

Cape Verde
Nights of International Tourists in Hotels and Similar Establishments (by residence)

	1995	2000	2003	2004	2005*	Market share (%)		Growth rate (%)		Average per year (%)
						2000	2005*	04/03	05*/04	2000-2005*
Total	..	602,344	819,726	786,771	850,297	100	100	-4.0	8.1	7.1
From Africa	..	51,536	31,922	11,110	10,794	8.6	1.3	-65.2	-2.8	-26.8
South Africa	..	51,536	31,922	11,110	10,794	8.6	1.3	-65.2	-2.8	-26.8
From other regions	..	517,129	757,771	741,914	794,848	85.9	93.5	-2.1	7.1	9.0
Italy	..	182,422	375,566	387,797	326,554	30.3	38.4	3.3	-15.8	12.4
Portugal	..	151,495	122,800	184,571	235,788	25.2	27.7	50.3	27.7	9.3
Germany	..	98,948	111,107	70,333	104,397	16.4	12.3	-36.7	48.4	1.1
France	..	35,106	40,345	32,494	47,188	5.8	5.5	-19.5	45.2	6.1
Spain	..	15,580	36,110	31,707	29,141	2.6	3.4	-12.2	-8.1	13.3
Belgium	..	9,097	54,231	20,251	25,526	1.5	3.0	-62.7	26.0	22.9
United Kingdom	..	2,202	3,565	3,296	8,039	0.4	0.9	-7.5	143.9	29.6
Switzerland	..	9,008	5,672	4,595	7,621	1.5	0.9	-19.0	65.9	-3.3
United States	..	5,696	5,015	4,693	7,087	0.9	0.8	-6.4	51.0	4.5
Austria	..	7,575	3,360	2,177	3,507	1.3	0.4	-35.2	61.1	-14.3
Other World/Not specified	..	33,679	30,033	33,747	44,655	5.6	5.3	12.4	32.3	5.8

Source: World Tourism Organization (UNWTO) ©   (Data as collected by UNWTO for TMT 2006 Edition)

III.2.4   Côte d'Ivoire   West Africa

Promotional: www.tourismeci.org
Institutional/corporate: www.virtuel.ci/production/tourisme (in progress)

Profile

Côte d'Ivoire

Africa
West Africa

Capital	Yamoussoukro
Year of entry in UNWTO	1975
Area (1000 km²)	322
Population (2005, million)	17.3
Gross Domestic Product (GDP) (2005, US$ million)	16,373
GDP per capita (2005, US$)	900
GDP growth (real, %)	
'-> 2004: 1.8; 2005: 1.9; 2006*: 1.9; 2007*: 3.0	

	2003	2004	2005*	2004/2003	2005*/2004
International Arrivals					
Tourists (overnight visitors) (1000)	180	..	..		
- per 100 of inhabitants	1	..	..		
Receipts and Expenditure for International Tourism					
International Tourism Receipts (US$ million)	69	82	83	18.8	1.2
- per Tourist Arrival (US$)	383	..	..		
- per capita (US$)	4	5	5		
International Fare Receipts (US$ million)	7	9	..	28.6	
International Tourism Expenditure (US$ million)	387	382	346	-1.3	-9.4
- per capita (US$)	23	23	20		
International Fare Expenditure (US$ million)	164	190	..	15.9	
Δ International Tourism Balance (US$ million)	-318	-300	-263		
Δ International Fare Balance (US$ million)	-157	-181	..		

Source: World Tourism Organization (UNWTO)   (Data as collected by UNWTO for TMT 2006 Edition)

See annex for methodological notes and reference of external sources used.

III.2.5   Gambia

West Africa

Promotional: www.visitthegambia.gm

Profile

Gambia

Capital	Banjul
Year of entry in UNWTO	1975
Area (100 km²)	113
Population (2005, million)	1.6
Gross Domestic Product (GDP) (2005, US$ million)	461
GDP per capita (2005, US$)	306

Africa
West Africa

GDP growth (real, %)
'-> 2004: 5.1;   2005: 5.0;   2006*: 4.5;   2007*: 5.0

	2003	2004	2005*	2004/2003	2005*/2004
International Arrivals					
Visitors (1000)	..	..	463		
Tourists (overnight visitors) (1000)	73	90	111	22.6	23.2
- per 100 of inhabitants	5	6	7		
Tourism accommodation					
Number of rooms	..	..	3,066		
Outbound Tourism					
Trips abroad (1000)	..	..	387		
- per 100 of inhabitants	..	..	24		
Receipts and Expenditure for International Tourism					
International Tourism Receipts (US$ million)	56	47	56	-16.1	19.1
- per Tourist Arrival (US$)	762	522	505	-31.5	-3.3
- per Visitor Arrival (US$)	..	..	121		
- per capita (US$)	37	30	35		
International Fare Receipts (US$ million)	2	4	1	100.0	-75.0
International Tourism Expenditure (US$ million)	4	4	5		25.0
- per trip (US$)	..	..	13		
- per capita (US$)	3	3	3		
International Fare Expenditure (US$ million)	4	2	2	-50.0	
Δ International Tourism Balance (US$ million)	52	43	51		
Δ International Fare Balance (US$ million)	-2	2	-1		

Source: World Tourism Organization (UNWTO)   (Data as collected by UNWTO for TMT 2006 Edition)

See annex for methodological notes and reference of external sources used.

International Tourism by Origin

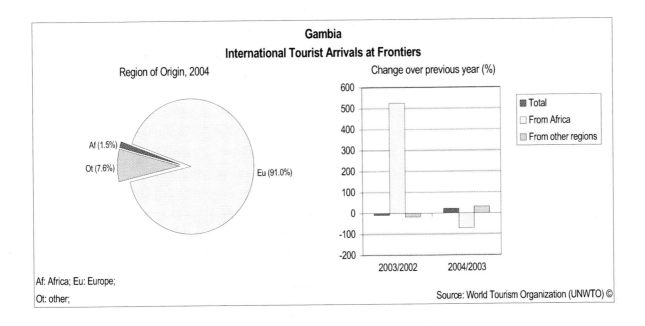

Gambia
International Tourist Arrivals at Frontiers

Region of Origin, 2004

Af (1.5%)
Ot (7.6%)
Eu (91.0%)

Change over previous year (%)

- Total
- From Africa
- From other regions

Af: Africa; Eu: Europe;
Ot: other;

Source: World Tourism Organization (UNWTO) ©

Gambia
International Tourist Arrivals at Frontiers (by nationality)

	1995	2000	2002	2003	2004	Market share (%) 2000	Market share (%) 2004	Growth rate (%) 03/02	Growth rate (%) 04/03	Average per year (%) 2000-2004
Total	**45,401**	**78,710**	**81,005**	**73,485**	**90,095**	**100**	**100**	**-9.3**	**22.6**	**3.4**
From Africa	*950*	*804*	*726*	*4,542*	*1,330*	*1.0*	*1.5*	*525.6*	*-70.7*	*13.4*
All Africa	950	804	726	4,542	1,330	1.0	1.5	525.6	-70.7	13.4
From other regions	*40,422*	*75,553*	*78,230*	*64,268*	*85,203*	*96.0*	*94.6*	*-17.8*	*32.6*	*3.1*
United Kingdom	14,171	37,594	48,894	40,872	48,297	47.8	53.6	-16.4	18.2	6.5
Netherlands	12,274	9,668	10,419	7,262	13,112	12.3	14.6	-30.3	80.6	7.9
Norway	296	654	711	999	5,513	0.8	6.1	40.5	451.9	70.4
Belgium	2,177	4,392	4,268	1,707	4,961	5.6	5.5	-60.0	190.6	3.1
Sweden	2,942	4,997	5,594	4,205	3,954	6.3	4.4	-24.8	-6.0	-5.7
United States	266	732	866	445	3,059	0.9	3.4	-48.6	587.4	43.0
Germany	6,018	12,156	3,707	4,253	2,891	15.4	3.2	14.7	-32.0	-30.2
Denmark	1,243	3,597	2,260	2,616	1,997	4.6	2.2	15.8	-23.7	-13.7
France	281	612	645	653	432	0.8	0.5	1.2	-33.8	-8.3
Switzerland	242	250	190	705	293	0.3	0.3	271.1	-58.4	4.0
Austria	265	506	257	153	275	0.6	0.3	-40.5	79.7	-14.1
Italy	157	217	210	200	230	0.3	0.3	-4.8	15.0	1.5
Canada	90	178	209	198	189	0.2	0.2	-5.3	-4.5	1.5
Other World/Not specified	*4,029*	*2,353*	*2,049*	*4,675*	*3,562*	*3.0*	*4.0*	*128.2*	*-23.8*	*10.9*

Source: World Tourism Organization (UNWTO) ©   (Data as collected by UNWTO for TMT 2006 Edition)

III.2.6   Ghana   West Africa

Promotional: www.ghanatourism.gov.gh
Institutional/corporate: www.ghanatourism.gov.gh

Profile

Ghana

Capital	Accra
Year of entry in UNWTO	1975
Area (1000 km²)	239
Population (2005, million)	22.0
Gross Domestic Product (GDP) (2005, US$ million)	10,694
GDP per capita (2005, US$)	512

Africa
West Africa

GDP growth (real, %)
'-> 2004: 5.8;   2005: 5.8;   2006*: 6.0;   2007*: 6.0

	2003	2004	2005*	2004/2003	2005*/2004
International Arrivals					
Tourists (overnight visitors) (1000)	531	584	429	10.0	-26.6
- per 100 of inhabitants	3	3	2		
Tourism accommodation					
Number of rooms	17,352	18,079	18,632	4.2	3.1
Receipts and Expenditure for International Tourism					
International Tourism Receipts (US$ million)	414	466	796	12.6	70.8
- per Tourist Arrival (US$)	780	798	1,857	2.3	132.7
- per capita (US$)	20	22	36		
International Fare Receipts (US$ million)	27	29	31	7.4	6.9
International Tourism Expenditure (US$ million)	138	186	303	34.8	62.9
- per capita (US$)	7	9	14		
International Fare Expenditure (US$ million)	78	84	169	7.7	101.2
Δ International Tourism Balance (US$ million)	276	280	493		
Δ International Fare Balance (US$ million)	-51	-55	-138		

Source: World Tourism Organization (UNWTO)   (Data as collected by UNWTO for TMT 2006 Edition)
See annex for methodological notes and reference of external sources used.

International Tourism by Origin

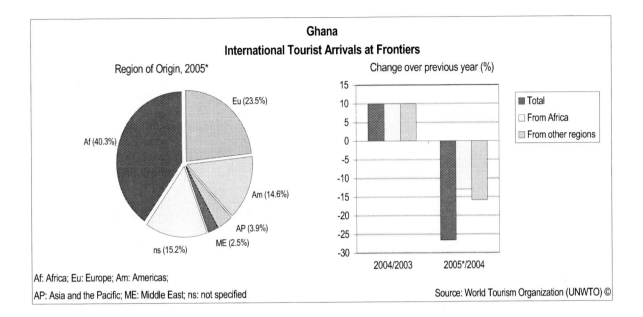

Ghana
International Tourist Arrivals at Frontiers

Region of Origin, 2005*

Af (40.3%)
Eu (23.5%)
Am (14.6%)
AP (3.9%)
ME (2.5%)
ns (15.2%)

Change over previous year (%)

Total
From Africa
From other regions

2004/2003   2005*/2004

Af: Africa; Eu: Europe; Am: Americas;
AP: Asia and the Pacific; ME: Middle East; ns: not specified

Source: World Tourism Organization (UNWTO) ©

Ghana

International Tourist Arrivals at Frontiers (by nationality)

	1995	2000	2003	2004	2005*	Market share (%) 2000	2005*	Growth rate (%) 04/03	05*/04	Average per year (%) 2000-2005*
Total	**286,000**	**398,998**	**530,827**	**583,819**	**428,533**	**100**	**100**	**10.0**	**-26.6**	**1.4**
From Africa	*97,309*	*135,754*	*180,609*	*198,638*	*172,913*	*34.0*	*40.3*	*10.0*	*-13.0*	*5.0*
Nigeria	39,254	54,764	72,857	80,131	74,983	13.7	17.5	10.0	-6.4	6.5
Côte d'Ivoire	13,750	19,183	25,521	28,069	25,155	4.8	5.9	10.0	-10.4	5.6
Liberia	7,500	10,463	13,920	15,310	14,472	2.6	3.4	10.0	-5.5	6.7
Togo	8,560	11,941	15,886	17,472	11,888	3.0	2.8	10.0	-32.0	-0.1
Burkina Faso	4,551	6,348	8,446	9,289	10,544	1.6	2.5	10.0	13.5	10.7
Benin	2,468	3,444	4,581	5,039	6,197	0.9	1.4	10.0	23.0	12.5
Niger	4,658	6,498	8,645	9,508	2,048	1.6	0.5	10.0	-78.5	-20.6
Mali	4,658	6,498	8,645	9,508	2,046	1.6	0.5	10.0	-78.5	-20.6
Other Africa	11,910	16,615	22,108	24,312	25,580	4.2	6.0	10.0	5.2	9.0
From other regions	*110,841*	*154,635*	*205,726*	*226,264*	*190,525*	*38.8*	*44.5*	*10.0*	*-15.8*	*4.3*
United States	18,864	26,317	35,013	38,508	50,475	6.6	11.8	10.0	31.1	13.9
United Kingdom	24,762	34,546	45,959	50,547	36,747	8.7	8.6	10.0	-27.3	1.2
Germany	13,799	19,251	25,611	28,168	14,094	4.8	3.3	10.0	-50.0	-6.0
Netherlands	6,924	9,659	12,850	14,133	13,663	2.4	3.2	10.0	-3.3	7.2
All Middle East	2,169	3,026	4,026	4,428	10,632	0.8	2.5	10.0	140.1	28.6
France	10,334	14,418	19,181	21,096	10,089	3.6	2.4	10.0	-52.2	-6.9
Canada	3,843	5,361	7,132	7,844	8,951	1.3	2.1	10.0	14.1	10.8
Scandinavia	3,817	5,325	7,085	7,792	8,751	1.3	2.0	10.0	12.3	10.4
Italy	3,473	4,845	6,445	7,089	6,716	1.2	1.6	10.0	-5.3	6.7
China	3,218	4,489	5,972	6,569	5,572	1.1	1.3	10.0	-15.2	4.4
Belgium	1,436	2,003	2,665	2,931	3,147	0.5	0.7	10.0	7.4	9.5
Switzerland	2,713	3,784	5,034	5,537	2,391	0.9	0.6	10.0	-56.8	-8.8
Japan	1,788	2,495	3,320	3,651	1,864	0.6	0.4	10.0	-48.9	-5.7
Other Americas	1,312	1,831	2,436	2,679	3,146	0.5	0.7	10.0	17.4	11.4
Other Europe	3,639	5,078	6,757	7,431	4,911	1.3	1.1	10.0	-33.9	-0.7
Other East Asia/Pacific	8,750	12,207	16,240	17,861	9,376	3.1	2.2	10.0	-47.5	-5.1
Nationals residing abroad	*77,850*	*108,609*	*144,492*	*158,917*	*59,821*	*27.2*	*14.0*	*10.0*	*-62.4*	*-11.2*
Other World/Not specified	*..*	*..*	*..*	*..*	*5,274*		*1.2*			

Source: World Tourism Organization (UNWTO) ©   (Data as collected by UNWTO for TMT 2006 Edition)

III.2.7   Guinea   West Africa

Promotional: http://ontguinee.free.fr
Institutional/corporate: http://ontguinee.free.fr ; www.ecovisionsguinée.com

Profile

Guinea

Africa
West Africa

		Conakry
Capital		Conakry
Year of entry in UNWTO		1985
Area (1000 km²)		246
Population (2005, million)		9.5
Gross Domestic Product (GDP) (2005, US$ million)		3,293
GDP per capita (2005, US$)		355
GDP growth (real, %)		
'-> 2004: 2.7; 2005: 3.3; 2006*: 5.0; 2007*: 5.4		

	2003	2004	2005*	2004/2003	2005*/2004
International Arrivals					
Tourists (overnight visitors) (1000)	44	45	45	1.5	1.6
- per 100 of inhabitants	0	0	0		
Tourism accommodation					
Number of rooms	3,747	3,886	..	3.7	
Nights spent in collective establishments (1000)					
by non-residents (inbound tourism)	928	1,233	1,318	32.9	6.9
Nights spent in hotels and similar establishments (1000)					
by non-residents (inbound tourism)	122	152	195	24.6	28.3
Receipts and Expenditure for International Tourism					
International Tourism Receipts (US$ million)	31	30	..	-3.2	
- per Tourist Arrival (US$)	705	672	..	-4.6	
- per capita (US$)	3	3	..		
International Fare Receipts (US$ million)	1	..	..		
International Tourism Expenditure (US$ million)	26	25	..	-3.8	
- per capita (US$)	3	3	..		
International Fare Expenditure (US$ million)	10	4	..	-60.0	
Δ International Tourism Balance (US$ million)	5	5	..		
Δ International Fare Balance (US$ million)	-9	..	..		

Source: World Tourism Organization (UNWTO)   (Data as collected by UNWTO for TMT 2006 Edition)
See annex for methodological notes and reference of external sources used.

International Tourism by Origin

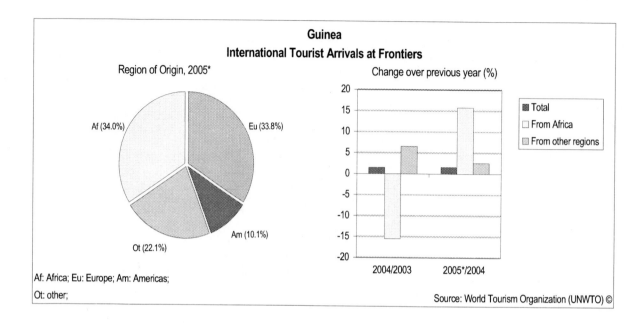

Guinea
International Tourist Arrivals at Frontiers

Region of Origin, 2005*

Af (34.0%)
Eu (33.8%)
Am (10.1%)
Ot (22.1%)

Change over previous year (%)

Total
From Africa
From other regions

2004/2003   2005*/2004

Af: Africa; Eu: Europe; Am: Americas;
Ot: other;

Source: World Tourism Organization (UNWTO) ©

World Tourism Organization ©

Guinea
International Tourist Arrivals at Frontiers (by nationality)

	1995	2000	2003	2004	2005*	Market share (%) 2000	Market share (%) 2005*	Growth rate (%) 04/03	Growth rate (%) 05*/04	Average per year (%) 2000-2005*
Total	..	**32,598**	**43,966**	**44,622**	**45,330**	**100**	**100**	**1.5**	**1.6**	**6.8**
From Africa	..	*12,679*	*15,771*	*13,330*	*15,427*	*38.9*	*34.0*	*-15.5*	*15.7*	*4.0*
All Africa	..	..	..	13,330	..					
Senegal	..	2,651	3,634	..	4,523	8.1	10.0			11.3
Côte d'Ivoire	..	2,081	2,078	..	2,453	6.4	5.4			3.3
Sierra Leone	..	2,948	3,135	..	1,328	9.0	2.9			-14.7
Mali	..	1,118	1,598	..	1,295	3.4	2.9			3.0
Nigeria	..	379	571	..	807	1.2	1.8			16.3
Gambia	..	284	530	..	541	0.9	1.2			13.8
Ghana	..	266	423	..	489	0.8	1.1			12.9
Liberia	..	254	528	..	434	0.8	1.0			11.3
Benin	..	247	271	..	386	0.8	0.9			9.3
Morocco	..	267	415	..	386	0.8	0.9			7.7
Togo	..	234	271	..	364	0.7	0.8			9.2
Burkina Faso	..	267	304	..	361	0.8	0.8			6.2
Mauritania	..	122	229	..	303	0.4	0.7			20.0
Cameroon	..	96	251	..	236	0.3	0.5			19.7
Guinea-Bissau	..	57	170	..	229	0.2	0.5			32.1
South Africa	..	133	163	..	203	0.4	0.4			8.8
Other intraregional	..	1,275	1,200	..	1,089	3.9	2.4			-3.1
From other regions	..	*19,919*	*22,422*	*23,883*	*24,495*	*61.1*	*54.0*	*6.5*	*2.6*	*4.2*
All Europe	..	..	..	15,500	..					
France	..	7,333	9,378	..	7,984	22.5	17.6			1.7
All Americas	..	..	..	4,378	..					
United States	..	2,532	2,495	..	3,237	7.8	7.1			5.0
All Asia	..	..	..	2,454	..					
China	..	549	1,041	..	1,575	1.7	3.5			23.5
Canada	..	1,006	897	..	1,135	3.1	2.5			2.4
Belgium	..	1,438	905	..	1,126	4.4	2.5			-4.8
Germany	..	949	841	..	1,029	2.9	2.3			1.6
All South Asia	..	..	..	985	..					
India	..	284	548	..	950	0.9	2.1			27.3
Russian Federation	..	294	661	..	919	0.9	2.0			25.6
Italy	..	811	631	..	767	2.5	1.7			-1.1
Netherlands	..	361	448	..	697	1.1	1.5			14.1
United Kingdom	..	1,316	628	..	629	4.0	1.4			-13.7
All Middle East	..	..	..	566	..					
Switzerland	..	537	329	..	471	1.6	1.0			-2.6
Japan	..	222	307	..	404	0.7	0.9			12.7
Lebanon	..	165	631	..	397	0.5	0.9			19.2
Pakistan	..	36	126	..	309	0.1	0.7			53.7
Spain	..	345	250	..	294	1.1	0.6			-3.1
Ukraine	..	101	190	..	245	0.3	0.5			19.4
Korea, D P Rp	..	31	232	..	239	0.1	0.5			50.5
Australia	..	129	191	..	224	0.4	0.5			11.7
Sweden	..	131	170	..	224	0.4	0.5			11.3
Other interregional	..	1,349	1,523	..	1,640	4.1	3.6			4.0
Nationals residing abroad	..	..	*5,583*	*4,828*	*5,214*		*11.5*	*-13.5*	*8.0*	
Other World/Not specified	..	..	*190*	*2,581*	*194*		*0.4*	*1258.4*	*-92.5*	

Source: World Tourism Organization (UNWTO) ©   (Data as collected by UNWTO for TMT 2006 Edition)

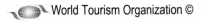

III.2.8   Guinea-Bissau   West Africa

Profile

Guinea-Bissau

Capital	Bissau
Year of entry in UNWTO	1991
Area (1000 km²)	36
Population (2005, million)	1.4
Gross Domestic Product (GDP) (2005, US$ million)	302
GDP per capita (2005, US$)	190

Africa
West Africa

GDP growth (real, %)
'-> 2004: 2.2;   2005: 3.2;   2006*: 4.6;   2007*: 5.2

	2003	2004	2005*	2004/2003	2005*/2004
International Arrivals					
Tourists (overnight visitors) (1000)	..	..	5		
- per 100 of inhabitants	..	..	0		
Tourism accommodation					
Number of rooms	..	3,533	..		
Receipts and Expenditure for International Tourism					
International Tourism Receipts (US$ million)	2	1	..	-50.0	
- per capita (US$)	1	1	..		
International Fare Receipts (US$ million)	1	1	..		
International Tourism Expenditure (US$ million)	13	13	..		
- per capita (US$)	10	9	..		
International Fare Expenditure (US$ million)	8	9	..	12.5	
Δ International Tourism Balance (US$ million)	-11	-12	..		
Δ International Fare Balance (US$ million)	-7	-8	..		

Source: World Tourism Organization (UNWTO)   (Data as collected by UNWTO for TMT 2006 Edition)
See annex for methodological notes and reference of external sources used.

International Tourism by Origin

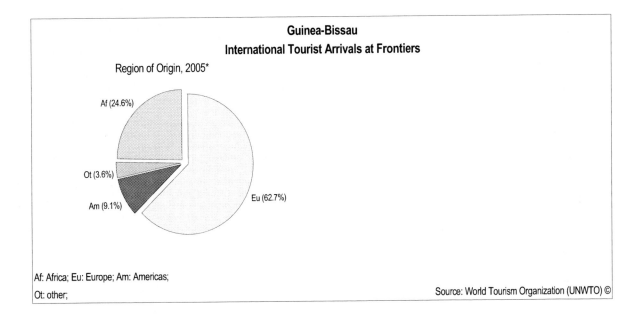

Guinea-Bissau
International Tourist Arrivals at Frontiers

Region of Origin, 2005*

Af (24.6%)

Ot (3.6%)

Am (9.1%)

Eu (62.7%)

Af: Africa; Eu: Europe; Am: Americas;
Ot: other;

Source: World Tourism Organization (UNWTO) ©

Guinea-Bissau

International Tourist Arrivals at Frontiers (by nationality)

	1995	2000	2003	2004	2005*	Market share (%) 2000	Market share (%) 2005*	Growth rate (%) 04/03	Growth rate (%) 05*/04	Average per year (%) 2000-2005*
Total	..	..	..	..	**4,978**		**100**			
From Africa	..	..	..	..	*1,224*		*24.6*			
Mali	..	..	..	..	252		5.1			
Senegal	..	..	..	..	235		4.7			
Cape Verde	..	..	..	..	159		3.2			
Cameroon	..	..	..	..	80		1.6			
Mozambique	..	..	..	..	70		1.4			
Nigeria	..	..	..	..	68		1.4			
Gambia	..	..	..	..	60		1.2			
Congo	..	..	..	..	49		1.0			
Uganda	..	..	..	..	39		0.8			
Guinea	..	..	..	..	34		0.7			
Mauritania	..	..	..	..	30		0.6			
Côte d'Ivoire	..	..	..	..	28		0.6			
Togo	..	..	..	..	26		0.5			
Sierra Leone	..	..	..	..	25		0.5			
Kenya	..	..	..	..	15		0.3			
Liberia	..	..	..	..	15		0.3			
Angola	..	..	..	..	14		0.3			
Benin	..	..	..	..	14		0.3			
Burkina Faso	..	..	..	..	11		0.2			
From other regions	..	..	..	..	*3,754*		*75.4*			
Portugal	..	..	..	..	1,552		31.2			
France	..	..	..	..	599		12.0			
Spain	..	..	..	..	324		6.5			
Italy	..	..	..	..	213		4.3			
Brazil	..	..	..	..	176		3.5			
India	..	..	..	..	66		1.3			
Germany	..	..	..	..	65		1.3			
Mexico	..	..	..	..	59		1.2			
Romania	..	..	..	..	58		1.2			
United States	..	..	..	..	57		1.1			
Colombia	..	..	..	..	55		1.1			
Czech Rep	..	..	..	..	50		1.0			
Serbia & Montenegro	..	..	..	..	49		1.0			
China	..	..	..	..	46		0.9			
Netherlands	..	..	..	..	41		0.8			
Finland	..	..	..	..	40		0.8			
Korea, Republic of	..	..	..	..	36		0.7			
Belgium	..	..	..	..	30		0.6			
Denmark	..	..	..	..	30		0.6			
Cuba	..	..	..	..	29		0.6			
Peru	..	..	..	..	27		0.5			
Switzerland	..	..	..	..	24		0.5			
Sweden	..	..	..	..	22		0.4			
Other interregional	..	..	..	..	106		2.1			

Source: World Tourism Organization (UNWTO) ©   (Data as collected by UNWTO for TMT 2006 Edition)

World Tourism Organization ©

III.2.9   Liberia   West Africa

Profile

Liberia

Africa
West Africa

Capital	Monrovia
Area (1000 km²)	111
Population (2005, million)	2.9
Gross Domestic Product (GDP) (2005, US$ million)	530
GDP per capita (2005, US$)	161
GDP growth (real, %)	
-> 2004: -5.2; 2005: 9.5; 2006*: 7.0; 2007*: 8.1	

Source: World Tourism Organization (UNWTO)   (Data as collected by UNWTO for TMT 2006 Edition)

See annex for methodological notes and reference of external sources used.

III.2.10 Mali | West Africa

Promotional: www.omatho.com
Institutional/corporate: www.malitourisme.com
Research and data: www.omatho.com

Profile

Mali

Africa
West Africa

Capital	Bamako
Year of entry in UNWTO	1975
Area (1000 km²)	1,240
Population (2005, million)	11.4
Gross Domestic Product (GDP) (2005, US$ million)	5,390
GDP per capita (2005, US$)	432
GDP growth (real, %)	
'-> 2004: 2.4; 2005: 6.1; 2006*: 5.1; 2007*: 5.4	

	2003	2004	2005*	2004/2003	2005*/2004
International Arrivals					
Tourists (overnight visitors) (1000)	110	113	143	2.1	26.8
- per 100 of inhabitants	1	1	1		
Tourism accommodation					
Number of rooms	3,907	4,659	5,311	19.2	14.0
Nights spent in hotels and similar establishments (1000)	283	355	381	25.4	7.3
by non-residents (inbound tourism)	229	291	310	27.1	6.5
by residents (domestic tourism)	54	64	71	18.5	10.9
Receipts and Expenditure for International Tourism					
International Tourism Receipts (US$ million)	128	140	148	9.4	5.7
- per Tourist Arrival (US$)	1,160	1,243	1,036	7.2	-16.6
- per capita (US$)	12	13	13		
International Fare Receipts (US$ million)	8	2	1	-75.0	-50.0
International Tourism Expenditure (US$ million)	48	66	77	37.5	16.7
- per capita (US$)	4	6	7		
International Fare Expenditure (US$ million)	46	59	56	28.3	-5.1
Δ International Tourism Balance (US$ million)	80	74	71		
Δ International Fare Balance (US$ million)	-38	-57	-55		

Source: World Tourism Organization (UNWTO)   (Data as collected by UNWTO for TMT 2006 Edition)
See annex for methodological notes and reference of external sources used.

World Tourism Organization ©

International Tourism by Origin

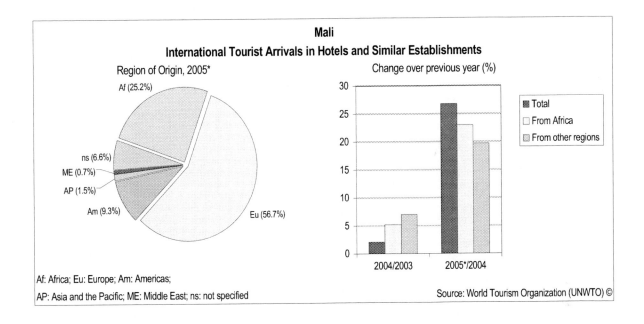

Af: Africa; Eu: Europe; Am: Americas;

AP: Asia and the Pacific; ME: Middle East; ns: not specified

Source: World Tourism Organization (UNWTO) ©

Mali

International Tourist Arrivals in Hotels and Similar Establishments (by nationality)

	1995	2000	2003	2004	2005*	Market share (%) 2000	Market share (%) 2005*	Growth rate (%) 04/03	Growth rate (%) 05*/04	Average per year (%) 2000-2005*
Total	**42,897**	**86,469**	**110,365**	**112,654**	**142,814**	**100**	**100**	**2.1**	**26.8**	**10.6**
From Africa	*12,026*	*18,962*	*27,816*	*29,256*	*35,985*	*21.9*	*25.2*	*5.2*	*23.0*	*13.7*
All West Africa	..	16,312	19,000	21,993	23,972	18.9	16.8	15.8	9.0	8.0
All Africa	12,026	..	..	..	..					
Other Africa	..	2,650	8,816	7,263	12,013	3.1	8.4	-17.6	65.4	35.3
From other regions	*27,748*	*60,836*	*76,049*	*81,387*	*97,409*	*70.4*	*68.2*	*7.0*	*19.7*	*9.9*
France	8,065	19,008	27,047	37,971	37,851	22.0	26.5	40.4	-0.3	14.8
United States	3,537	6,841	6,113	8,951	9,641	7.9	6.8	46.4	7.7	7.1
Benelux	1,662	7,858	9,046	6,591	9,002	9.1	6.3	-27.1	36.6	2.8
Spain	1,027	3,060	4,692	4,322	7,069	3.5	4.9	-7.9	63.6	18.2
Italy	1,250	9,638	11,570	6,087	7,066	11.1	4.9	-47.4	16.1	-6.0
Germany	1,833	2,776	3,200	3,676	5,885	3.2	4.1	14.9	60.1	16.2
United Kingdom	438	1,211	1,752	560	5,180	1.4	3.6	-68.0	825.0	33.7
Canada	1,152	2,465	3,280	3,543	3,646	2.9	2.6	8.0	2.9	8.1
Switzerland	7,214	917	1,345	1,236	2,384	1.1	1.7	-8.1	92.9	21.1
Austria	298	73	636	1,167	2,175	0.1	1.5	83.5	86.4	97.2
Japan	728	1,020	1,200	3,117	2,090	1.2	1.5	159.8	-32.9	15.4
Scandinavia	224	2,316	2,728	800	1,946	2.7	1.4	-70.7	143.3	-3.4
All Middle East	176	2,206	2,712	1,524	1,064	2.6	0.7	-43.8	-30.2	-13.6
Former U.S.S.R.	129	615	728	1,842	524	0.7	0.4	153.0	-71.6	-3.2
Other Central/Eastern Europe	15	832	..	..	1,886	1.0	1.3			17.8
Other World/Not specified	*3,123*	*6,671*	*6,500*	*2,011*	*9,420*	*7.7*	*6.6*	*-69.1*	*368.4*	*7.1*

Source: World Tourism Organization (UNWTO) ©   (Data as collected by UNWTO for TMT 2006 Edition)

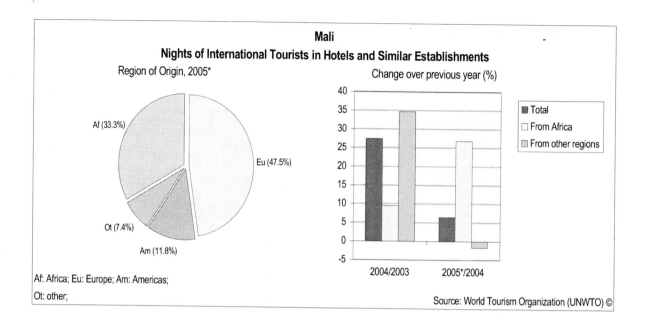

Mali
Nights of International Tourists in Hotels and Similar Establishments

Region of Origin, 2005*

Af (33.3%)
Eu (47.5%)
Ot (7.4%)
Am (11.8%)

Af: Africa; Eu: Europe; Am: Americas;
Ot: other;

Change over previous year (%)

Total
From Africa
From other regions

2004/2003   2005*/2004

Source: World Tourism Organization (UNWTO) ©

Mali

Nights of International Tourists in Hotels and Similar Establishments (by nationality)

	1995	2000	2003	2004	2005*	Market share (%) 2000	Market share (%) 2005*	Growth rate (%) 04/03	Growth rate (%) 05*/04	Average per year (%) 2000-2005*
Total	**102,678**	**173,560**	**228,663**	**291,447**	**310,202**	**100**	**100**	**27.5**	**6.4**	**12.3**
From Africa	*29,713*	*51,548*	*74,291*	*81,352*	*103,149*	*29.7*	*33.3*	*9.5*	*26.8*	*14.9*
All West Africa	..	47,236	43,830	60,658	75,701	27.2	24.4	38.4	24.8	9.9
All Africa	29,713	..	..	..	..					
Other Africa	..	4,312	30,461	20,694	27,448	2.5	8.8	-32.1	32.6	44.8
From other regions	*66,476*	*115,195*	*143,256*	*192,967*	*189,636*	*66.4*	*61.1*	*34.7*	*-1.7*	*10.5*
France	20,734	50,995	54,335	63,776	71,953	29.4	23.2	17.4	12.8	7.1
United States	9,501	7,100	14,119	63,776	27,047	4.1	8.7	351.7	-57.6	30.7
Benelux	4,569	14,968	15,446	10,794	15,466	8.6	5.0	-30.1	43.3	0.7
Spain	1,854	7,621	8,387	6,382	10,411	4.4	3.4	-23.9	63.1	6.4
Italy	2,455	11,687	15,525	10,519	10,209	6.7	3.3	-32.2	-2.9	-2.7
Germany	3,831	4,817	6,406	5,990	10,082	2.8	3.3	-6.5	68.3	15.9
Canada	3,830	4,644	8,094	9,376	9,675	2.7	3.1	15.8	3.2	15.8
United Kingdom	1,077	2,136	2,480	1,030	8,891	1.2	2.9	-58.5	763.2	33.0
Switzerland	14,529	1,026	2,736	2,823	6,286	0.6	2.0	3.2	122.7	43.7
Scandinavia	1,040	3,511	5,287	2,158	5,365	2.0	1.7	-59.2	148.6	8.8
Austria	408	207	1,048	1,690	3,812	0.1	1.2	61.3	125.6	79.1
Japan	1,666	1,413	2,421	5,052	3,294	0.8	1.1	108.7	-34.8	18.4
All Middle East	607	2,822	4,322	2,605	2,342	1.6	0.8	-39.7	-10.1	-3.7
Former U.S.S.R.	44	801	1,580	3,258	855	0.5	0.3	106.2	-73.8	1.3
Other Central/Eastern Europe	331	1,447	1,070	3,738	3,948	0.8	1.3	249.3	5.6	22.2
Other World/Not specified	*6,489*	*6,817*	*11,116*	*17,128*	*17,417*	*3.9*	*5.6*	*54.1*	*1.7*	*20.6*

Source: World Tourism Organization (UNWTO) ©   (Data as collected by UNWTO for TMT 2006 Edition)

World Tourism Organization ©

III.2.11 Mauritania   West Africa

Promotional: www.mauritania.mr

Profile

Mauritania

Africa
West Africa

Capital	Nouakchott
Year of entry in UNWTO	1976
Area (1000 km²)	1,026
Population (2005, million)	3.1
Gross Domestic Product (GDP) (2005, US$ million)	1,871
GDP per capita (2005, US$)	663
GDP growth (real, %)	

· 2004: 5.2;   2005: 5.4;   2006*: 14.1;   2007*: 10.6

Source: World Tourism Organization (UNWTO)   (Data as collected by UNWTO for TMT 2006 Edition)

See annex for methodological notes and reference of external sources used.

III.2.12 Niger   West Africa

Profile

Niger

Capital	Niamey
Year of entry in UNWTO	1979
Area (1000 km²)	1,267
Population (2005, million)	12.2
Gross Domestic Product (GDP) (2005, US$ million)	3,439
GDP per capita (2005, US$)	274

Africa
West Africa

GDP growth (real, %)
'-> 2004: -0.6;   2005: 7.0;   2006*: 3.5;   2007*: 4.2

	2003	2004	2005*	2004/2003	2005*/2004
International Arrivals					
Tourists (overnight visitors) (1000)	55	57	63	3.0	11.3
- per 100 of inhabitants	0	0	1		
Tourism accommodation					
Number of rooms	1,472	1,741	1,873	18.3	7.6
Nights spent in collective establishments (1000)					
by non-residents (inbound tourism)	253	263	298	4.0	13.3
Nights spent in hotels and similar establishments (1000)	146	139	158	-4.8	13.7
by non-residents (inbound tourism)	121	124	140	2.5	12.9
by residents (domestic tourism)	25	15	18	-40.0	20.0
Receipts and Expenditure for International Tourism					
International Tourism Receipts (US$ million)	28	31	34	10.7	9.7
- per Tourist Arrival (US$)	506	544	536	7.5	-1.5
- per capita (US$)	2	3	3		
International Fare Receipts (US$ million)	1	1	..		
International Tourism Expenditure (US$ million)	22	22	32		45.5
- per capita (US$)	2	2	3		
International Fare Expenditure (US$ million)	17	20	23	17.6	15.0
Δ International Tourism Balance (US$ million)	6	9	2		
Δ International Fare Balance (US$ million)	-16	-19	..		

Source: World Tourism Organization (UNWTO)   (Data as collected by UNWTO for TMT 2006 Edition)
See annex for methodological notes and reference of external sources used.

International Tourism by Origin

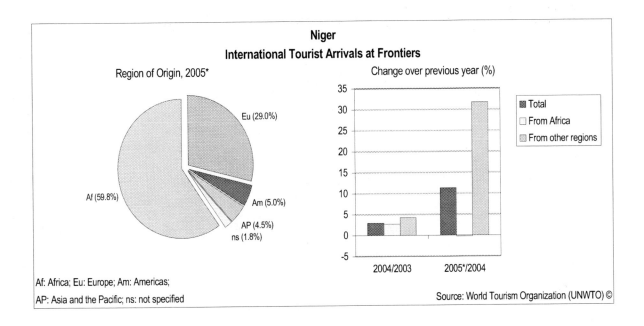

Niger
International Tourist Arrivals at Frontiers

Region of Origin, 2005*

Eu (29.0%)
Af (59.8%)
Am (5.0%)
AP (4.5%)
ns (1.8%)

Change over previous year (%)

Total
From Africa
From other regions

2004/2003   2005*/2004

Af: Africa; Eu: Europe; Am: Americas;
AP: Asia and the Pacific; ns: not specified

Source: World Tourism Organization (UNWTO) ©

Niger
International Tourist Arrivals at Frontiers (by nationality)

	1995	2000	2003	2004	2005*	Market share (%) 2000	Market share (%) 2005*	Growth rate (%) 04/03	Growth rate (%) 05*/04	Average per year (%) 2000-2005*
Total	**35,132**	**50,263**	**55,344**	**57,000**	**63,451**	**100**	**100**	**3.0**	**11.3**	**4.8**
From Africa	*7,151*	*28,181*	*37,000*	*38,000*	*37,926*	*56.1*	*59.8*	*2.7*	*-0.2*	*6.1*
All Africa	7,151	28,181	37,000	38,000	37,926	56.1	59.8	2.7	-0.2	6.1
From other regions	*8,948*	*17,975*	*17,744*	*18,500*	*24,373*	*35.8*	*38.4*	*4.3*	*31.7*	*6.3*
France	4,611	12,231	11,000	12,000	14,588	24.3	23.0	9.1	21.6	3.6
All Americas	1,701	2,500	2,000	2,500	3,150	5.0	5.0	25.0	26.0	4.7
All Asia	472	1,392	1,400	1,500	2,835	2.8	4.5	7.1	89.0	15.3
Germany	..	..	1,500	1,000	1,500		2.4	-33.3	50.0	
Benelux	..	..	1,300	1,000	1,300		2.0	-23.1	30.0	
Italy	..	..	400	500	1,000		1.6	25.0	100.0	
Other Europe	2,164	1,852	144	..	..	3.7				
Other World/Not specified	*19,033*	*4,107*	*600*	*500*	*1,152*	*8.2*	*1.8*	*-16.7*	*130.4*	*-22.4*

Source: World Tourism Organization (UNWTO) ©   (Data as collected by UNWTO for TMT 2006 Edition)
Note: air arrivals

III.2.13 Nigeria | West Africa

Profile

Nigeria

Capital	Abuja
Year of entry in UNWTO	1975
Area (1000 km²)	924
Population (2005, million)	129
Gross Domestic Product (GDP) (2005, US$ million)	99,147
GDP per capita (2005, US$)	678

Africa

West Africa

GDP growth (real, %)

'-> 2004: 6.0;   2005: 6.9;   2006*: 5.2;   2007*: 6.4

	2003	2004	2005*	2004/2003	2005*/2004
International Arrivals					
Visitors (1000)	2,253	2,646	2,778	17.5	5.0
Tourists (overnight visitors) (1000)	924	962	1,010	4.1	5.0
- per 100 of inhabitants	1	1	1		
Tourism accommodation					
Number of bed-places	37,528	37,738	38,870	0.6	3.0
Receipts and Expenditure for International Tourism					
International Tourism Receipts (US$ million)	49	21	18	-57.6	-14.2
- per Tourist Arrival (US$)	54	22	18	-59.3	-18.3
- per Visitor Arrival (US$)	22	8	6	-63.9	-18.3
- per capita (US$)	0	0	0		
International Fare Receipts (US$ million)	63	28	28	-55.3	-0.8
International Tourism Expenditure (US$ million)	1,793	1,156	1,109	-35.5	-4.1
- per capita (US$)	15	9	9		
International Fare Expenditure (US$ million)	281	307	276	9.3	-10.1
Δ International Tourism Balance (US$ million)	-1,743	-1,135	-1,091		
Δ International Fare Balance (US$ million)	-218	-279	-248		

Source: World Tourism Organization (UNWTO)   (Data as collected by UNWTO for TMT 2006 Edition)

See annex for methodological notes and reference of external sources used.

World Tourism Organization ©

International Tourism by Origin

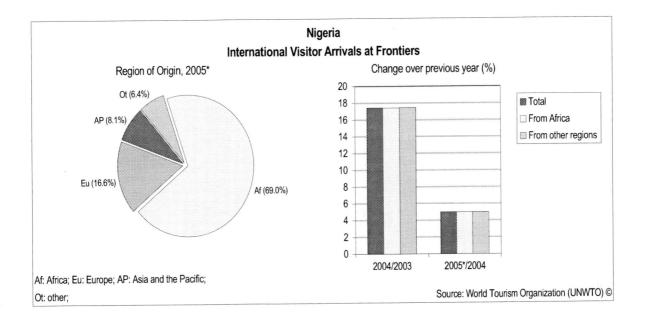

Nigeria
International Visitor Arrivals at Frontiers

Region of Origin, 2005*

Ot (6.4%)
AP (8.1%)
Eu (16.6%)
Af (69.0%)

Change over previous year (%)

Total
From Africa
From other regions

2004/2003   2005*/2004

Af: Africa; Eu: Europe; AP: Asia and the Pacific;
Ot: other;

Source: World Tourism Organization (UNWTO) ©

Nigeria
International Visitor Arrivals at Frontiers (by nationality)

	1995	2000	2003	2004	2005*	Market share (%)		Growth rate (%)		Average per year (%)
						2000	2005*	04/03	05*/04	2000-2005*
Total	1,030,739	1,491,767	2,253,115	2,646,411	2,778,365	100	100	17.5	5.0	13.2
From Africa	*737,762*	*1,050,993*	*1,554,308*	*1,825,312*	*1,916,246*	*70.5*	*69.0*	*17.4*	*5.0*	*12.8*
Niger	213,271	310,106	503,066	591,103	620,658	20.8	22.3	17.5	5.0	14.9
Benin	130,225	196,468	318,716	374,491	393,215	13.2	14.2	17.5	5.0	14.9
Liberia	39,671	53,663	87,053	102,287	107,401	3.6	3.9	17.5	5.0	14.9
Cameroon	39,651	53,516	86,815	102,008	107,108	3.6	3.9	17.5	5.0	14.9
Chad	32,555	42,508	68,958	81,026	85,077	2.8	3.1	17.5	5.0	14.9
Sudan	18,875	31,500	51,101	60,044	63,046	2.1	2.3	17.5	5.0	14.9
Morocco	15,509	28,790	46,704	54,877	57,620	1.9	2.1	17.5	5.0	14.9
Côte d'Ivoire	18,711	25,316	41,069	48,256	50,668	1.7	1.8	17.5	5.0	14.9
Ethiopia	13,289	18,546	30,085	35,350	37,117	1.2	1.3	17.5	5.0	14.9
Mali	12,091	18,480	29,979	35,225	36,986	1.2	1.3	17.5	5.0	14.9
Algeria	9,758	18,276	29,648	34,836	36,577	1.2	1.3	17.5	5.0	14.9
Togo	35,612	17,006	27,588	32,416	34,036	1.1	1.2	17.5	5.0	14.9
Burkina Faso	11,801	15,910	25,809	30,326	31,842	1.1	1.1	17.5	5.0	14.9
Tunisia	7,513	12,864	20,868	24,520	25,746	0.9	0.9	17.5	5.0	14.9
Senegal	8,721	10,924	17,721	20,822	21,548	0.7	0.8	17.5	3.5	14.6
Ghana	70,272	103,048	16,767	19,701	20,686	6.9	0.7	17.5	5.0	-27.5
Guinea	6,996	9,791	15,882	18,661	19,594	0.7	0.7	17.5	5.0	14.9
Kenya	7,301	10,115	16,409	18,281	19,195	0.7	0.7	11.4	5.0	13.7
Gambia	5,367	9,003	14,605	17,161	18,019	0.6	0.6	17.5	5.0	14.9
Namibia	4,982	8,349	13,544	15,914	16,709	0.6	0.6	17.5	5.0	14.9
Sierra Leone	5,701	8,266	13,409	15,756	16,543	0.6	0.6	17.5	5.0	14.9
Other intraregional	29,890	48,548	78,512	92,251	96,855	3.3	3.5	17.5	5.0	14.8
From other regions	*292,163*	*439,567*	*690,691*	*811,561*	*852,105*	*29.5*	*30.7*	*17.5*	*5.0*	*14.2*
Italy	25,718	32,770	53,166	62,470	65,593	2.2	2.4	17.5	5.0	14.9
France	21,294	30,913	50,149	58,925	61,871	2.1	2.2	17.5	5.0	14.9
Germany	19,950	30,153	48,915	57,475	60,348	2.0	2.2	17.5	5.0	14.9
Mexico	5,580	20,858	33,836	39,757	41,744	1.4	1.5	17.5	5.0	14.9
United Kingdom	12,256	19,800	31,310	36,789	38,628	1.3	1.4	17.5	5.0	14.3
China	11,835	16,633	26,983	31,705	33,290	1.1	1.2	17.5	5.0	14.9
Pakistan	8,578	13,841	22,453	26,382	27,701	0.9	1.0	17.5	5.0	14.9
India	9,891	14,666	21,031	24,711	25,946	1.0	0.9	17.5	5.0	12.1
Taiwan (pr. of China)	8,578	11,300	18,332	21,540	22,617	0.8	0.8	17.5	5.0	14.9
Romania	7,590	10,916	17,708	20,807	21,847	0.7	0.8	17.5	5.0	14.9
Spain	7,760	10,400	16,886	19,841	20,833	0.7	0.7	17.5	5.0	14.9
Lebanon	6,016	9,503	15,416	18,114	19,019	0.6	0.7	17.5	5.0	14.9
Finland	6,904	9,112	14,783	17,370	18,238	0.6	0.7	17.5	5.0	14.9
United States	13,301	9,098	14,759	17,342	18,209	0.6	0.7	17.5	5.0	14.9
Malaysia	5,041	8,748	14,192	16,676	17,509	0.6	0.6	17.5	5.0	14.9
Hungary	5,024	8,516	13,814	16,232	17,043	0.6	0.6	17.5	5.0	14.9
Indonesia	6,293	8,509	13,804	16,220	17,031	0.6	0.6	17.5	5.0	14.9
Hong Kong (China)	5,916	8,364	13,569	15,944	16,741	0.6	0.6	17.5	5.0	14.9
Denmark	5,412	8,163	13,243	15,561	16,339	0.5	0.6	17.5	5.0	14.9
Egypt	4,191	8,138	13,201	15,511	16,286	0.5	0.6	17.5	5.0	14.9
Other interregional	95,035	149,166	223,141	262,189	275,272	10.0	9.9	17.5	5.0	13.0
Other World/Not specified	*814*	*1,207*	*8,116*	*9,538*	*10,014*	*0.1*	*0.4*	*17.5*	*5.0*	*52.7*

Source: World Tourism Organization (UNWTO) ©

(Data as collected by UNWTO for TMT 2006 Edition)

World Tourism Organization ©

III.2.14 Senegal   West Africa

Promotional: www.primature.sn/tour
Institutional/corporate: www.tourisme.gouv.sn

Profile

Senegal

Capital	Dakar
Year of entry in UNWTO	1975
Area (1000 km²)	197
Population (2005, million)	11.9
Gross Domestic Product (GDP) (2005, US$ million)	8,609
GDP per capita (2005, US$)	738

Africa
West Africa

GDP growth (real, %)
'-> 2004: 5.6;   2005: 5.5;   2006*: 4.0;   2007*: 5.3

	2003	2004	2005*	2004/2003	2005*/2004
International Arrivals					
Visitors (1000)	502	677	779	34.9	15.1
Tourists (overnight visitors) (1000)	495	667	769	34.7	15.3
- per 100 of inhabitants	4	6	6		
Cruise passengers (1000)	7	10	9	42.9	-10.0
Tourism accommodation					
Number of rooms	10,268	10,884	15,842	6.0	45.6
Nights spent in hotels and similar establishments (1000)	1,607	1,508	1,595	-6.2	5.8
by non-residents (inbound tourism)	1,451	1,349	1,397	-7.0	3.6
by residents (domestic tourism)	156	159	198	1.9	24.5
Receipts and Expenditure for International Tourism					
International Tourism Receipts (US$ million)	209	212	..	1.4	
- per Tourist Arrival (US$)	422	318	..	-24.7	
- per Visitor Arrival (US$)	416	313	..	-24.8	
- per capita (US$)	19	18	..		
International Fare Receipts (US$ million)	60	75	..	25.0	
International Tourism Expenditure (US$ million)	55	57	..	3.6	
- per capita (US$)	5	5	..		
International Fare Expenditure (US$ million)	74	81	..	9.5	
Δ International Tourism Balance (US$ million)	154	155	..		
Δ International Fare Balance (US$ million)	-14	-6	..		

Source: World Tourism Organization (UNWTO)   (Data as collected by UNWTO for TMT 2006 Edition)

See annex for methodological notes and reference of external sources used.

International Tourism by Origin

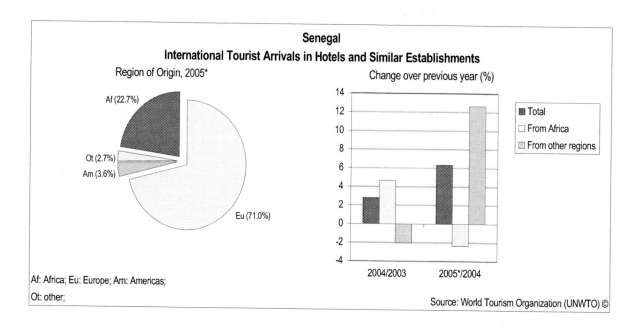

Senegal
International Tourist Arrivals in Hotels and Similar Establishments

Region of Origin, 2005*

Change over previous year (%)

Af (22.7%)
Ot (2.7%)
Am (3.6%)
Eu (71.0%)

Total
From Africa
From other regions

2004/2003   2005*/2004

Af: Africa; Eu: Europe; Am: Americas;
Ot: other;

Source: World Tourism Organization (UNWTO) ©

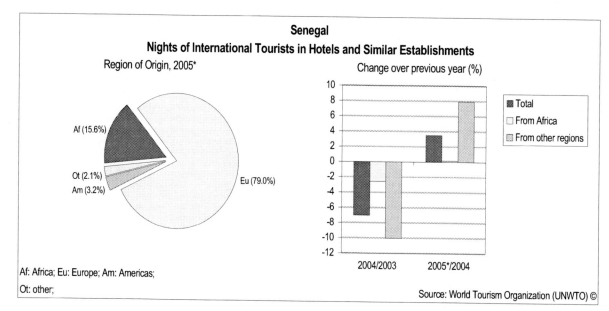

Senegal
Nights of International Tourists in Hotels and Similar Establishments

Region of Origin, 2005*

Change over previous year (%)

Af (15.6%)
Ot (2.1%)
Am (3.2%)
Eu (79.0%)

Total
From Africa
From other regions

2004/2003   2005*/2004

Af: Africa; Eu: Europe; Am: Americas;
Ot: other;

Source: World Tourism Organization (UNWTO) ©

Senegal
International Tourist Arrivals in Hotels and Similar Establishments (by nationality)

	1995	2000	2003	2004	2005*	Market share (%) 2000	Market share (%) 2005*	Growth rate (%) 04/03	Growth rate (%) 05*/04	Average per year (%) 2000-2005*
Total	280,000	389,433	353,539	363,490	386,564	100	100	2.8	6.3	-0.1
From Africa	*56,651*	*96,834*	*85,664*	*89,660*	*87,565*	*24.9*	*22.7*	*4.7*	*-2.3*	*-2.0*
All Africa	56,651	96,834	85,664	89,660	87,565	24.9	22.7	4.7	-2.3	-2.0
From other regions	*220,872*	*290,884*	*266,119*	*260,752*	*293,732*	*74.7*	*76.0*	*-2.0*	*12.6*	*0.2*
France	146,718	193,135	181,470	172,878	191,580	49.6	49.6	-4.7	10.8	-0.2
Benelux	11,294	15,233	17,025	16,160	21,712	3.9	5.6	-5.1	34.4	7.3
Spain	5,526	20,614	12,680	13,415	15,353	5.3	4.0	5.8	14.4	-5.7
Italy	14,871	13,923	9,279	9,413	11,493	3.6	3.0	1.4	22.1	-3.8
United States	8,867	12,017	8,518	10,422	11,080	3.1	2.9	22.4	6.3	-1.6
Germany	13,955	8,199	7,985	8,374	9,615	2.1	2.5	4.9	14.8	3.2
United Kingdom	3,063	4,533	3,063	4,092	4,380	1.2	1.1	33.6	7.0	-0.7
All Central/Eastern Europe	569	507	532	995	2,334	0.1	0.6	87.0	134.6	35.7
Canada	2,018	900	1,158	1,605	2,272	0.2	0.6	38.6	41.6	20.3
Portugal	681	892	1,511	1,729	1,817	0.2	0.5	14.4	5.1	15.3
Switzerland	3,396	2,068	1,475	1,370	1,513	0.5	0.4	-7.1	10.4	-6.1
All Middle East	1,174	988	1,253	1,672	1,467	0.3	0.4	33.4	-12.3	8.2
Sweden	454	264	276	338	660	0.1	0.2	22.5	95.3	20.1
Finland	134	160	119	136	390	0.0	0.1	14.3	186.8	19.5
Denmark	193	199	639	298	374	0.1	0.1	-53.4	25.5	13.4
Norway	190	163	415	219	257	0.0	0.1	-47.2	17.4	9.5
Other Americas	359	275	349	404	637	0.1	0.2	15.8	57.7	18.3
Other Europe	4,477	14,145	16,099	13,527	12,961	3.6	3.4	-16.0	-4.2	-1.7
All East Asia/Pacific	2,933	2,669	2,273	3,705	3,837	0.7	1.0	63.0	3.6	7.5
Other World/Not specified	*2,477*	*1,715*	*1,756*	*13,078*	*5,267*	*0.4*	*1.4*	*644.8*	*-59.7*	*25.2*

Source: World Tourism Organization (UNWTO) ©   (Data as collected by UNWTO for TMT 2006 Edition)

Senegal

Nights of International Tourists in Hotels and Similar Establishments (by nationality)

	1995	2000	2003	2004	2005*	Market share (%)		Growth rate (%)		Average per year (%)
						2000	2005*	04/03	05*/04	2000-2005*
Total	**1,139,258**	**1,401,470**	**1,451,213**	**1,349,397**	**1,396,673**	**100**	**100**	**-7.0**	**3.5**	**-0.1**
From Africa	*155,297*	*208,408*	*223,917*	*218,151*	*218,487*	*14.9*	*15.6*	*-2.6*	*0.2*	*0.9*
All Africa	155,297	208,408	223,917	218,151	218,487	14.9	15.6	-2.6	0.2	0.9
From other regions	*980,825*	*1,188,965*	*1,200,802*	*1,080,513*	*1,166,239*	*84.8*	*83.5*	*-10.0*	*7.9*	*-0.4*
France	646,656	849,103	852,973	766,034	794,315	60.6	56.9	-10.2	3.7	-1.3
Benelux	44,301	83,124	87,277	90,741	100,896	5.9	7.2	4.0	11.2	4.0
Germany	121,418	73,786	41,608	47,493	50,475	5.3	3.6	14.1	6.3	-7.3
Italy	54,934	45,858	41,608	30,608	43,254	3.3	3.1	-26.4	41.3	-1.2
Spain	13,952	40,415	32,703	30,402	37,491	2.9	2.7	-7.0	23.3	-1.5
United States	31,673	23,824	53,990	26,737	35,908	1.7	2.6	-50.5	34.3	8.6
United Kingdom	7,413	12,814	10,565	9,535	11,896	0.9	0.9	-9.7	24.8	-1.5
All Central/Eastern Europe	1,800	1,351	1,531	2,865	9,019	0.1	0.6	87.1	214.8	46.2
Canada	6,477	2,704	3,781	5,411	7,510	0.2	0.5	43.1	38.8	22.7
Switzerland	18,408	14,267	6,487	6,085	7,372	1.0	0.5	-6.2	21.2	-12.4
Portugal	4,690	3,492	5,372	5,249	5,808	0.2	0.4	-2.3	10.6	10.7
All Middle East	4,013	3,351	2,928	7,358	5,808	0.2	0.4	151.3	-21.1	11.6
Sweden	1,654	831	655	890	2,494	0.1	0.2	35.9	180.2	24.6
Denmark	709	417	1,205	904	1,072	0.0	0.1	-25.0	18.6	20.8
Finland	301	371	331	390	952	0.0	0.1	17.8	144.1	20.7
Norway	482	415	1,015	781	715	0.0	0.1	-23.1	-8.5	11.5
Other Americas	1,119	617	853	1,361	1,854	0.0	0.1	59.6	36.2	24.6
Other Europe	10,624	25,941	48,774	38,093	37,703	1.9	2.7	-21.9	-1.0	7.8
All East Asia/Pacific	10,201	6,284	7,146	9,576	11,697	0.4	0.8	34.0	22.1	13.2
Other World/Not specified	*3,136*	*4,097*	*26,494*	*50,733*	*11,947*	*0.3*	*0.9*	*91.5*	*-76.5*	*23.9*

Source: World Tourism Organization (UNWTO) ©

(Data as collected by UNWTO for TMT 2006 Edition)

III.2.15 Sierra Leone　　　　　　West Africa

Promotional:　　　www.welcometosierraleone.org ; www.visitsierraleone.org

Profile

Sierra Leone

Capital	Freetown
Year of entry in UNWTO	1975
Area (1000 km²)	72
Population (2005, million)	5.9
Gross Domestic Product (GDP) (2005, US$ million)	1,213
GDP per capita (2005, US$)	223

Africa
West Africa

GDP growth (real, %)
'-> 2004: 7.4;　2005: 7.2;　2006*: 7.4;　2007*: 6.5

	2003	2004	2005*	2004/2003	2005*/2004
International Arrivals					
Tourists (overnight visitors) (1000)	38	44	40	14.3	-8.1
- per 100 of inhabitants	1	1	1		
Tourism accommodation					
Number of rooms	1,457	1,622	2,012	11.3	24.0
Nights spent in hotels and similar establishments (1000)					
by non-residents (inbound tourism)	191	218	280	14.1	28.4
Outbound Tourism					
Trips abroad (1000)	13	28	63	115.4	125.0
- per 100 of inhabitants	0	0	1		
Receipts and Expenditure for International Tourism					
International Tourism Receipts (US$ million)	60	58	64	-3.3	10.3
- per Tourist Arrival (US$)	1,575	1,331	1,599	-15.4	20.1
- per capita (US$)	11	10	11		
International Tourism Expenditure (US$ million)	37	30	32	-18.9	6.7
- per trip (US$)	2,846	1,071	508	-62.4	-52.6
- per capita (US$)	7	5	5		
International Fare Expenditure (US$ million)	1	0	2	-62.5	433.3
Δ International Tourism Balance (US$ million)	23	28	32		

Source: World Tourism Organization (UNWTO)　　　　　　(Data as collected by UNWTO for TMT 2006 Edition)

See annex for methodological notes and reference of external sources used.

International Tourism by Origin

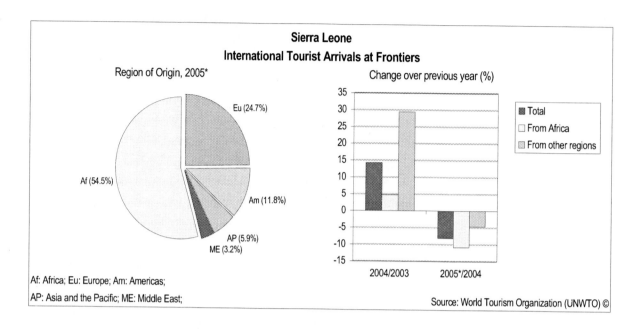

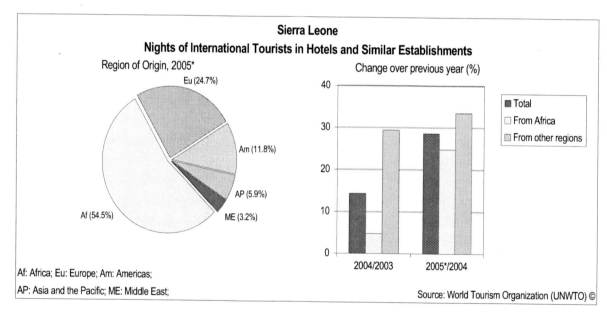

Sierra Leone
International Tourist Arrivals at Frontiers (by residence)

	1995	2000	2003	2004	2005*	Market share (%) 2000	Market share (%) 2005*	Growth rate (%) 04/03	Growth rate (%) 05*/04	Average per year (%) 2000-2005*
Total	**13,765**	**15,713**	**38,107**	**43,560**	**40,023**	**100**	**100**	**14.3**	**-8.1**	**20.6**
From Africa	*5,087*	*4,810*	*23,341*	*24,446*	*21,798*	*30.6*	*54.5*	*4.7*	*-10.8*	*35.3*
All Africa	5,087	4,810	23,341	24,446	21,798	30.6	54.5	4.7	-10.8	35.3
From other regions	*4,670*	*10,903*	*14,766*	*19,114*	*18,225*	*69.4*	*45.5*	*29.4*	*-4.7*	*10.8*
All Europe	2,553	5,658	6,460	9,476	9,879	36.0	24.7	46.7	4.3	11.8
All Americas	2,117	2,454	4,699	4,790	4,713	15.6	11.8	1.9	-1.6	13.9
All Asia	..	1,923	1,995	2,257	2,343	12.2	5.9	13.1	3.8	4.0
All Middle East	..	868	1,612	2,591	1,290	5.5	3.2	60.7	-50.2	8.2
Other World/Not specified	*4,008*	*..*	*..*	*..*	*..*					

Source: World Tourism Organization (UNWTO) ©   (Data as collected by UNWTO for TMT 2006 Edition)

Sierra Leone
Nights of International Tourists in Hotels and Similar Establishments (by residence)

	1995	2000	2003	2004	2005*	Market share (%) 2000	Market share (%) 2005*	Growth rate (%) 04/03	Growth rate (%) 05*/04	Average per year (%) 2000-2005*
Total	**309,007**	**78,565**	**190,535**	**217,800**	**280,161**	**100**	**100**	**14.3**	**28.6**	**29.0**
From Africa	*114,209*	*24,050*	*116,705*	*122,230*	*152,586*	*30.6*	*54.5*	*4.7*	*24.8*	*44.7*
All Africa	114,209	24,050	116,705	122,230	152,586	30.6	54.5	4.7	24.8	44.7
From other regions	*104,815*	*54,515*	*73,830*	*95,570*	*127,575*	*69.4*	*45.5*	*29.4*	*33.5*	*18.5*
All Europe	57,290	28,290	32,300	47,380	69,153	36.0	24.7	46.7	46.0	19.6
All Americas	47,525	12,270	23,495	23,950	32,991	15.6	11.8	1.9	37.7	21.9
All Asia	..	9,615	9,975	11,285	16,401	12.2	5.9	13.1	45.3	11.3
All Middle East	..	4,340	8,060	12,955	9,030	5.5	3.2	60.7	-30.3	15.8
Other World/Not specified	*89,983*	*..*	*..*	*..*	*..*					

Source: World Tourism Organization (UNWTO) ©   (Data as collected by UNWTO for TMT 2006 Edition)

III.2.16   Togo West Africa

Profile

Togo

Africa
West Africa

Capital	Lomé
Year of entry in UNWTO	1975
Area (1000 km²)	57
Population (2005, million)	5.4
Gross Domestic Product (GDP) (2005, US$ million)	2,107
GDP per capita (2005, US$)	377
GDP growth (real, %)	

'-> 2004: 3.0;   2005: 0.8;   2006*: 4.2;   2007*: 4.5

	2003	2004	2005*	2004/2003	2005*/2004
International Arrivals					
Tourists (overnight visitors) (1000)	61	83	81	36.5	-2.3
- per 100 of inhabitants	1	2	1		
Tourism accommodation					
Number of rooms	4,480	4,728	4,944	5.5	4.6
Nights spent in hotels and similar establishments (1000)	154	212	182	37.7	-14.2
by non-residents (inbound tourism)	136	183	157	34.6	-14.2
by residents (domestic tourism)	18	29	25	61.1	-13.8
Receipts and Expenditure for International Tourism					
International Tourism Receipts (US$ million)	15	19	..	26.7	
- per Tourist Arrival (US$)	248	230	..	-7.2	
- per capita (US$)	3	4	..		
International Fare Receipts (US$ million)	11	6	..	-45.5	
International Tourism Expenditure (US$ million)	7	8	..	14.3	
- per capita (US$)	1	2	..		
International Fare Expenditure (US$ million)	30	30	..		
Δ International Tourism Balance (US$ million)	8	11	..		
Δ International Fare Balance (US$ million)	-19	-24	..		

Source: World Tourism Organization (UNWTO)   (Data as collected by UNWTO for TMT 2006 Edition)
See annex for methodological notes and reference of external sources used.

International Tourism by Origin

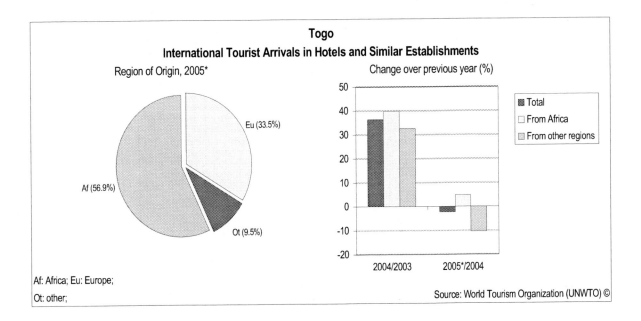

Togo
International Tourist Arrivals in Hotels and Similar Establishments

Region of Origin, 2005*

Change over previous year (%)

Af: Africa; Eu: Europe;
Ot: other;

Source: World Tourism Organization (UNWTO) ©

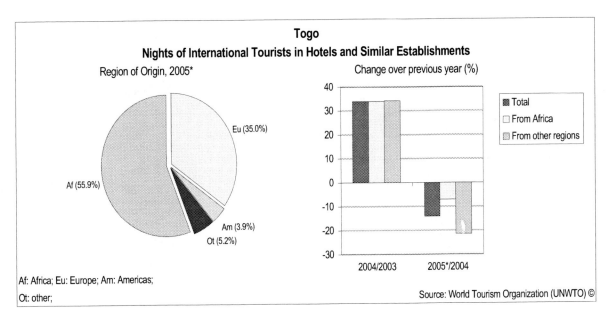

Togo
Nights of International Tourists in Hotels and Similar Establishments

Region of Origin, 2005*

Change over previous year (%)

Af: Africa; Eu: Europe; Am: Americas;
Ot: other;

Source: World Tourism Organization (UNWTO) ©

Togo

International Tourist Arrivals in Hotels and Similar Establishments (by residence)

	1995	2000	2003	2004	2005*	Market share (%)		Growth rate (%)		Average per year (%)
						2000	2005*	04/03	05*/04	2000-2005*
Total	53,061	59,541	60,592	82,686	80,763	100	100	36.5	-2.3	6.3
From Africa	28,016	29,546	31,334	43,842	45,967	49.6	56.9	39.9	4.8	9.2
Burkina Faso	6,164	6,079	5,953	8,132	8,069	10.2	10.0	36.6	-0.8	5.8
Côte d'Ivoire	4,259	2,415	4,134	5,860	5,916	4.1	7.3	41.8	1.0	19.6
Benin	3,699	4,964	5,111	7,434	5,909	8.3	7.3	45.5	-20.5	3.5
Nigeria	3,473	3,179	3,152	3,572	3,356	5.3	4.2	13.3	-6.0	1.1
Ghana	1,568	1,530	1,585	2,161	1,880	2.6	2.3	36.3	-13.0	4.2
Other Africa	8,853	11,379	11,399	16,683	20,837	19.1	25.8	46.4	24.9	12.9
From other regions	24,968	29,900	29,216	38,748	34,723	50.2	43.0	32.6	-10.4	3.0
France	9,516	9,690	14,154	17,674	16,511	16.3	20.4	24.9	-6.6	11.2
Benelux	2,114	1,127	509	1,024	3,517	1.9	4.4	101.2	243.5	25.6
All Middle East	959	1,203	1,495	2,500	2,371	2.0	2.9	67.2	-5.2	14.5
United States	1,821	1,688	1,384	2,097	2,141	2.8	2.7	51.5	2.1	4.9
Germany	2,467	1,391	830	879	1,092	2.3	1.4	5.9	24.2	-4.7
Italy	995	524	570	960	674	0.9	0.8	68.4	-29.8	5.2
United Kingdom	621	414	655	879	619	0.7	0.8	34.2	-29.6	8.4
Canada	554	249	315	443	398	0.4	0.5	40.6	-10.2	9.8
Switzerland	663	418	274	464	297	0.7	0.4	69.3	-36.0	-6.6
Former U.S.S.R.	2,675	87	79	567	168	0.1	0.2	617.7	-70.4	14.1
Japan	110	104	60	97	141	0.2	0.2	61.7	45.4	6.3
Scandinavia	210	63	24	70	34	0.1	0.0	191.7	-51.4	-11.6
Other Americas	226	113	86	198	94	0.2	0.1	130.2	-52.5	-3.6
Other Asia	565	1,167	1,392	3,395	2,486	2.0	3.1	143.9	-26.8	16.3
Other Europe	1,472	11,662	7,389	7,501	4,180	19.6	5.2	1.5	-44.3	-18.6
Other World/Not specified	77	95	42	96	73	0.2	0.1	128.6	-24.0	-5.1

Source: World Tourism Organization (UNWTO) ©

(Data as collected by UNWTO for TMT 2006 Edition)

Togo
Nights of International Tourists in Hotels and Similar Establishments (by residence)

	1995	2000	2003	2004	2005*	Market share (%)		Growth rate (%)		Average per year (%) 2000-2005*
						2000	2005*	04/03	05*/04	
Total	126,675	132,211	136,422	182,628	157,003	100	100	33.9	-14.0	3.5
From Africa	*59,689*	*69,262*	*70,552*	*94,440*	*87,755*	*52.4*	*55.9*	*33.9*	*-7.1*	*4.8*
Burkina Faso	15,221	14,634	13,743	16,704	15,907	11.1	10.1	21.5	-4.8	1.7
Côte d'Ivoire	9,013	6,249	11,373	16,321	12,167	4.7	7.7	43.5	-25.5	14.3
Benin	6,088	8,475	8,293	12,410	9,521	6.4	6.1	49.6	-23.3	2.4
Nigeria	6,029	6,302	5,961	8,147	6,519	4.8	4.2	36.7	-20.0	0.7
Ghana	2,686	3,055	3,181	3,977	3,687	2.3	2.3	25.0	-7.3	3.8
Other Africa	20,652	30,547	28,001	36,881	39,954	23.1	25.4	31.7	8.3	5.5
From other regions	*66,487*	*62,723*	*65,575*	*87,975*	*69,111*	*47.4*	*44.0*	*34.2*	*-21.4*	*2.0*
France	25,780	18,754	27,765	41,652	30,778	14.2	19.6	50.0	-26.1	10.4
Benelux	5,703	2,984	1,827	2,757	7,560	2.3	4.8	50.9	174.2	20.4
United States	4,045	5,088	3,740	5,135	4,735	3.8	3.0	37.3	-7.8	-1.4
All Middle East	..	1,672	1,779	2,809	3,142	1.3	2.0	57.9	11.9	13.4
Germany	7,247	3,281	2,199	3,080	2,363	2.5	1.5	40.1	-23.3	-6.4
United Kingdom	1,654	996	2,114	2,873	1,696	0.8	1.1	35.9	-41.0	11.2
Italy	3,992	1,259	1,538	1,857	1,453	1.0	0.9	20.7	-21.8	2.9
Canada	1,474	777	1,015	1,323	1,215	0.6	0.8	30.3	-8.2	9.4
Switzerland	2,452	1,422	1,350	1,212	638	1.1	0.4	-10.2	-47.4	-14.8
Former U.S.S.R.	5,646	168	373	256	574	0.1	0.4	-31.4	124.2	27.9
Japan	343	231	263	213	440	0.2	0.3	-19.0	106.6	13.8
Scandinavia	684	172	8	71	66	0.1	0.0	787.5	-7.0	-17.4
Other Americas	782	307	1,269	952	202	0.2	0.1	-25.0	-78.8	-8.0
Other North-East Asia	1,522	..	..	..	..					
Other Asia	1,285	2,276	2,809	5,582	4,415	1.7	2.8	98.7	-20.9	14.2
Other Europe	3,878	23,336	17,526	18,203	9,834	17.7	6.3	3.9	-46.0	-15.9
Other World/Not specified	*499*	*226*	*295*	*213*	*137*	*0.2*	*0.1*	*-27.8*	*-35.7*	*-9.5*

Source: World Tourism Organization (UNWTO) ©   (Data as collected by UNWTO for TMT 2006 Edition)

III.3 Central Africa

III.3.1 Angola   Central Africa

Profile

Angola

Africa
Central Africa

Capital	Luanda
Year of entry in UNWTO	1989
Area (1000 km²)	1,247
Population (2005, million)	11.7
Gross Domestic Product (GDP) (2005, US$ million)	32,810
GDP per capita (2005, US$)	2,129
GDP growth (real, %)	

GDP growth (real, %)
2004: 11.2;   2005: 20.6;   2006*: 14.3;   2007*: 31.4

	2003	2004	2005*	2004/2003	2005*/2004
International Arrivals					
Tourists (overnight visitors) (1000)	107	194	210	82.3	8.0
- per 100 of inhabitants	1	2	2		
Tourism accommodation					
Number of rooms	9,244	9,358	9,593	1.2	2.5
Nights spent in collective establishments (1000)	341	236	306	-30.8	29.7
by non-residents (inbound tourism)	217	149	182	-31.3	22.1
by residents (domestic tourism)	124	87	124	-29.8	42.5
Nights spent in hotels and similar establishments (1000)	290	204	248	-29.7	21.6
by non-residents (inbound tourism)	212	143	176	-32.5	23.1
by residents (domestic tourism)	78	61	72	-21.8	18.0
Receipts and Expenditure for International Tourism					
International Tourism Receipts (US$ million)	49	66	88	34.3	34.0
- per Tourist Arrival (US$)	460	339	420	-26.3	24.1
- per capita (US$)	4	6	8		
International Fare Receipts (US$ million)	14	16	15	14.3	-6.3
International Tourism Expenditure (US$ million)	12	39	74	220.7	90.7
- per capita (US$)	1	3	6		
International Fare Expenditure (US$ million)	37	47	61	27.0	29.8
Δ International Tourism Balance (US$ million)	37	27	14		
Δ International Fare Balance (US$ million)	-23	-31	-46		

Source: World Tourism Organization (UNWTO)   (Data as collected by UNWTO for TMT 2006 Edition)
See annex for methodological notes and reference of external sources used.

International Tourism by Origin

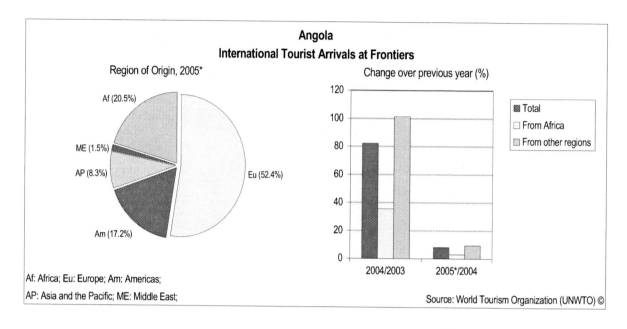

Angola
International Tourist Arrivals at Frontiers

Region of Origin, 2005*

Change over previous year (%)

Af: Africa; Eu: Europe; Am: Americas;
AP: Asia and the Pacific; ME: Middle East;

Source: World Tourism Organization (UNWTO) ©

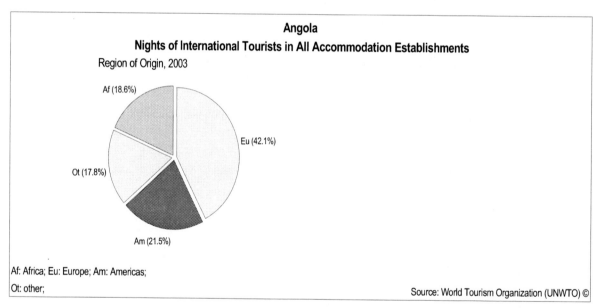

Angola
Nights of International Tourists in All Accommodation Establishments

Region of Origin, 2003

Af: Africa; Eu: Europe; Am: Americas;
Ot: other;

Source: World Tourism Organization (UNWTO) ©

Angola
International Tourist Arrivals at Frontiers (by residence)

	1995	2000	2003	2004	2005*	Market share (%) 2000	Market share (%) 2005*	Growth rate (%) 04/03	Growth rate (%) 05*/04	Average per year (%) 2000-2005*
Total	**9,546**	**50,765**	**106,625**	**194,329**	**209,956**	**100**	**100**	**82.3**	**8.0**	**32.8**
From Africa	*2,115*	*8,343*	*30,915*	*41,873*	*43,138*	*16.4*	*20.5*	*35.4*	*3.0*	*38.9*
All Africa	..	..	30,915	41,873	..			35.4		
South Africa	700	3,774	..	..	13,294	7.4	6.3			28.6
Congo	429	683	..	..	4,191	1.3	2.0			43.7
Dem.R.Congo	307	345	..	..	4,147	0.7	2.0			64.4
Mozambique	126	340	..	..	2,227	0.7	1.1			45.6
Sao Tome Prn	269	392	..	..	1,876	0.8	0.9			36.8
Zimbabwe	..	305	..	..	1,837	0.6	0.9			43.2
Nigeria	28	312	..	..	1,799	0.6	0.9			42.0
Cape Verde	..	239	..	..	1,788	0.5	0.9			49.6
Namibia	118	207	..	..	1,429	0.4	0.7			47.2
Zambia	72	179	..	..	1,095	0.4	0.5			43.7
Cameroon	..	140	..	..	1,030	0.3	0.5			49.1
Gabon	..	69	..	..	990	0.1	0.5			70.4
Morocco	..	38	..	..	906	0.1	0.4			88.6
Equatorial Guinea	..	56	..	..	810	0.1	0.4			70.6
Algeria	..	53	..	..	779	0.1	0.4			71.2
Tunisia	..	17	..	..	744	0.0	0.4			112.9
Other intraregional	66	1,194	..	..	4,196	2.4	2.0			28.6
From other regions	*7,431*	*42,422*	*75,710*	*152,456*	*166,818*	*83.6*	*79.5*	*101.4*	*9.4*	*31.5*
All Europe	..	..	55,190	101,180	..			83.3		
All Americas	..	..	14,770	34,045	..			130.5		
Portugal	3,357	15,601	..	..	29,527	30.7	14.1			13.6
France	1,413	4,577	..	..	17,658	9.0	8.4			31.0
All Asia	..	..	4,613	14,556	..			215.5		
United States	107	3,013	..	..	13,896	5.9	6.6			35.8
United Kingdom	..	3,648	..	..	11,157	7.2	5.3			25.1
Brazil	1,038	3,272	..	..	11,053	6.4	5.3			27.6
Belgium	938	597	..	..	7,459	1.2	3.6			65.7
Spain	..	1,361	..	..	7,368	2.7	3.5			40.2
China	..	475	..	..	5,849	0.9	2.8			65.2
Italy	93	935	..	..	5,250	1.8	2.5			41.2
Philippines	..	1,175	..	..	4,697	2.3	2.2			31.9
Netherlands	..	285	..	..	4,530	0.6	2.2			73.9
Israel	..	190	..	..	3,886	0.4	1.9			82.9
Norway	..	520	..	..	3,747	1.0	1.8			48.4
Cuba	..	303	..	..	3,673	0.6	1.7			64.7
Germany	..	359	..	..	3,399	0.7	1.6			56.8
Russian Federation	..	1,243	..	..	2,788	2.4	1.3			17.5
Sweden	..	94	..	..	2,465	0.2	1.2			92.2
Ireland	..	26	..	..	2,257	0.1	1.1			144.2
Denmark	..	246	..	..	1,686	0.5	0.8			47.0
Japan	..	347	..	..	1,661	0.7	0.8			36.8
India	..	561	..	..	1,642	1.1	0.8			24.0
Canada	..	451	..	..	1,566	0.9	0.7			28.3
Other interregional	485	3,143	1,137	2,675	19,604	6.2	9.3	135.3	632.9	44.2

Source: World Tourism Organization (UNWTO) ©   (Data as collected by UNWTO for TMT 2006 Edition)

Angola

Nights of International Tourists in All Accommodation Establishments (by residence)

	1995	2000	2002	2003	2004	Market share (%) 2000	Market share (%) 2004	Growth rate (%) 03/02	Growth rate (%) 04/03	Average per year (%) 2000-2004
Total	..	77,063	..	216,549	..	100				
From Africa	..	*8,994*	..	*40,175*	..	*11.7*				
South Africa	..	3,460	..	29,366	..	4.5				
Namibia	..	288	..	1,417	..	0.4				
Zimbabwe	..	438	..	1,310	..	0.6				
Mozambique	..	425	..	1,108	..	0.6				
Congo	..	361	..	777	..	0.5				
Dem.R.Congo	..	199	..	596	..	0.3				
Sao Tome Prn	..	246	..	522	..	0.3				
Senegal	..	86	..	518	..	0.1				
Cameroon	..	222	..	426	..	0.3				
Zambia	..	146	..	402	..	0.2				
Nigeria	..	335	..	279	..	0.4				
Other intraregional	..	2,788	..	3,454	..	3.6				
From other regions	..	*46,466*	..	*147,609*	..	*60.3*				
United Kingdom	..	2,687	..	29,987	..	3.5				
Brazil	..	3,508	..	20,502	..	4.6				
Portugal	..	18,467	..	14,996	..	24.0				
United States	..	6,266	..	13,502	..	8.1				
France	..	4,249	..	12,923	..	5.5				
Norway	..	357	..	9,987	..	0.5				
Cuba	..	431	..	4,536	..	0.6				
Italy	..	581	..	3,319	..	0.8				
Canada	..	1,007	..	2,809	..	1.3				
India	..	170	..	2,566	..	0.2				
Ukraine	..	253	..	1,876	..	0.3				
Ireland	..	64	..	1,769	..	0.1				
Sweden	..	109	..	1,756	..	0.1				
Argentina	..	123	..	1,638	..	0.2				
Russian Federation	..	775	..	1,432	..	1.0				
Japan	..	828	..	1,172	..	1.1				
Bulgaria	..	136	..	1,112	..	0.2				
Spain	..	972	..	1,097	..	1.3				
Israel	..	..	..	988	..					
Germany	..	1,305	..	984	..	1.7				
Netherlands	..	..	..	976	..					
China	..	438	..	975	..	0.6				
Australia	..	685	..	949	..	0.9				
Greece	..	72	..	921	..	0.1				
Belarus	..	..	..	920	..					
Other interregional	..	2,983	..	13,917	..	3.9				
Nationals residing abroad	..	*21,603*	..	*28,765*	..	*28.0*				

Source: World Tourism Organization (UNWTO) ©   (Data as collected by UNWTO for TMT 2006 Edition)

III.3.2   Cameroon   Central Africa

Promotional: www.cameroun-infotourisme.com

Profile

Cameroon

Capital	Yaoundé
Year of entry in UNWTO	1975
Area (1000 km²)	475
Population (2005, million)	17.3
Gross Domestic Product (GDP) (2005, US$ million)	16,991
GDP per capita (2005, US$)	952

Africa
Central Africa

GDP growth (real, %)
'-> 2004: 3.7;   2005: 2.6;   2006*: 4.2;   2007*: 4.3

	2003	2004	2005*	2004/2003	2005*/2004
International Arrivals					
Tourists (overnight visitors) (1000)	..	190	176		-7.1
- per 100 of inhabitants	..	1	1		
Tourism accommodation					
Number of rooms	..	..	22,112		
Nights spent in hotels and similar establishments (1000)		1,807	1,754		-2.9
by non-residents (inbound tourism)	..	414	355		-14.3
by residents (domestic tourism)	..	1,393	1,399		0.4
Receipts and Expenditure for International Tourism					
International Tourism Receipts (US$ million)	114	..	..		
- per capita (US$)	7	..	..		
International Fare Receipts (US$ million)	48	..	..		
International Tourism Expenditure (US$ million)	212	..	..		
- per capita (US$)	13	..	..		
International Fare Expenditure (US$ million)	82	..	..		
Δ International Tourism Balance (US$ million)	-98	..	..		
Δ International Fare Balance (US$ million)	-34	..	..		

Source: World Tourism Organization (UNWTO)   (Data as collected by UNWTO for TMT 2006 Edition)

See annex for methodological notes and reference of external sources used.

International Tourism by Origin

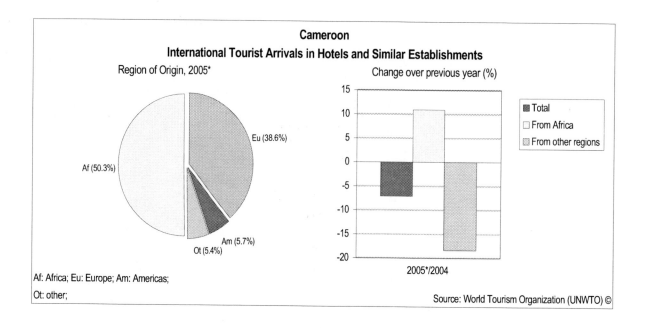

Cameroon
International Tourist Arrivals in Hotels and Similar Establishments

Region of Origin, 2005*

Change over previous year (%)

- Total
- From Africa
- From other regions

Af (50.3%)
Eu (38.6%)
Am (5.7%)
Ot (5.4%)

2005*/2004

Af: Africa; Eu: Europe; Am: Americas;
Ot: other;

Source: World Tourism Organization (UNWTO) ©

Cameroon

International Tourist Arrivals in Hotels and Similar Establishments (by nationality)

	1995	2000	2003	2004	2005*	Market share (%) 2000	Market share (%) 2005*	Growth rate (%) 04/03	Growth rate (%) 05*/04	Average per year (%) 2000-2005*
Total	99,749	277,070	..	189,856	176,372	100	100		-7.1	-8.6
From Africa	26,551	88,618	..	80,013	88,739	32.0	50.3		10.9	0.0
All Africa	26,551	88,618	..	80,013	88,739	32.0	50.3		10.9	0.0
From other regions	72,176	187,067	..	103,696	84,647	67.5	48.0		-18.4	-14.7
France	35,612	38,771	..	40,611	33,650	14.0	19.1		-17.1	-2.8
United States	4,974	12,462	..	9,194	7,242	4.5	4.1		-21.2	-10.3
Germany	6,211	16,616	..	7,127	5,581	6.0	3.2		-21.7	-19.6
United Kingdom	3,798	13,847	..	5,818	5,076	5.0	2.9		-12.8	-18.2
All Asia	1,849	8,308	..	4,248	4,580	3.0	2.6		7.8	-11.2
Italy	4,237	5,537	..	4,426	4,211	2.0	2.4		-4.9	-5.3
Switzerland	2,516	11,077	..	5,668	3,715	4.0	2.1		-34.5	-19.6
Belgium	2,562	41,540	..	3,885	3,046	15.0	1.7		-21.6	-40.7
Netherlands	1,580	9,970	..	4,217	2,951	3.6	1.7		-30.0	-21.6
Canada	2,650	10,662	..	2,399	2,760	3.8	1.6		15.0	-23.7
All Middle East	1,310	5,539	..	4,583	2,007	2.0	1.1		-56.2	-18.4
Former U.S.S.R.	421	830	..	1,325	1,242	0.3	0.7		-6.3	8.4
Sweden	378	831	..	982	1,026	0.3	0.6		4.5	4.3
Other Europe	4,078	11,077	..	9,213	7,560	4.0	4.3		-17.9	-7.4
Other World/Not specified	1,022	1,385	..	6,147	2,986	0.5	1.7		-51.4	16.6

Source: World Tourism Organization (UNWTO) ©

(Data as collected by UNWTO for TMT 2006 Edition)

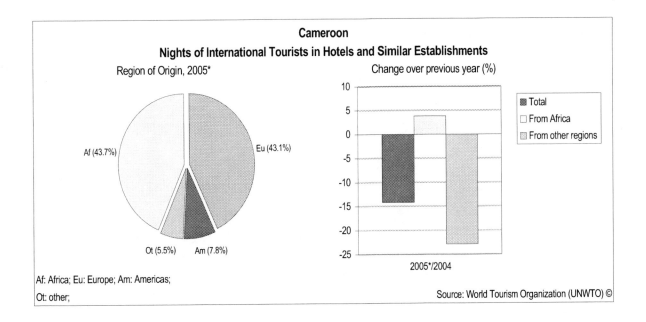

Cameroon
Nights of International Tourists in Hotels and Similar Establishments

Region of Origin, 2005*

Af (43.7%)
Eu (43.1%)
Ot (5.5%)   Am (7.8%)

Change over previous year (%)

Total
From Africa
From other regions

2005*/2004

Af: Africa; Eu: Europe; Am: Americas;
Ot: other;

Source: World Tourism Organization (UNWTO) ©

Cameroon
Nights of International Tourists in Hotels and Similar Establishments (by nationality)

	1995	2000	2003	2004	2005*	Market share (%) 2000	Market share (%) 2005*	Growth rate (%) 04/03	Growth rate (%) 05*/04	Average per year (%) 2000-2005*
Total	**224,394**	**492,894**	..	**413,958**	**355,322**	**100**	**100**		**-14.2**	**-6.3**
From Africa	58,795	157,648	..	149,369	155,109	32.0	43.7		3.8	-0.3
All Africa	58,795	157,648	..	149,369	155,109	32.0	43.7		3.8	-0.3
From other regions	163,709	332,783	..	253,408	195,476	67.5	55.0		-22.9	-10.1
France	80,759	68,971	..	95,742	80,057	14.0	22.5		-16.4	3.0
United States	13,324	22,169	..	27,044	21,779	4.5	6.1		-19.5	-0.4
United Kingdom	9,592	24,632	..	16,412	11,618	5.0	3.3		-29.2	-14.0
Germany	14,388	29,559	..	14,018	11,266	6.0	3.2		-19.6	-17.5
All Asia	4,456	14,779	..	9,983	10,643	3.0	3.0		6.6	-6.4
Italy	7,560	9,853	..	9,792	8,915	2.0	2.5		-9.0	-2.0
Switzerland	4,277	19,706	..	9,883	7,188	4.0	2.0		-27.3	-18.3
Netherlands	3,183	17,735	..	11,480	6,959	3.6	2.0		-39.4	-17.1
Belgium	6,307	73,897	..	8,236	6,454	15.0	1.8		-21.6	-38.6
Canada	6,543	18,967	..	6,285	5,918	3.8	1.7		-5.8	-20.8
All Middle East	3,073	9,853	..	8,493	4,157	2.0	1.2		-51.1	-15.9
Former U.S.S.R.	741	1,478	..	2,961	3,123	0.3	0.9		5.5	16.1
Sweden	873	1,478	..	1,948	2,239	0.3	0.6		14.9	8.7
Other Europe	8,633	19,706	..	31,131	15,160	4.0	4.3		-51.3	-5.1
Other World/Not specified	1,890	2,463	..	11,181	4,737	0.5	1.3		-57.6	14.0

Source: World Tourism Organization (UNWTO) ©   (Data as collected by UNWTO for TMT 2006 Edition)

III.3.3   Central African Republic   Central Africa

Institutional/corporate: www.kodro.net

Profile

Central African Republic

Africa
Central Africa

Capital	Bangui
Year of entry in UNWTO	1995
Area (1000 km²)	623
Population (2005, million)	4.2
Gross Domestic Product (GDP) (2005, US$ million)	1,377
GDP per capita (2005, US$)	335
GDP growth (real, %)	
'-> 2004: 1.3; 2005: 2.2; 2006*: 3.2; 2007*: 3.8	

	2003	2004	2005*	2004/2003	2005*/2004
International Arrivals					
Tourists (overnight visitors) (1000)	6	8	12	43.4	46.8
- per 100 of inhabitants	0	0	0		
Tourism accommodation					
Number of rooms	201	235	241	16.9	2.6
Nights spent in hotels and similar establishments (1000)	45	26		-42.2	
by non-residents (inbound tourism)	42	23	33	-45.2	43.5
by residents (domestic tourism)	3	3	..		
Outbound Tourism					
Trips abroad (1000)	6	7	..	16.7	
- per 100 of inhabitants	0	0	..		
Receipts and Expenditure for International Tourism					
International Tourism Receipts (US$ million)	4	4	..		
- per Tourist Arrival (US$)	703	490	..	-30.3	
- per capita (US$)	1	1	..		
International Tourism Expenditure (US$ million)	31	32	..	3.2	
- per trip (US$)	5,167	4,571	..	-11.5	
- per capita (US$)	8	8	..		
Δ International Tourism Balance (US$ million)	-27	-28	..		

Source: World Tourism Organization (UNWTO)   (Data as collected by UNWTO for TMT 2006 Edition)

See annex for methodological notes and reference of external sources used.

International Tourism by Origin

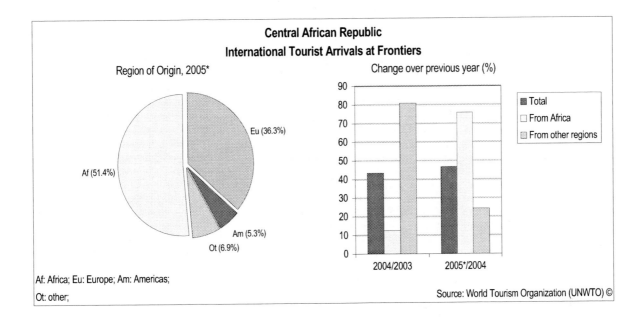

Central African Republic
International Tourist Arrivals at Frontiers

Region of Origin, 2005*

Af (51.4%)
Eu (36.3%)
Am (5.3%)
Ot (6.9%)

Change over previous year (%)

- Total
- From Africa
- From other regions

2004/2003   2005*/2004

Af: Africa; Eu: Europe; Am: Americas;
Ot: other;

Source: World Tourism Organization (UNWTO) ©

Central African Republic
International Tourist Arrivals at Frontiers (by nationality)

	1995	2000	2003	2004	2005*	Market share (%)		Growth rate (%)		Average per year (%)
						2000	2005*	04/03	05*/04	2000-2005*
Total	..	**11,217**	**5,687**	**8,156**	**11,969**	**100**	**100**	**43.4**	**46.8**	**1.3**
From Africa	..	*5,379*	*3,111*	*3,501*	*6,156*	*48.0*	*51.4*	*12.5*	*75.8*	*2.7*
Cameroon	..	1,066	604	904	1,165	9.5	9.7	49.7	28.9	1.8
Chad	..	578	212	352	566	5.2	4.7	66.0	60.8	-0.4
Congo	..	713	411	418	468	6.4	3.9	1.7	12.0	-8.1
Senegal	..	331	139	315	383	3.0	3.2	126.6	21.6	3.0
Côte d'Ivoire	..	216	182	127	280	1.9	2.3	-30.2	120.5	5.3
Gabon	..	192	32	166	251	1.7	2.1	418.8	51.2	5.5
Dem.R.Congo	..	168	103	142	248	1.5	2.1	37.9	74.6	8.1
Benin	..	215	54	119	190	1.9	1.6	120.4	59.7	-2.4
Nigeria	..	194	72	107	182	1.7	1.5	48.6	70.1	-1.3
Togo	..	191	164	81	119	1.7	1.0	-50.6	46.9	-9.0
South Africa	..	45	45	73	108	0.4	0.9	62.2	47.9	19.1
Mali	..	133	37	65	106	1.2	0.9	75.7	63.1	-4.4
Sudan	..	176	58	72	44	1.6	0.4	24.1	-38.9	-24.2
Rwanda	..	55	45	18	43	0.5	0.4	-60.0	138.9	-4.8
Other East Africa	..	22	..	33	126	0.2	1.1		281.8	41.8
Other Central Africa	..	483	110	41	134	4.3	1.1	-62.7	226.8	-22.6
Other North Africa	..	188	89	146	181	1.7	1.5	64.0	24.0	-0.8
Other Southern Africa	..	69	67	74	88	0.6	0.7	10.4	18.9	5.0
Other West Africa	..	344	687	248	665	3.1	5.6	-63.9	168.1	14.1
Other Africa	..	..	..	..	809		6.8			
From other regions	..	*5,788*	*2,561*	*4,632*	*5,758*	*51.6*	*48.1*	*80.9*	*24.3*	*-0.1*
France	..	2,344	1,010	2,492	2,913	20.9	24.3	146.7	16.9	4.4
Italy	..	266	130	383	475	2.4	4.0	194.6	24.0	12.3
United States	..	593	120	264	377	5.3	3.1	120.0	42.8	-8.7
Lebanon	..	117	18	192	255	1.0	2.1	966.7	32.8	16.9
Belgium	..	220	153	196	219	2.0	1.8	28.1	11.7	-0.1
China	..	257	141	134	150	2.3	1.3	-5.0	11.9	-10.2
Germany	..	150	80	117	132	1.3	1.1	46.3	12.8	-2.5
Canada	..	193	180	104	104	1.7	0.9	-42.2	0.0	-11.6
Switzerland	..	113	68	59	87	1.0	0.7	-13.2	47.5	-5.1
Japan	..	168	112	32	48	1.5	0.4	-71.4	50.0	-22.2
United Kingdom	..	141	50	42	42	1.3	0.4	-16.0	0.0	-21.5
Other Americas	..	118	74	81	158	1.1	1.3	9.5	95.1	6.0
Other Middle East	..	..	..	..	142		1.2			
Other Asia	..	738	35	151	175	6.6	1.5	331.4	15.9	-25.0
Other Europe	..	370	390	385	481	3.3	4.0	-1.3	24.9	5.4
Other World/Not specified	..	*50*	*15*	*23*	*55*	*0.4*	*0.5*	*53.3*	*139.1*	*1.9*

Source: World Tourism Organization (UNWTO) ©   (Data as collected by UNWTO for TMT 2006 Edition)

III.3.4   Chad   Central Africa

Profile

Chad

Africa
Central Africa

Capital	N'Djamena
Year of entry in UNWTO	1985
Area (1000 km²)	1,284
Population (2005, million)	9.7
Gross Domestic Product (GDP) (2005, US$ million)	5,907
GDP per capita (2005, US$)	654
GDP growth (real, %)	
‣ 2004: 31.3; 2005: 12.2; 2006*: 0.1; 2007*: 2.5	

	2003	2004	2005*	2004/2003	2005*/2004
International Arrivals					
Visitors (1000)	101	106	59	5.0	-44.3
Tourists (overnight visitors) (1000)	21	26	29	23.5	13.3
- per 100 of inhabitants	0	0	0		
Tourism accommodation					
Number of rooms	835	835	922		10.4
Nights spent in hotels and similar establishments (1000)	64	81	68	26.6	-16.0
by non-residents (inbound tourism)	60	76	64	26.7	-15.8
by residents (domestic tourism)	4	5	4	25.0	-20.0

Source: World Tourism Organization (UNWTO)   (Data as collected by UNWTO for TMT 2006 Edition)

See annex for methodological notes and reference of external sources used.

International Tourism by Origin

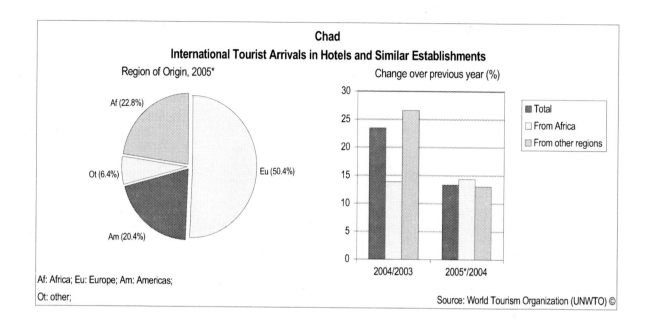

Chad
International Tourist Arrivals in Hotels and Similar Establishments

Region of Origin, 2005*

Af (22.8%)
Ot (6.4%)
Eu (50.4%)
Am (20.4%)

Change over previous year (%)

Total
From Africa
From other regions

2004/2003   2005*/2004

Af: Africa; Eu: Europe; Am: Americas;
Ot: other;

Source: World Tourism Organization (UNWTO) ©

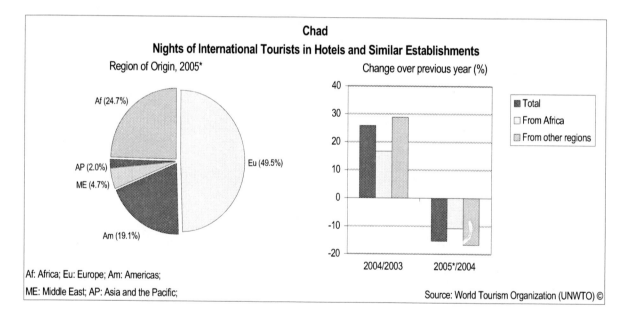

Chad
Nights of International Tourists in Hotels and Similar Establishments

Region of Origin, 2005*

Af (24.7%)
AP (2.0%)
ME (4.7%)
Eu (49.5%)
Am (19.1%)

Change over previous year (%)

Total
From Africa
From other regions

2004/2003   2005*/2004

Af: Africa; Eu: Europe; Am: Americas;
ME: Middle East; AP: Asia and the Pacific;

Source: World Tourism Organization (UNWTO) ©

Chad

International Tourist Arrivals in Hotels and Similar Establishments (by nationality)

	1995	2000	2003	2004	2005*	Market share (%) 2000	2005*	Growth rate (%) 04/03	05*/04	Average per year (%) 2000-2005*
Total	**18,821**	**43,034**	**20,974**	**25,899**	**29,356**	**100**	**100**	**23.5**	**13.3**	**-7.4**
From Africa	*2,137*	*12,542*	*5,141*	*5,855*	*6,695*	*29.1*	*22.8*	*13.9*	*14.3*	*-11.8*
All Central Africa	769	6,621	3,004	3,397	3,559	15.4	12.1	13.1	4.8	-11.7
All West Africa	921	4,137	1,603	1,854	2,334	9.6	8.0	15.7	25.9	-10.8
All North Africa	176	369	256	296	357	0.9	1.2	15.6	20.6	-0.7
All East Africa	220	1,277	182	209	329	3.0	1.1	14.8	57.4	-23.8
Other Africa	51	138	96	99	116	0.3	0.4	3.1	17.2	-3.4
From other regions	*5,245*	*30,492*	*15,833*	*20,044*	*22,661*	*70.9*	*77.2*	*26.6*	*13.1*	*-5.8*
France	2,861	13,707	7,897	9,986	11,757	31.9	40.0	26.5	17.7	-3.0
United States	594	5,320	3,206	3,433	3,693	12.4	12.6	7.1	7.6	-7.0
Canada	44	2,470	1,044	1,942	1,935	5.7	6.6	86.0	-0.4	-4.8
Libyan Arab Jamahiriya	..	190	473	563	549	0.4	1.9	19.0	-2.5	23.6
Germany	86	1,361	405	508	547	3.2	1.9	25.4	7.7	-16.7
Switzerland	28	710	303	381	458	1.6	1.6	25.7	20.2	-8.4
Egypt	..	49	370	440	426	0.1	1.5	18.9	-3.2	54.1
United Kingdom	25	585	270	336	363	1.4	1.2	24.4	8.0	-9.1
Italy	134	1,254	166	202	246	2.9	0.8	21.7	21.8	-27.8
Belgium	50	645	164	219	241	1.5	0.8	33.5	10.0	-17.9
China	46	40	96	128	183	0.1	0.6	33.3	43.0	35.5
Saudi Arabia	80	70	121	143	149	0.2	0.5	18.2	4.2	16.3
Netherlands	17	220	34	51	87	0.5	0.3	50.0	70.6	-16.9
Scandinavia	..	115	26	42	67	0.3	0.2	61.5	59.5	-10.2
Japan	18	75	34	45	45	0.2	0.2	32.4	0.0	-9.7
Korea, Republic of	4	20	16	22	42	0.0	0.1	37.5	90.9	16.0
Lebanon	30	..	50	43	40		0.1	-14.0	-7.0	
Syrian Arab Republic	8	..	17	36	32		0.1	111.8	-11.1	
Other Americas	5	426	118	234	348	1.0	1.2	98.3	48.7	-4.0
Other Middle East	125	225	108	122	134	0.5	0.5	13.0	9.8	-9.8
Other Europe	940	2,709	764	965	1,039	6.3	3.5	26.3	7.7	-17.4
Other East Asia/Pacific	150	301	151	203	280	0.7	1.0	34.4	37.9	-1.4
Other World/Not specified	*11,439*	*..*	*..*	*..*	*..*					

Source: World Tourism Organization (UNWTO) ©   (Data as collected by UNWTO for TMT 2006 Edition)

Chad

Nights of International Tourists in Hotels and Similar Establishments (by nationality)

	1995	2000	2003	2004	2005*	Market share (%)		Growth rate (%)		Average per year (%)
						2000	2005*	04/03	05*/04	2000-2005*
Total	**38,518**	**107,195**	**60,395**	**75,967**	**64,293**	**100**	**100**	**25.8**	**-15.4**	**-9.7**
From Africa	*7,024*	*59,519*	*15,241*	*17,787*	*15,875*	*55.5*	*24.7*	*16.7*	*-10.7*	*-23.2*
All Central Africa	2,588	28,876	8,884	10,232	8,334	26.9	13.0	15.2	-18.5	-22.0
All West Africa	3,106	19,964	4,733	5,681	5,768	18.6	9.0	20.0	1.5	-22.0
All East Africa	739	5,820	562	637	779	5.4	1.2	13.3	22.3	-33.1
All North Africa	591	1,640	757	874	712	1.5	1.1	15.5	-18.5	-15.4
Other Africa	..	3,219	305	363	282	3.0	0.4	19.0	-22.3	-38.6
From other regions	*19,386*	*47,676*	*45,154*	*58,180*	*48,418*	*44.5*	*75.3*	*28.8*	*-16.8*	*0.3*
France	11,804	20,040	21,707	28,514	24,968	18.7	38.8	31.4	-12.4	4.5
United States	1,883	8,714	9,191	10,414	7,634	8.1	11.9	13.3	-26.7	-2.6
Canada	268	1,917	2,974	5,716	4,090	1.8	6.4	92.2	-28.4	16.4
Germany	293	1,948	1,227	1,279	1,310	1.8	2.0	4.2	2.4	-7.6
Libyan Arab Jamahiriya	..	1,312	1,188	1,659	1,209	1.2	1.9	39.6	-27.1	-1.6
Switzerland	178	710	896	1,083	1,154	0.7	1.8	20.9	6.6	10.2
Egypt	..	184	1,196	1,224	913	0.2	1.4	2.3	-25.4	37.8
United Kingdom	110	680	802	901	821	0.6	1.3	12.3	-8.9	3.8
Italy	247	1,050	546	618	555	1.0	0.9	13.2	-10.2	-12.0
Belgium	234	820	479	528	496	0.8	0.8	10.2	-6.1	-9.6
China	214	143	385	401	418	0.1	0.7	4.2	4.2	23.9
Saudi Arabia	277	..	369	482	374		0.6	30.6	-22.4	
Netherlands	83	164	123	183	219	0.2	0.3	48.8	19.7	6.0
Scandinavia	..	80	72	150	166	0.1	0.3	108.3	10.7	15.7
Japan	94	237	124	159	99	0.2	0.2	28.2	-37.7	-16.0
Lebanon	190	..	166	140	88		0.1	-15.7	-37.1	
Korea, Republic of	8	56	62	74	75	0.1	0.1	19.4	1.4	6.0
Syrian Arab Republic	35	257	53	112	66	0.2	0.1	111.3	-41.1	-23.8
Other Americas	55	686	343	686	553	0.6	0.9	100.0	-19.4	-4.2
Other Middle East	280	1,126	350	363	375	1.1	0.6	3.7	3.3	-19.7
Other Europe	2,808	5,386	2,242	2,905	2,147	5.0	3.3	29.6	-26.1	-16.8
Other East Asia/Pacific	325	2,166	659	589	688	2.0	1.1	-10.6	16.8	-20.5
Other World/Not specified	*12,108*	*..*	*..*	*..*	*..*					

Source: World Tourism Organization (UNWTO) ©

(Data as collected by UNWTO for TMT 2006 Edition)

III.3.5   Congo   Central Africa

Profile

Congo

Capital	Brazzaville
Year of entry in UNWTO	1979
Area (1000 km²)	342
Population (2005, million)	3.6
Gross Domestic Product (GDP) (2005, US$ million)	5,980
GDP per capita (2005, US$)	1,785

Africa

Central Africa

GDP growth (real, %)

'-> 2004: 3.6;   2005: 7.9;   2006*: 7.4;   2007*: 2.1

	2003	2004	2005*	2004/2003	2005*/2004
Receipts and Expenditure for International Tourism					
International Tourism Receipts (US$ million)	29	22	34	-24.1	54.5
- per capita (US$)	8	6	9		
International Fare Receipts (US$ million)	1	1	..	10.0	
International Tourism Expenditure (US$ million)	78	103	103	32.1	
- per capita (US$)	23	29	29		
International Fare Expenditure (US$ million)	40	73	..	82.5	
Δ International Tourism Balance (US$ million)	-49	-81	-69		
Δ International Fare Balance (US$ million)	-39	-72	..		

Source: World Tourism Organization (UNWTO)   (Data as collected by UNWTO for TMT 2006 Edition)

See annex for methodological notes and reference of external sources used.

International Tourism by Origin

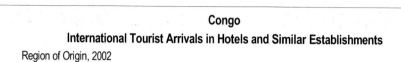

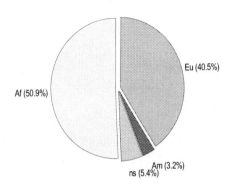

Congo
International Tourist Arrivals in Hotels and Similar Establishments
Region of Origin, 2002

Eu (40.5%)

Af (50.9%)

Am (3.2%)
ns (5.4%)

Af: Africa; Eu: Europe; Am: Americas;
ns: not specified

Source: World Tourism Organization (UNWTO) ©

Congo
International Tourist Arrivals in Hotels and Similar Establishments (by residence)

	1995	2000	2002	2003	2004	Market share (%) 2000	Market share (%) 2004	Growth rate (%) 03/02	Growth rate (%) 04/03	Average per year (%) 2000-2004
Total	**37,432**	**18,797**	**21,611**	..	..	**100**				
From Africa	*16,872*	*9,300*	*11,006*	..	..	*49.5*				
Dem.R.Congo	7,121	2,172	2,402	..	..	11.6				
Angola	1,203	1,747	2,169	..	..	9.3				
Cameroon	1,146	591	950	..	..	3.1				
Gabon	1,218	906	907	..	..	4.8				
Côte d'Ivoire	994	401	633	..	..	2.1				
All North Africa	244	242	257	..	..	1.3				
Senegal	626	354	253	..	..	1.9				
Cent.Afr.Rep.	646	238	172	..	..	1.3				
Togo	265	270	58	..	..	1.4				
Other Central Africa	498	239	239	..	..	1.3				
Other West Africa	1,366	642	918	..	..	3.4				
Other Africa	1,545	1,498	2,048	..	..	8.0				
From other regions	*19,510*	*9,079*	*9,446*	..	..	*48.3*				
France	10,708	4,831	6,196	..	..	25.7				
United Kingdom	1,352	640	505	..	..	3.4				
Belgium	831	230	477	..	..	1.2				
United States	1,705	518	414	..	..	2.8				
Italy	1,248	869	382	..	..	4.6				
Former U.S.S.R.	252	41	294	..	..	0.2				
Canada	271	124	126	..	..	0.7				
Germany	593	230	103	..	..	1.2				
Other Americas	159	143	154	..	..	0.8				
Other Europe	2,391	1,453	795	..	..	7.7				
Other World/Not specified	*1,050*	*418*	*1,159*	..	..	*2.2*				

Source: World Tourism Organization (UNWTO) ©   (Data as collected by UNWTO for TMT 2006 Edition)

World Tourism Organization ©

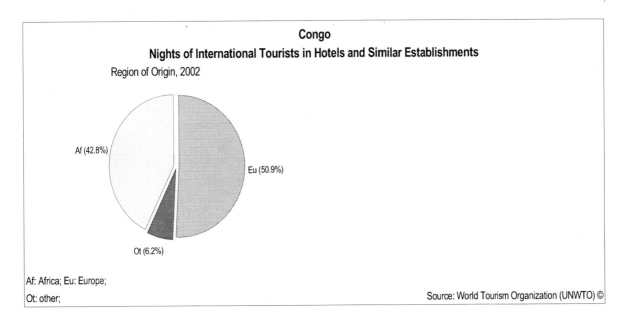

Congo
Nights of International Tourists in Hotels and Similar Establishments (by residence)

	1995	2000	2002	2003	2004	Market share (%) 2000	Market share (%) 2004	Growth rate (%) 03/02	Growth rate (%) 04/03	Average per year (%) 2000-2004
Total	110,434	75,761	87,754	..	..	100				
From Africa	47,377	32,090	37,562	..	..	42.4				
Dem.R.Congo	14,596	6,557	5,340	..	..	8.7				
Cameroon	3,678	2,396	3,938	..	..	3.2				
Angola	3,438	4,504	3,921	..	..	5.9				
Gabon	3,764	3,816	3,093	..	..	5.0				
Côte d'Ivoire	3,544	1,761	2,017	..	..	2.3				
All North Africa	2,356	894	1,668	..	..	1.2				
Senegal	1,789	1,304	1,424	..	..	1.7				
Cent.Afr.Rep.	1,812	883	611	..	..	1.2				
Togo	879	1,097	204	..	..	1.4				
Other Central Africa	1,723	1,027	1,164	..	..	1.4				
Other West Africa	4,325	2,452	2,758	..	..	3.2				
Other Africa	5,473	5,399	11,424	..	..	7.1				
From other regions	59,774	41,893	47,249	..	..	55.3				
France	33,363	22,707	27,491	..	..	30.0				
Former U.S.S.R.	1,065	158	7,257	..	..	0.2				
Belgium	2,241	1,006	2,195	..	..	1.3				
Italy	4,034	5,060	1,899	..	..	6.7				
United Kingdom	3,838	2,748	1,758	..	..	3.6				
United States	5,051	2,380	1,405	..	..	3.1				
Canada	709	523	501	..	..	0.7				
Germany	1,848	943	372	..	..	1.2				
Other Americas	447	684	634	..	..	0.9				
Other Europe	7,178	5,684	3,737	..	..	7.5				
Other World/Not specified	3,283	1,778	2,943	..	..	2.3				

Source: World Tourism Organization (UNWTO) ©   (Data as collected by UNWTO for TMT 2006 Edition)

III.3.6 Democratic Republic of the Congo

Central Africa

Profile

Democratic Republic of the Congo

Africa
Central Africa

	Capital	Kinshasa
	Year of entry in UNWTO	1975
	Area (1000 km²)	2,345
	Population (2005, million)	60.8
	Gross Domestic Product (GDP) (2005, US$ million)	7,094
	GDP growth (real, %)	
	'-> 2004: 6.6; 2005: 6.5; 2006*: 6.5; 2007*: 7.2	

	2003	2004	2005*	2004/2003	2005*/2004
International Arrivals					
Tourists (overnight visitors) (1000)	35	36	61	3.1	68.3
- per 100 of inhabitants	0	0	0		
Same-day visitors (1000)	20	..	..		
Tourism accommodation					
Number of rooms	5,829	..	..		
Nights spent in collective establishments (1000)	190	184	321	-3.2	74.5
by non-residents (inbound tourism)	150	99	165	-34.0	66.7
by residents (domestic tourism)	40	85	156	112.5	83.5
Receipts and Expenditure for International Tourism					
International Tourism Receipts (US$ million)	1	1	..	1.1	
- per Tourist Arrival (US$)	25	24	..	-2.0	
- per capita (US$)	0	0	..		

Source: World Tourism Organization (UNWTO)

(Data as collected by UNWTO for TMT 2006 Edition)

See annex for methodological notes and reference of external sources used.

International Tourism by Origin

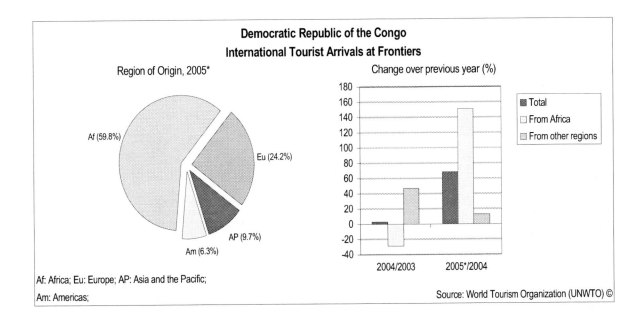

Af: Africa; Eu: Europe; AP: Asia and the Pacific;

Am: Americas;

Source: World Tourism Organization (UNWTO) ©

Democratic Republic of the Congo

International Tourist Arrivals at Frontiers (by nationality)

	1995	2000	2003	2004	2005*	Market share (%) 2000	Market share (%) 2005*	Growth rate (%) 04/03	Growth rate (%) 05*/04	Average per year (%) 2000-2005*
Total	**35,700**	**102,770**	**35,141**	**36,238**	**61,007**	**100**	**100**	**3.1**	**68.4**	**-9.9**
From Africa	*20,000*	*96,594*	*20,380*	*14,531*	*36,489*	*94.0*	*59.8*	*-28.7*	*151.1*	*-17.7*
Congo	15,000	96,594	121	109	437	94.0	0.7	-9.9	300.9	-66.0
Other Central Africa	..	..	551	559	1,472		2.4	1.5	163.3	
Other Africa	5,000	..	19,708	13,863	34,580		56.7	-29.7	149.4	
From other regions	*15,700*	*6,176*	*14,761*	*21,707*	*24,518*	*6.0*	*40.2*	*47.1*	*12.9*	*31.8*
All Asia	..	..	3,018	3,865	5,654		9.3	28.1	46.3	
Belgium	5,000	1,644	2,337	4,446	4,788	1.6	7.8	90.2	7.7	23.8
All Americas	500	495	2,568	4,592	3,824	0.5	6.3	78.8	-16.7	50.5
France	4,000	1,759	2,012	3,348	3,245	1.7	5.3	66.4	-3.1	13.0
Italy	500	1,020	475	785	1,038	1.0	1.7	65.3	32.2	0.4
Germany	500	558	384	637	951	0.5	1.6	65.9	49.3	11.3
All Oceania	..	..	138	133	289		0.5	-3.6	117.3	
Other Europe	5,000	700	3,829	3,901	4,729	0.7	7.8	1.9	21.2	46.5
All East Asia/Pacific	200	..	..	..	..					

Source: World Tourism Organization (UNWTO) ©   (Data as collected by UNWTO for TMT 2006 Edition)

III.3.7   Equatorial Guinea   Central Africa

Profile

Equatorial Guinea

Africa
Central Africa

Capital	Malabo
Year of entry in UNWTO	1995
Area (1000 km²)	28
Population (2005, 1000)	529
Gross Domestic Product (GDP) (2005, US$ million)	7,062
GDP per capita (2005, US$)	6,205
GDP growth (real, %)	
> 2004: 32.4; 2005: 6.0; 2006*: -1.0; 2007*: 9.4	

Source: World Tourism Organization (UNWTO)   (Data as collected by UNWTO for TMT 2006 Edition)

See annex for methodological notes and reference of external sources used.

III.3.8   Gabon   Central Africa

Profile

Gabon

Africa
Central Africa

Capital	Libreville
Year of entry in UNWTO	1975
Area (1000 km²)	268
Population (2005, million)	1.4
Gross Domestic Product (GDP) (2005, US$ million)	8,724
GDP per capita (2005, US$)	6,397
GDP growth (real, %)	
'-> 2004: 1.4; 2005: 2.9; 2006*: 2.2; 2007*: 2.5	

	2003	2004	2005*	2004/2003	2005*/2004
International Arrivals					
Visitors (1000)	234	..	..		
Tourists (overnight visitors) (1000)	222	..	..		
- per 100 of inhabitants	17	..	..		
Same-day visitors (1000)	12	..	..		
Outbound Tourism					
Trips abroad (1000)	236	..	..		
- per 100 of inhabitants	18	..	..		
Receipts and Expenditure for International Tourism					
International Tourism Receipts (US$ million)	15	10	..	-33.3	
- per Tourist Arrival (US$)	68	..	..		
- per Visitor Arrival (US$)	64	..	..		
- per capita (US$)	11	7	..		
International Fare Receipts (US$ million)	69	64	..	-7.2	
International Tourism Expenditure (US$ million)	194	214	..	10.3	
- per trip (US$)	822	..	..		
- per capita (US$)	146	157	..		
International Fare Expenditure (US$ million)	45	61	..	35.6	
Δ International Tourism Balance (US$ million)	-179	-204	..		
Δ International Fare Balance (US$ million)	24	3	..		

Source: World Tourism Organization (UNWTO)   (Data as collected by UNWTO for TMT 2006 Edition)

See annex for methodological notes and reference of external sources used.

International Tourism by Origin

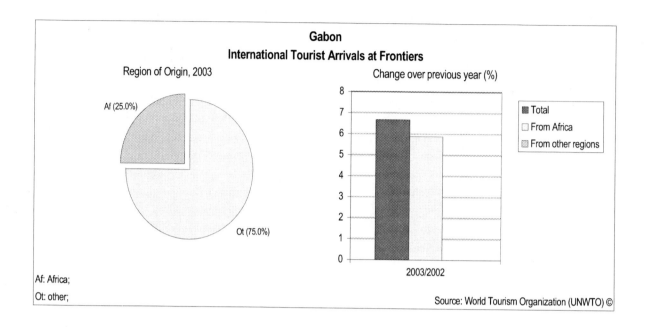

Gabon
International Tourist Arrivals at Frontiers

Region of Origin, 2003

Af (25.0%)
Ot (75.0%)

Change over previous year (%)

Total
From Africa
From other regions

2003/2002

Af: Africa;
Ot: other;

Source: World Tourism Organization (UNWTO) ©

Gabon
International Tourist Arrivals at Frontiers (by nationality)

	1995	2000	2002	2003	2004	Market share (%) 2000	Market share (%) 2004	Growth rate (%) 03/02	Growth rate (%) 04/03	Average per year (%) 2000-2004
Total	**124,685**	**155,432**	**208,348**	**222,257**	..	**100**		**6.7**		
From Africa	*21,363*	*37,712*	*52,408*	*55,487*	..	*24.3*		*5.9*		
All Africa	21,363	37,712	52,408	55,487	..	24.3		5.9		
From other regions	*94,394*	*117,000*	..	..	..	*75.3*				
All Europe	72,325	112,000	..	..	..	72.1				
All Middle East	2,479	2,000	..	..	..	1.3				
All Americas	18,598	2,000	..	..	..	1.3				
All Asia	992	1,000	..	..	..	0.6				
Other World/Not specified	*8,928*	*720*	*155,940*	*166,770*	..	*0.5*		*6.9*		

Source: World Tourism Organization (UNWTO) ©   (Data as collected by UNWTO for TMT 2006 Edition)

III.3.9   Sao Tome and Principe   Central Africa

Profile

Sao Tome and Principe

Africa
Central Africa

Capital	São Tomé
Year of entry in UNWTO	1985
Area (10 km²)	96
Population (2005, 1000)	187
Gross Domestic Product (GDP) (2005, US$ million)	70
GDP per capita (2005, US$)	430
GDP growth (real, %)	
'-> 2004: 3.8; 2005: 3.8; 2006*: 5.5; 2007*: 5.5	

	2003	2004	2005*	2004/2003	2005*/2004
International Arrivals					
Tourists (overnight visitors) (1000)	14	11	11	-21.6	-1.9
- per 100 of inhabitants	8	..	..		
Receipts and Expenditure for International Tourism					
International Tourism Receipts (US$ million)	11	13	14	20.8	6.3
- per Tourist Arrival (US$)	777	1,196	1,295	54.0	8.3
- per capita (US$)	60	70	73		

Source: World Tourism Organization (UNWTO)   (Data as collected by UNWTO for TMT 2006 Edition)

See annex for methodological notes and reference of external sources used.

International Tourism by Origin

Sao Tome and Principe
International Tourist Arrivals at Frontiers (by residence)

	1995	2000	2002	2003	2004	Market share (%) 2000	Market share (%) 2004	Growth rate (%) 03/02	Growth rate (%) 04/03	Average per year (%) 2000-2004
Total	**6,160**	**7,137**	..	..	..	**100**				
From Africa	*1,657*	*1,141*	..	..	..	*16.0*				
All Africa	..	1,141	..	..	..	16.0				
Angola	471	..	..	..	..					
Nigeria	338	..	..	..	..					
Gabon	154	..	..	..	..					
Cape Verde	189	..	..	..	..					
Cameroon	138	..	..	..	..					
South Africa	70	..	..	..	..					
Guinea-Bissau	60	..	..	..	..					
Other intraregional	237	..	..	..	..					
From other regions	*4,503*	*3,818*	..	..	..	*53.5*				
All Europe	..	3,818	..	..	..	53.5				
Portugal	1,841	..	..	..	..					
France	950	..	..	..	..					
United States	321	..	..	..	..					
Spain, Portugal	318	..	..	..	..					
Spain	207	..	..	..	..					
Germany	116	..	..	..	..					
United Kingdom	86	..	..	..	..					
Belgium	59	..	..	..	..					
Italy	111	..	..	..	..					
Netherlands	39	..	..	..	..					
Philippines	48	..	..	..	..					
Japan	46	..	..	..	..					
Lebanon	38	..	..	..	..					
Brazil	37	..	..	..	..					
Switzerland	34	..	..	..	..					
China	29	..	..	..	..					
Other interregional	223	..	..	..	..					
Other World/Not specified	..	*2,178*	..	..	..	*30.5*				

Source: World Tourism Organization (UNWTO) ©   (Data as collected by UNWTO for TMT 2006 Edition)

III.4   East Africa

III.4.1   Burundi   East Africa

Profile

Burundi

Capital		Bujumbura
Year of entry in UNWTO		1975
Area (1000 km²)		28
Population (2005, million)		7.8
Gross Domestic Product (GDP) (2005, US$ million)		799
GDP per capita (2005, US$)		107

Africa
East Africa

GDP growth (real, %)
'-> 2004: 4.8;   2005: 0.9;   2006*: 6.1;   2007*: 6.6

	2003	2004	2005*	2004/2003	2005*/2004
International Arrivals					
Tourists (overnight visitors) (1000)	74	133	148	79.8	11.4
- per 100 of inhabitants	1	2	2		
Tourism accommodation					
Number of rooms	130	130	130		
Receipts and Expenditure for International Tourism					
International Tourism Receipts (US$ million)	1	1	2	71.4	25.0
- per Tourist Arrival (US$)	9	9	10	-4.6	12.2
- per capita (US$)	0	0	0		
International Fare Receipts (US$ million)	1	1	0	20.0	-33.3
International Tourism Expenditure (US$ million)	15	24	60	60.0	150.0
- per capita (US$)	2	3	8		
International Fare Expenditure (US$ million)	..	6	2		-66.7
Δ International Tourism Balance (US$ million)	-14	-23	-59		
Δ International Fare Balance (US$ million)	..	-5	-2		

Source: World Tourism Organization (UNWTO)   (Data as collected by UNWTO for TMT 2006 Edition)
See annex for methodological notes and reference of external sources used.

International Tourism by Origin

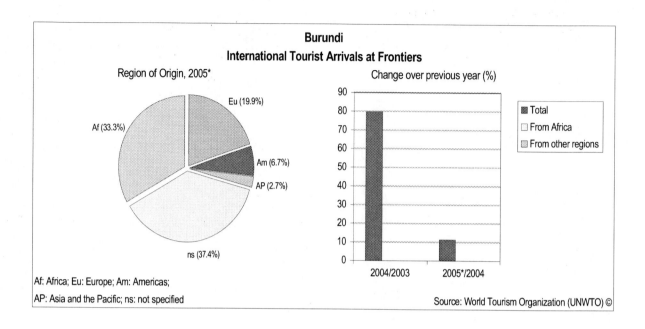

Burundi

International Tourist Arrivals at Frontiers (by nationality)

	1995	2000	2003	2004	2005*	Market share (%) 2000	Market share (%) 2005*	Growth rate (%) 04/03	Growth rate (%) 05*/04	Average per year (%) 2000-2005*
Total	**34,125**	**29,000**	**74,116**	**133,228**	**148,418**	**100**	**100**	**79.8**	**11.4**	**38.6**
From Africa	*16,201*	*14,000*	*24,706*	*1,333*	*49,473*	*48.3*	*33.3*	*-94.6*	*3611.4*	*28.7*
All Africa	16,201	14,000	24,706	1,333	49,473	48.3	33.3	-94.6	3611.4	28.7
From other regions	*17,924*	*15,000*	*11,090*	*39,845*	*43,465*	*51.7*	*29.3*	*259.3*	*9.1*	*23.7*
All Europe	13,099	12,000	7,620	29,409	29,486	41.4	19.9	285.9	0.3	19.7
All Americas	2,068	2,000	2,308	5,908	9,956	6.9	6.7	156.0	68.5	37.9
All Asia	2,757	1,000	1,162	4,528	4,023	3.4	2.7	289.7	-11.2	32.1
Other World/Not specified	*..*	*..*	*38,320*	*92,050*	*55,480*		*37.4*	*140.2*	*-39.7*	

Source: World Tourism Organization (UNWTO) ©   (Data as collected by UNWTO for TMT 2006 Edition)

III.4.2 Comoros — East Africa

Profile

Comoros

Capital		Moroni
Area (10 km²)		223
Population (2005, 1000)		671
Gross Domestic Product (GDP) (2005, US$ million)		369
GDP per capita (2005, US$)		615
GDP growth (real, %)		

Africa
East Africa

-> 2004: -0.2; 2005: 4.2; 2006*: 1.2; 2007*: 3.0

	2003	2004	2005*	2004/2003	2005*/2004
International Arrivals					
Tourists (overnight visitors) (1000)	14	18	20	23.7	11.1
- per 100 of inhabitants	2	3	3		
Tourism accommodation					
Number of rooms	375	418	418	11.5	
Nights spent in collective establishments (1000)					
by non-residents (inbound tourism)	123	123	137		11.4
Receipts and Expenditure for International Tourism					
International Tourism Receipts (US$ million)	11	13	14	16.8	12.8
- per Tourist Arrival (US$)	752	710	721	-5.6	1.6
- per capita (US$)	17	19	21		

Source: World Tourism Organization (UNWTO)   (Data as collected by UNWTO for TMT 2006 Edition)

See annex for methodological notes and reference of external sources used.

International Tourism by Origin

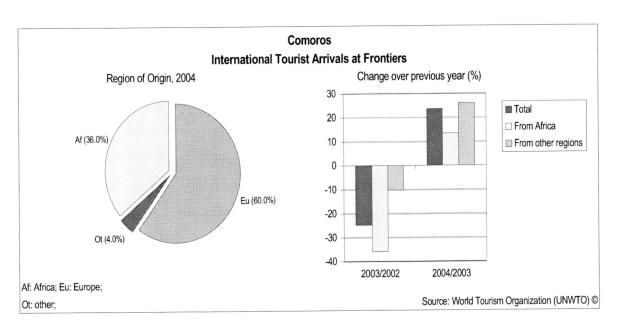

Comoros — International Tourist Arrivals at Frontiers

Af: Africa; Eu: Europe; Ot: other;

Source: World Tourism Organization (UNWTO) ©

Comoros

International Tourist Arrivals at Frontiers (by nationality)

	1995	2000	2002	2003	2004	Market share (%)		Growth rate (%)		Average per year (%)
						2000	2004	03/02	04/03	2000-2004
Total	**22,838**	**23,893**	**18,936**	**14,229**	**17,603**	**100**	**100**	**-24.9**	**23.7**	**-7.4**
From Africa	*7,949*	*15,812*	*8,715*	*5,590*	*6,344*	*66.2*	*36.0*	*-35.9*	*13.5*	*-20.4*
Reunion	..	1,403	2,164	1,670	1,429	5.9	8.1	-22.8	-14.4	0.5
Zimbabwe	..	494	..	613	786	2.1	4.5		28.2	12.3
Madagascar	659	779	789	269	656	3.3	3.7	-65.9	143.9	-4.2
Mauritius	..	392	135	180	360	1.6	2.0	33.3	100.0	-2.1
South Africa	6,526	9,146	1,247	36	71	38.3	0.4	-97.1	97.2	-70.3
Other East Africa	236	2,881	3,592	456	346	12.1	2.0	-87.3	-24.1	-41.1
Other Africa	528	717	788	2,366	2,696	3.0	15.3	200.3	13.9	39.3
From other regions	*14,889*	*7,623*	*9,614*	*8,639*	*10,889*	*31.9*	*61.9*	*-10.1*	*26.0*	*9.3*
France	9,455	5,836	9,076	7,883	9,460	24.4	53.7	-13.1	20.0	12.8
Belgium	294	..	..	..	..					
Italy	444	239	..	..	..	1.0				
United Kingdom	1,231	712	172	..	..	3.0				
All Americas	292	230	60	26	162	1.0	0.9	-56.7	523.1	-8.4
All Asia	278	109	13	609	114	0.5	0.6	4584.6	-81.3	1.1
All Oceania	168	44	51	1	51	0.2	0.3	-98.0	5000.0	3.8
Germany	2,006	208	39	..	..	0.9				
Turkey	..	28	..	..	..	0.1				
Other Europe	721	217	203	120	1,102	0.9	6.3	-40.9	818.3	50.1
Other World/Not specified	*..*	*458*	*607*	*..*	*370*	*1.9*	*2.1*			*-5.2*

Source: World Tourism Organization (UNWTO) ©   (Data as collected by UNWTO for TMT 2006 Edition)

Comoros

Nights of International Tourists in All Accommodation Establishments (by nationality)

	1995	2000	2002	2003	2004	Market share (%)		Growth rate (%)		Average per year (%)
						2000	2004	03/02	04/03	2000-2004
Total	**181,360**	..	..	..	..					
From Africa	*63,592*	..	..	..	..					
All Africa	63,592	..	..	..	..					
From other regions	*117,768*	..	..	..	..					
All Europe	113,208	..	..	..	..					
All Americas	2,336	..	..	..	..					
All East Asia/Pacific	2,224	..	..	..	..					

Source: World Tourism Organization (UNWTO) ©   (Data as collected by UNWTO for TMT 2006 Edition)

III.4.3   Djibouti   East Africa

Promotional: www.office-tourism.dj

Profile

Djibouti

Africa
East Africa

Capital	Djibouti
Year of entry in UNWTO	1997
Area (1000 km²)	23
Population (2005, 1000)	477
Gross Domestic Product (GDP) (2005, US$ million)	709
GDP per capita (2005, US$)	973
GDP growth (real, %)	
'-> 2004: 3.0; 2005: 3.2; 2006*: 4.2; 2007*: 5.0	

	2003	2004	2005*	2004/2003	2005*/2004
International Arrivals					
Tourists (overnight visitors) (1000)	23	26	30	13.4	14.8
- per 100 of inhabitants	5	6	6		
Tourism accommodation					
Number of rooms	450	450	450		
Nights spent in hotels and similar establishments (1000)					
by non-residents (inbound tourism)	64	67	59	5.0	-11.8
Receipts and Expenditure for International Tourism					
International Tourism Receipts (US$ million)	7	7	7	-1.8	4.3
- per Tourist Arrival (US$)	299	259	235	-13.4	-9.2
- per capita (US$)	15	15	15		
International Tourism Expenditure (US$ million)	3	3	3	-3.0	3.2
- per capita (US$)	6	6	6		
Δ International Tourism Balance (US$ million)	4	4	4		

Source: World Tourism Organization (UNWTO)   (Data as collected by UNWTO for TMT 2006 Edition)

See annex for methodological notes and reference of external sources used.

III.4.4 Eritrea East Africa

Profile

Eritrea

Africa
East Africa

				Capital	Asmara
				Year of entry in UNWTO	1995
				Area (1000 km²)	118
				Population (2005, million)	4.7
				Gross Domestic Product (GDP) (2005, US$ million)	970
				GDP per capita (2005, US$)	209

GDP growth (real, %)
'-> 2004: 3.5; 2005: 4.8; 2006*: 2.0; 2007*: 4.0

	2003	**2004**	**2005***	**2004/2003**	**2005*/2004**
International Arrivals					
Visitors (1000)	80	87	83	9.1	-4.6
- per 100 of inhabitants	2	2	2		
Tourism accommodation					
Number of rooms	4,139	4,712	5,447	13.8	15.6
Nights spent in hotels and similar establishments (1000)			845		
by non-residents (inbound tourism)	..	..	176		
by residents (domestic tourism)	..	..	669		
Receipts and Expenditure for International Tourism					
International Tourism Receipts (US$ million)	74	73	66	-1.4	-9.6
- per Visitor Arrival (US$)	925	836	792	-9.6	-5.3
- per capita (US$)	17	16	14		

Source: World Tourism Organization (UNWTO)   (Data as collected by UNWTO for TMT 2006 Edition)

See annex for methodological notes and reference of external sources used.

International Tourism by Origin

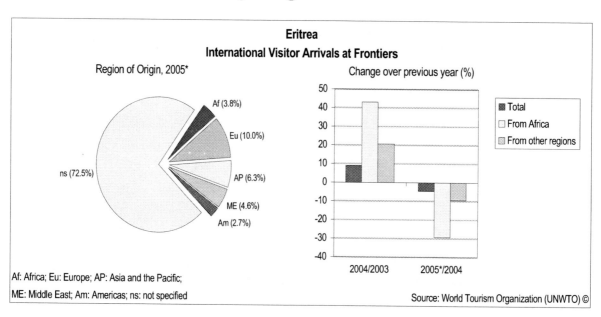

Eritrea
International Visitor Arrivals at Frontiers

Region of Origin, 2005*

Change over previous year (%)

- Af (3.8%)
- Eu (10.0%)
- AP (6.3%)
- ME (4.6%)
- Am (2.7%)
- ns (72.5%)

Legend: Total; From Africa; From other regions

Af: Africa; Eu: Europe; AP: Asia and the Pacific;
ME: Middle East; Am: Americas; ns: not specified

Source: World Tourism Organization (UNWTO) ©

Eritrea
International Visitor Arrivals at Frontiers (by nationality)

	1995	2000	2003	2004	2005*	Market share (%) 2000	Market share (%) 2005*	Growth rate (%) 04/03	Growth rate (%) 05*/04	Average per year (%) 2000-2005*
Total	315,417	70,355	80,029	87,298	83,307	100	100	9.1	-4.6	3.4
From Africa	181,955	4,023	3,147	4,503	3,182	5.7	3.8	43.1	-29.3	-4.6
Kenya	199	311	695	1,481	796	0.4	1.0	113.1	-46.3	20.7
Sudan	3,893	2,875	717	992	664	4.1	0.8	38.4	-33.1	-25.4
South Africa	..	97	232	263	220	0.1	0.3	13.4	-16.3	17.8
Uganda	..	40	117	196	169	0.1	0.2	67.5	-13.8	33.4
Tanzania	..	29	59	106	138	0.0	0.2	79.7	30.2	36.6
Ethiopia	170,783	35	76	77	109	0.0	0.1	1.3	41.6	25.5
Zimbabwe	..	24	48	69	69	0.0	0.1	43.8	0.0	23.5
Somalia	6,004	66	92	107	59	0.1	0.1	16.3	-44.9	-2.2
Zambia	..	14	50	71	51	0.0	0.1	42.0	-28.2	29.5
Malawi	..	7	4	16	28	0.0	0.0	300.0	75.0	32.0
Botswana	..	1	5	19	26	0.0	0.0	280.0	36.8	91.9
Mozambique	..	1	21	28	16	0.0	0.0	33.3	-42.9	74.1
Namibia	..	2	10	16	15	0.0	0.0	60.0	-6.3	49.6
Madagascar	..	..	4	2	1		0.0	-50.0	-50.0	
Mauritius	..	2	..	..	1	0.0	0.0			-12.9
Other Africa	1,076	519	1,017	1,060	820	0.7	1.0	4.2	-22.6	9.6
From other regions	16,843	13,403	18,078	21,801	19,741	19.1	23.7	20.6	-9.4	8.1
Italy	3,168	1,691	2,334	3,476	3,246	2.4	3.9	48.9	-6.6	13.9
India	193	562	2,580	2,420	2,985	0.8	3.6	-6.2	23.3	39.7
United States	1,708	1,464	1,745	1,611	1,611	2.1	1.9	-7.7	0.0	1.9
Germany	1,423	469	1,252	1,005	1,045	0.7	1.3	-19.7	4.0	17.4
Japan	525	1,214	103	1,063	1,018	1.7	1.2	932.0	-4.2	-3.5
United Kingdom	1,326	582	1,106	1,079	888	0.8	1.1	-2.4	-17.7	8.8
Scandinavia	989	842	1,210	1,598	835	1.2	1.0	32.1	-47.7	-0.2
Egypt	..	475	537	698	678	0.7	0.8	30.0	-2.9	7.4
Saudi Arabia	903	415	550	484	600	0.6	0.7	-12.0	24.0	7.7
France	636	325	461	416	410	0.5	0.5	-9.8	-1.4	4.8
Canada	301	566	367	731	357	0.8	0.4	99.2	-51.2	-8.8
Netherlands	458	..	..	487	353		0.4		-27.5	
Yemen	2,183	369	342	402	349	0.5	0.4	17.5	-13.2	-1.1
China	204	166	279	340	245	0.2	0.3	21.9	-27.9	8.1
Australia	278	206	237	260	239	0.3	0.3	9.7	-8.1	3.0
Switzerland	242	164	187	299	237	0.2	0.3	59.9	-20.7	7.6
Philippines	..	101	76	123	127	0.1	0.2	61.8	3.3	4.7
Israel	157	114	147	231	115	0.2	0.1	57.1	-50.2	0.2
Korea, Republic of	..	296	658	91	84	0.4	0.1	-86.2	-7.7	-22.3
Benelux	..	1,435	622	77	84	2.0	0.1	-87.6	9.1	-43.3
New Zealand	..	29	100	57	39	0.0	0.0	-43.0	-31.6	6.1
Malaysia	..	4	18	36	28	0.0	0.0	100.0	-22.2	47.6
Indonesia	..	4	15	7	19	0.0	0.0	-53.3	171.4	36.6
Singapore	..	11	8	16	17	0.0	0.0	100.0	6.3	9.1
Other Americas	56	63	209	217	295	0.1	0.4	3.8	35.9	36.2
Other interregional	2,093	1,836	2,935	4,577	3,837	2.6	4.6	55.9	-16.2	15.9
Nationals residing abroad	105,404	52,929	58,804	60,994	60,384	75.2	72.5	3.7	-1.0	2.7
Other World/Not specified	11,215	..	..	..	..					

Source: World Tourism Organization (UNWTO) ©   (Data as collected by UNWTO for TMT 2006 Edition)

III.4.5   Ethiopia East Africa

Promotional: www.visitethiopia.com

Profile

Ethiopia

Capital	Addis Ababa
Year of entry in UNWTO	1975
Area (1000 km²)	1,104
Population (2005, million)	73.1
Gross Domestic Product (GDP) (2005, US$ million)	11,174
GDP per capita (2005, US$)	153

Africa

East Africa

GDP growth (real, %)

-> 2004: 12.3;   2005: 8.7;   2006*: 5.4;   2007*: 5.5

	2003	2004	2005*	2004/2003	2005*/2004
International Arrivals					
Tourists (overnight visitors) (1000)	180	184	227	2.3	23.5
- per 100 of inhabitants	0	0	0		
Tourism accommodation					
Number of rooms	3,497	..	3,387		
Receipts and Expenditure for International Tourism					
International Tourism Receipts (US$ million)	114	174	168	52.6	-3.3
- per Tourist Arrival (US$)	634	945	740	49.2	-21.7
- per capita (US$)	2	2	2		
International Fare Receipts (US$ million)	222	284	365	27.9	28.5
International Tourism Expenditure (US$ million)	50	58	77	16.0	32.3
- per capita (US$)	1	1	1		
International Fare Expenditure (US$ million)	13	1	..	-92.3	
Δ International Tourism Balance (US$ million)	64	116	92		
Δ International Fare Balance (US$ million)	209	283	..		

Source: World Tourism Organization (UNWTO)   (Data as collected by UNWTO for TMT 2006 Edition)

See annex for methodological notes and reference of external sources used.

World Tourism Organization ©

International Tourism by Origin

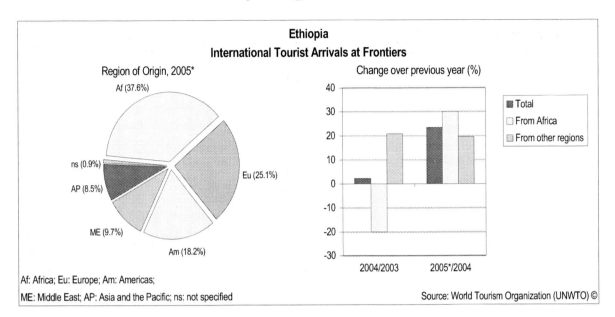

Ethiopia
International Tourist Arrivals at Frontiers

Region of Origin, 2005*

Change over previous year (%)

Af: Africa; Eu: Europe; Am: Americas;
ME: Middle East; AP: Asia and the Pacific; ns: not specified

Source: World Tourism Organization (UNWTO) ©

Ethiopia
International Tourist Arrivals at Frontiers (by nationality)

	1995	2000	2003	2004	2005*	Market share (%) 2000	Market share (%) 2005*	Growth rate (%) 04/03	Growth rate (%) 05*/04	Average per year (%) 2000-2005*
Total	**103,336**	**135,954**	**179,910**	**184,079**	**227,398**	**100**	**100**	**2.3**	**23.5**	**10.8**
From Africa	*30,595*	*48,796*	*82,152*	*65,744*	*85,501*	*35.9*	*37.6*	*-20.0*	*30.1*	*11.9*
Kenya	6,893	3,437	7,072	7,217	9,277	2.5	4.1	2.1	28.5	22.0
Sudan	5,035	4,723	3,769	3,787	5,343	3.5	2.3	0.5	41.1	2.5
Djibouti	5,004	14,512	21,708	14,627	4,179	10.7	1.8	-32.6	-71.4	-22.0
Other Africa	13,663	26,124	49,603	40,113	66,702	19.2	29.3	-19.1	66.3	20.6
From other regions	*64,792*	*68,256*	*96,716*	*116,934*	*139,958*	*50.2*	*61.5*	*20.9*	*19.7*	*15.4*
United States	7,545	11,318	22,496	28,112	32,282	8.3	14.2	25.0	14.8	23.3
United Kingdom	5,994	7,074	8,978	10,627	11,254	5.2	4.9	18.4	5.9	9.7
Canada	3,306	2,597	4,434	5,169	8,396	1.9	3.7	16.6	62.4	26.5
Italy	6,820	4,395	6,348	7,696	7,983	3.2	3.5	21.2	3.7	12.7
India	2,172	3,480	3,602	4,641	7,125	2.6	3.1	28.8	53.5	15.4
Germany	4,753	4,665	5,719	6,256	6,731	3.4	3.0	9.4	7.6	7.6
France	3,266	5,856	5,482	4,501	5,899	4.3	2.6	-17.9	31.1	0.1
Saudi Arabia	3,484	1,967	6,283	9,778	5,382	1.4	2.4	55.6	-45.0	22.3
Netherlands	2,274	2,717	3,044	3,227	4,387	2.0	1.9	6.0	35.9	10.1
Yemen	2,923	3,897	2,651	2,975	3,102	2.9	1.4	12.2	4.3	-4.5
Switzerland	3,245	1,663	2,072	1,854	1,962	1.2	0.9	-10.5	5.8	3.4
Japan	2,168	1,193	1,622	1,658	1,708	0.9	0.8	2.2	3.0	7.4
Russian Federation	3,513	385	430	682	654	0.3	0.3	58.6	-4.1	11.2
Other Americas	2,892	364	526	614	702	0.3	0.3	16.7	14.3	14.0
Other Middle East	2,893	2,741	5,432	7,865	13,678	2.0	6.0	44.8	73.9	37.9
Other Asia	1,757	5,758	6,023	8,167	10,480	4.2	4.6	35.6	28.3	12.7
Other Europe	5,787	8,186	11,574	13,112	18,233	6.0	8.0	13.3	39.1	17.4
Nationals residing abroad	*7,846*	*18,827*	*..*	*..*	*..*	*13.8*				
Other World/Not specified	*103*	*75*	*1,042*	*1,401*	*1,939*	*0.1*	*0.9*	*34.5*	*38.4*	*91.6*

Source: World Tourism Organization (UNWTO) ©   (Data as collected by UNWTO for TMT 2006 Edition)

III.4.6   Kenya   East Africa

Promotional: www.magicalkenya.com ; www.ktdc.co.ke ; www.katokenya.org ;
                      kenyatourism.org
Institutional/corporate: www.cbs.co.ke ; www.ktdc.co.ke ; www.ipckenya.org ; esok.org ;
                      www.kws.org
Research and data: www.cbs.go.ke ; www.magicalkenya.com

Profile

Kenya

Capital	Nairobi
Year of entry in UNWTO	1975
Area (1000 km²)	580
Population (2005, million)	34.9
Gross Domestic Product (GDP) (2005, US$ million)	18,730
GDP per capita (2005, US$)	560

Africa
East Africa

GDP growth (real, %)

'-> 2004: 4.6;   2005: 5.7;   2006*: 5.4;   2007*: 5.2

	2003	2004	2005*	2004/2003	2005*/2004
International Arrivals					
Visitors (1000)	1,146	1,359	1,675	18.6	23.3
Tourists (overnight visitors) (1000)	927	1,193	1,536	28.7	28.8
- per 100 of inhabitants	3	4	4		
Same-day visitors (1000)	216	162	135	-25.0	-16.7
Cruise passengers (1000)	3	4	5	33.3	25.0
Tourism accommodation					
Number of rooms	15,320	19,660	20,037	28.3	1.9
Nights spent in hotels and similar establishments (1000)	2,661	5,840	7,672	119.5	31.4
by non-residents (inbound tourism)	1,890	5,060	6,832	167.7	35.0
by residents (domestic tourism)	771	780	840	1.2	7.7
Receipts and Expenditure for International Tourism					
International Tourism Receipts (US$ million)	347	486	579	39.8	19.2
- per Tourist Arrival (US$)	375	407	377	8.6	-7.4
- per Visitor Arrival (US$)	303	357	346	17.9	-3.3
- per capita (US$)	11	14	17		
International Fare Receipts (US$ million)	272	313	390	15.1	24.6
International Tourism Expenditure (US$ million)	127	107	124	-15.4	15.2
- per capita (US$)	4	3	4		
Δ International Tourism Balance (US$ million)	220	378	455		

Source: World Tourism Organization (UNWTO)   (Data as collected by UNWTO for TMT 2006 Edition)
See annex for methodological notes and reference of external sources used.

World Tourism Organization ©

International Tourism by Origin

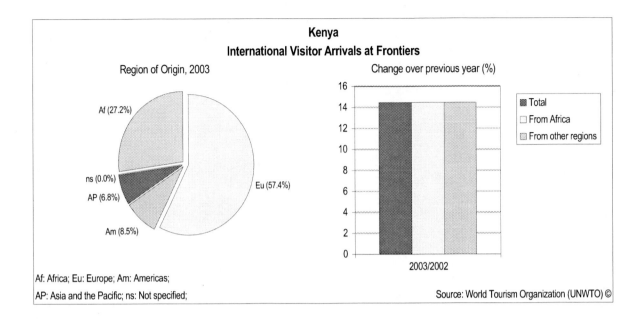

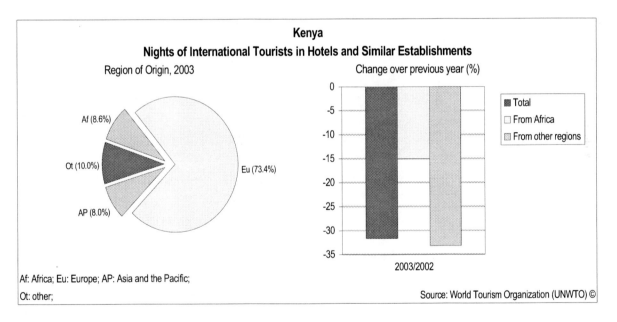

Kenya

International Visitor Arrivals at Frontiers (by residence)

	1995	2000	2002	2003	2004	Market share (%) 2000	Market share (%) 2004	Growth rate (%) 03/02	Growth rate (%) 04/03	Average per year (%) 2000-2004
Total	973,600	1,036,628	1,001,297	1,146,099	..	100		14.5		
From Africa	*188,170*	*282,458*	*272,429*	*311,819*	..	*27.2*		*14.5*		
All Africa	188,170	..	..	..	..					
Tanzania	..	116,574	112,435	128,695	..	11.2		14.5		
Uganda	..	72,803	70,218	80,373	..	7.0		14.5		
Zambia	..	9,562	9,223	10,557	..	0.9		14.5		
Other Africa	..	83,519	80,553	92,194	..	8.1		14.5		
From other regions	*497,890*	*754,170*	*728,565*	*833,933*	..	*72.8*		*14.5*		
Germany	108,700	163,168	157,394	180,156	..	15.7		14.5		
United Kingdom	105,640	158,574	154,933	177,339	..	15.3		14.5		
United States	45,310	68,014	65,599	75,086	..	6.6		14.5		
Italy	37,060	55,631	53,662	61,428	..	5.4		14.5		
France	33,220	49,866	48,101	55,057	..	4.8		14.5		
Switzerland	27,160	40,769	39,326	45,013	..	3.9		14.5		
Sweden	23,890	35,860	34,591	39,593	..	3.5		14.5		
India	..	24,889	24,007	27,479	..	2.4		14.5		
Austria	13,850	20,789	20,054	22,954	..	2.0		14.5		
Canada	12,920	19,393	18,704	21,410	..	1.9		14.5		
Netherlands	12,380	18,583	17,926	20,518	..	1.8		14.5		
Japan	10,650	15,986	15,421	17,651	..	1.5		14.5		
Spain	7,040	10,567	10,193	11,667	..	1.0		14.5		
Denmark	6,320	9,486	9,151	10,474	..	0.9		14.5		
Israel	..	8,564	7,383	8,451	..	0.8		14.5		
Finland	4,740	7,114	6,863	7,855	..	0.7		14.5		
Belgium	4,480	6,723	6,486	7,424	..	0.6		14.5		
Australia	3,160	4,744	4,575	5,237	..	0.5		14.5		
New Zealand	2,600	3,902	3,764	4,308	..	0.4		14.5		
Ireland	..	3,782	3,648	4,176	..	0.4		14.5		
Norway	1,360	2,042	1,969	2,254	..	0.2		14.5		
Greece	..	1,530	1,476	1,689	..	0.1		14.4		
Portugal	..	584	565	647	..	0.1		14.5		
Brazil	120	180	174	199	..	0.0		14.4		
Mexico	40	59	56	64	..	0.0		14.3		
Other interregional	37,250	23,371	22,544	25,804	..	2.3		14.5		
Other World/Not specified	*287,540*	..	*303*	*347*	..			*14.5*		

Source: World Tourism Organization (UNWTO) ©

(Data as collected by UNWTO for TMT 2006 Edition)

Kenya
Nights of International Tourists in Hotels and Similar Establishments (by residence)

	1995	2000	2002	2003	2004	Market share (%) 2000	2004	Growth rate (%) 03/02	04/03	Average per year (%) 2000-2004
Total	**4,365,500**	**2,873,300**	**2,766,000**	**1,889,900**	..	**100**		**-31.7**		
From Africa	*266,500*	*264,100*	*191,500*	*162,700*	..	*9.2*		*-15.0*		
All Southern Africa	23,100	38,700	42,700	34,400	..	1.3		-19.4		
Tanzania	40,600	41,400	26,700	30,400	..	1.4		13.9		
Uganda	30,800	30,000	26,900	26,200	..	1.0		-2.6		
All North Africa	12,000	15,900	12,700	16,500	..	0.6		29.9		
All West Africa	28,200	22,600	25,100	15,400	..	0.8		-38.6		
Other Africa	131,800	115,500	57,400	39,800	..	4.0		-30.7		
From other regions	*3,963,000*	*2,561,500*	*2,549,500*	*1,703,000*	..	*89.1*		*-33.2*		
Germany	1,201,400	605,100	721,300	420,400	..	21.1		-41.7		
United Kingdom	984,600	558,600	591,400	324,300	..	19.4		-45.2		
Italy	305,700	202,400	211,900	144,000	..	7.0		-32.0		
Switzerland	312,000	174,800	218,300	125,900	..	6.1		-42.3		
France	310,100	212,800	164,800	113,900	..	7.4		-30.9		
United States	265,900	228,900	149,800	109,600	..	8.0		-26.8		
Australia, New Zealand	25,100	26,900	21,900	76,800	..	0.9		250.7		
Scandinavia	86,300	69,900	56,300	45,600	..	2.4		-19.0		
India	27,800	34,700	25,000	29,200	..	1.2		16.8		
Japan	33,400	55,900	44,200	26,200	..	1.9		-40.7		
All Middle East	29,600	50,500	37,700	20,300	..	1.8		-46.2		
Canada	51,600	26,800	22,400	17,600	..	0.9		-21.4		
Other Americas	15,000	27,700	22,300	17,500	..	1.0		-21.5		
Other Asia	25,500	27,200	17,300	18,200	..	0.9		5.2		
Other Europe	289,000	259,300	244,900	213,500	..	9.0		-12.8		
Other World/Not specified	*136,000*	*47,700*	*25,000*	*24,200*	..	*1.7*		*-3.2*		

Source: World Tourism Organization (UNWTO) ©   (Data as collected by UNWTO for TMT 2006 Edition)

III.4.7   Madagascar   East Africa

Promotional: www.tourisme.gov.mg
Institutional/corporate: En construction

Profile

Madagascar

Africa
East Africa

Capital		Antananarivo
Year of entry in UNWTO		1975
Area (1000 km²)		587
Population (2005, million)		18.3
Gross Domestic Product (GDP) (2005, US$ million)		5,033
GDP per capita (2005, US$)		282
GDP growth (real, %)		
'-> 2004: 5.3; 2005: 4.6; 2006*: 4.7; 2007*: 5.6		

	2003	2004	2005*	2004/2003	2005*/2004
International Arrivals					
Tourists (overnight visitors) (1000)	139	229	277	64.6	21.3
- per 100 of inhabitants	1	1	2		
Tourism accommodation					
Number of rooms	9,325	10,230	10,879	9.7	6.3
Nights spent in hotels and similar establishments (1000)					
by non-residents (inbound tourism)	1,970	3,536	5,221	79.5	47.7
Outbound Tourism					
Trips abroad (1000)	..	67	41		-38.8
- per 100 of inhabitants	..	0	0		
Receipts and Expenditure for International Tourism					
International Tourism Receipts (US$ million)	44	56	62	27.3	10.7
- per Tourist Arrival (US$)	317	245	223	-22.7	-8.7
- per capita (US$)	3	3	3		
International Fare Receipts (US$ million)	25	28	36	12.0	28.6
International Tourism Expenditure (US$ million)	37	35	25	-5.4	-28.6
- per trip (US$)	..	522	610		16.7
- per capita (US$)	2	2	1		
International Fare Expenditure (US$ million)	2	6	2	200.0	-66.7
Δ International Tourism Balance (US$ million)	7	21	37		
Δ International Fare Balance (US$ million)	23	22	34		

Source: World Tourism Organization (UNWTO)   (Data as collected by UNWTO for TMT 2006 Edition)
See annex for methodological notes and reference of external sources used.

World Tourism Organization ©

International Tourism by Origin

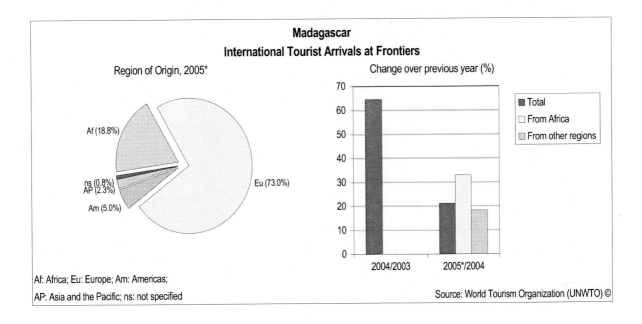

Madagascar
International Tourist Arrivals at Frontiers

Region of Origin, 2005*

Af (18.8%)
ns (0.8%)
AP (2.3%)
Am (5.0%)
Eu (73.0%)

Change over previous year (%)

Total
From Africa
From other regions

Af: Africa; Eu: Europe; Am: Americas;
AP: Asia and the Pacific; ns: not specified

Source: World Tourism Organization (UNWTO) ©

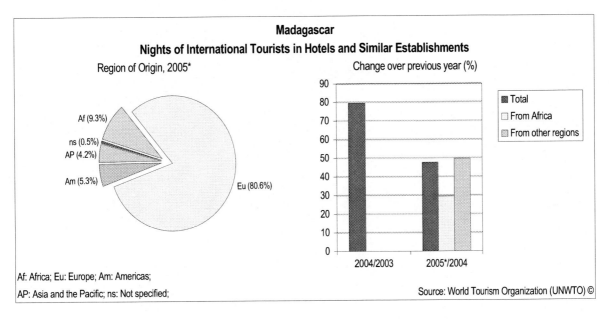

Madagascar
Nights of International Tourists in Hotels and Similar Establishments

Region of Origin, 2005*

Af (9.3%)
ns (0.5%)
AP (4.2%)
Am (5.3%)
Eu (80.6%)

Change over previous year (%)

Total
From Africa
From other regions

Af: Africa; Eu: Europe; Am: Americas;
AP: Asia and the Pacific; ns: Not specified;

Source: World Tourism Organization (UNWTO) ©

Madagascar
International Tourist Arrivals at Frontiers (by nationality)

	1995	2000	2003	2004	2005*	Market share (%) 2000	Market share (%) 2005*	Growth rate (%) 04/03	Growth rate (%) 05*/04	Average per year (%) 2000-2005*
Total	**74,619**	**160,071**	**139,000**	**228,785**	**277,422**	**100**	**100**	**64.6**	**21.3**	**11.6**
From Africa	*8,331*	*24,534*	*17,000*	*39,302*	*52,277*	*15.3*	*18.8*	*131.2*	*33.0*	*16.3*
Reunion	4,414	14,406	..	22,878	31,861	9.0	11.5		39.3	17.2
All Africa	..	..	17,000	..	..					
Mauritius	1,362	4,526	..	9,609	9,825	2.8	3.5		2.2	16.8
South Africa	689	..	..	3,203	5,860		2.1		83.0	
Comoros	1,458	..	..	125	201		0.1		60.8	
Kenya	345	..	..	55	78		0.0		41.8	
Seychelles	63	..	..	..	..					
Other Africa	..	5,602	..	3,432	4,452	3.5	1.6		29.7	-4.5
From other regions	*66,288*	*118,906*	*106,000*	*188,339*	*222,787*	*74.3*	*80.3*	*77.7*	*18.3*	*13.4*
France	23,616	88,039	..	129,263	145,192	55.0	52.3		12.3	10.5
All Europe	..	..	100,000	..	..					
Italy	6,002	8,004	..	17,159	22,657	5.0	8.2		32.0	23.1
Canada, USA	5,148	6,402	..	9,151	13,808	4.0	5.0		50.9	16.6
Germany	15,362	6,403	..	9,609	12,025	4.0	4.3		25.1	13.4
Benelux	980	..	..	8,236	9,879		3.6		19.9	
United Kingdom	4,458	4,802	..	6,864	6,732	3.0	2.4		-1.9	7.0
Japan	415	2,055	..	3,432	5,952	1.3	2.1		73.4	23.7
Switzerland	5,801	3,201	..	4,576	4,987	2.0	1.8		9.0	9.3
All Americas	..	..	4,000	..	..					
Spain	568	..	..	..	370		0.1			
Scandinavia	510	..	..	20	237		0.1		1085.0	
Other Americas	87	..	..	29	45		0.0		55.2	
Other Asia	3,252	..	..	..	452		0.2			
Other Europe	89	..	..	..	451		0.2			
All East Asia/Pacific	..	..	2,000	..	..					
Other World/Not specified	*..*	*16,631*	*16,000*	*1,144*	*2,358*	*10.4*	*0.8*	*-92.9*	*106.1*	*-32.3*

Source: World Tourism Organization (UNWTO) ©   (Data as collected by UNWTO for TMT 2006 Edition)

Madagascar
Nights of International Tourists in Hotels and Similar Establishments (by nationality)

	1995	2000	2003	2004	2005*	Market share (%) 2000	Market share (%) 2005*	Growth rate (%) 04/03	Growth rate (%) 05*/04	Average per year (%) 2000-2005*
Total	1,248,574	3,041,349	1,970,000	3,536,098	5,221,156	100	100	79.5	47.7	11.4
From Africa	101,668	466,146	..	374,844	485,523	15.3	9.3		29.5	0.8
Reunion	59,380	273,714	..	137,268	223,027	9.0	4.3		62.5	-4.0
Mauritius	12,176	85,994	..	67,263	68,775	2.8	1.3		2.2	-4.4
South Africa	7,896	..	..	48,045	52,740		1.0		9.8	
Comoros	19,653	..	..	1,598	6,231		0.1		289.9	
Kenya	2,132	..	..	550	1,170		0.0		112.7	
Seychelles	431	..	..	..	..					
Other Africa	..	106,438	..	120,120	133,580	3.5	2.6		11.2	4.6
From other regions	1,146,906	2,259,214	..	3,144,094	4,707,337	74.3	90.2		49.7	15.8
France	234,588	1,672,741	..	2,304,589	3,629,800	55.0	69.5		57.5	16.8
Canada, USA	66,776	121,638	..	183,020	276,160	4.0	5.3		50.9	17.8
Japan	44,731	39,045	..	102,960	208,230	1.3	4.0		102.2	39.8
Italy	60,018	152,076	..	240,226	178,296	5.0	3.4		-25.8	3.2
Germany	142,797	121,657	..	86,481	132,275	4.0	2.5		53.0	1.7
United Kingdom	41,912	91,238	..	102,960	121,178	3.0	2.3		17.7	5.8
Benelux	6,909	..	..	90,596	88,911		1.7		-1.9	
Switzerland	47,985	60,819	..	32,032	49,870	2.0	1.0		55.7	-3.9
Scandinavia	7,651	..	..	360	3,318		0.1		821.7	
Spain	5,248	..	..	..	2,590		0.0			
Other Americas	6,021	..	..	870	1,350		0.0		55.2	
Other Asia	2,714	..	..	..	11,300		0.2			
Other Europe	479,556	..	..	..	4,059		0.1			
Other World/Not specified	..	315,989	1,970,000	17,160	28,296	10.4	0.5	-99.1	64.9	-38.3

Source: World Tourism Organization (UNWTO) ©   (Data as collected by UNWTO for TMT 2006 Edition)

III.4.8   Malawi   East Africa

Profile

Malawi

Capital		Lilongwe
Year of entry in UNWTO		1975
Area (1000 km²)		118
Population (2005, million)		13.0
Gross Domestic Product (GDP) (2005, US$ million)		2,076
GDP per capita (2005, US$)		161

Africa
East Africa

GDP growth (real, %)
'-> 2004: 5.1;   2005: 2.1;   2006*: 8.4;   2007*: 5.6

	2003	2004	2005*	2004/2003	2005*/2004
International Arrivals					
Tourists (overnight visitors) (1000)	424	427	438	0.8	2.4
- per 100 of inhabitants	3	3	3		
Tourism accommodation					
Number of rooms	20,871	20,871	..		
Nights spent in collective establishments (1000)					
by non-residents (inbound tourism)	3,259	3,617	..	11.0	
Receipts and Expenditure for International Tourism					
International Tourism Receipts (US$ million)	23	24	24	2.9	-0.1
- per Tourist Arrival (US$)	55	56	55	2.1	-2.5
- per capita (US$)	2	2	2		
International Fare Receipts (US$ million)	12	12	13	4.1	10.4
International Tourism Expenditure (US$ million)	48	50	50	4.3	-0.1
- per capita (US$)	4	4	4		
International Fare Expenditure (US$ million)	13	12	12	-5.3	-0.1
Δ International Tourism Balance (US$ million)	-24	-25	-25		
Δ International Fare Balance (US$ million)	-1	0	1		

Source: World Tourism Organization (UNWTO)   (Data as collected by UNWTO for TMT 2006 Edition)
See annex for methodological notes and reference of external sources used.

International Tourism by Origin

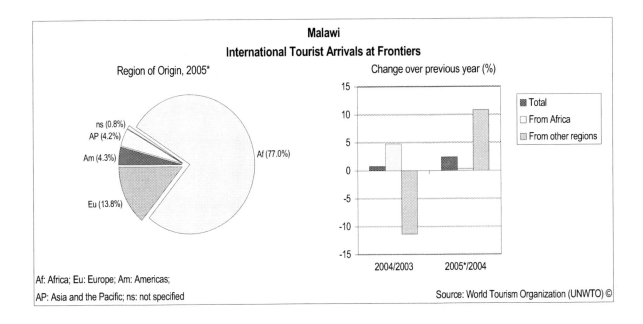

Malawi

International Tourist Arrivals at Frontiers (by residence)

	1995	2000	2003	2004	2005*	Market share (%) 2000	2005*	Growth rate (%) 04/03	05*/04	Average per year (%) 2000-2005*
Total	**192,169**	**227,576**	**424,000**	**427,360**	**437,718**	**100**	**100**	**0.8**	**2.4**	**14.0**
From Africa	*139,602*	*171,317*	*320,360*	*335,651*	*336,856*	*75.3*	*77.0*	*4.8*	*0.4*	*14.5*
Mozambique	32,846	48,400	92,200	104,698	95,019	21.3	21.7	13.6	-9.2	14.4
Zimbabwe	25,412	29,003	63,910	57,518	60,807	12.7	13.9	-10.0	5.7	16.0
All Southern Africa	17,001	28,390	49,200	54,230	48,155	12.5	11.0	10.2	-11.2	11.1
Zambia	38,830	24,029	50,540	45,817	43,855	10.6	10.0	-9.3	-4.3	12.8
Other East Africa	..	36,181	58,920	67,704	82,618	15.9	18.9	14.9	22.0	18.0
Other Africa	25,513	5,314	5,590	5,684	6,402	2.3	1.5	1.7	12.6	3.8
From other regions	*52,567*	*48,605*	*99,130*	*87,885*	*97,409*	*21.4*	*22.3*	*-11.3*	*10.8*	*14.9*
United Kingdom/Ireland	21,576	17,693	31,220	17,030	28,157	7.8	6.4	-45.5	65.3	9.7
Canada, USA	6,397	10,744	17,210	19,431	17,278	4.7	3.9	12.9	-11.1	10.0
All South Asia	2,172	..	3,620	6,815	9,549		2.2	88.3	40.1	
All Asia	7,686	..	9,940	11,313	8,698		2.0	13.8	-23.1	
All Middle East	192	..	..	..	..					
Other Americas	..	..	860	1,397	1,447		0.3	62.4	3.6	
Other Europe	14,544	20,168	36,280	31,899	32,280	8.9	7.4	-12.1	1.2	9.9
Other World/Not specified	*..*	*7,654*	*4,510*	*3,824*	*3,453*	*3.4*	*0.8*	*-15.2*	*-9.7*	*-14.7*

Source: World Tourism Organization (UNWTO) ©   (Data as collected by UNWTO for TMT 2006 Edition)

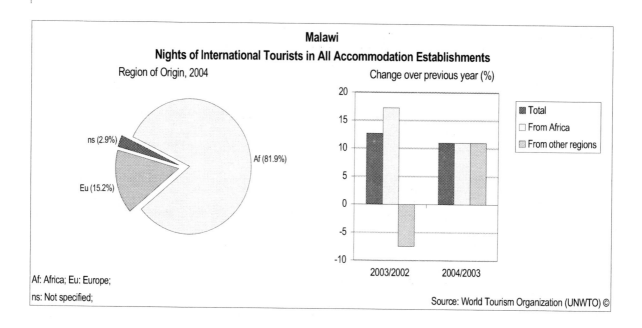

Malawi

Nights of International Tourists in All Accommodation Establishments (by residence)

	1995	2000	2002	2003	2004	Market share (%) 2000	Market share (%) 2004	Growth rate (%) 03/02	Growth rate (%) 04/03	Average per year (%) 2000-2004
Total	**1,345,183**	**1,325,000**	**2,892,726**	**3,258,728**	**3,617,187**	**100**	**100**	**12.7**	**11.0**	**28.5**
From Africa	*977,081*	*860,000*	*2,276,085*	*2,668,424*	*2,961,950*	*64.9*	*81.9*	*17.2*	*11.0*	*36.2*
Mozambique	229,922	149,600	631,286	740,097	821,508	11.3	22.7	17.2	11.0	53.1
Zimbabwe	177,884	146,400	410,970	481,812	534,811	11.0	14.8	17.2	11.0	38.2
All Southern Africa	119,007	120,000	355,338	416,591	462,416	9.1	12.8	17.2	11.0	40.1
Zambia	271,810	273,600	297,836	349,175	387,584	20.6	10.7	17.2	11.0	9.1
Other East Africa	166,509	160,000	540,413	633,566	703,258	12.1	19.4	17.2	11.0	44.8
Other Africa	11,949	10,400	40,242	47,183	52,373	0.8	1.4	17.2	11.0	49.8
From other regions	*297,619*	*219,200*	*536,522*	*496,376*	*550,977*	*16.5*	*15.2*	*-7.5*	*11.0*	*25.9*
United Kingdom/Ireland	151,032	137,600	157,267	184,372	204,653	10.4	5.7	17.2	11.0	10.4
Canada, USA	44,779	24,000	113,126	..	..	1.8				
Other Europe	101,808	57,600	266,129	312,004	346,324	4.3	9.6	17.2	11.0	56.6
Other World/Not specified	*70,483*	*245,800*	*80,119*	*93,928*	*104,260*	*18.6*	*2.9*	*17.2*	*11.0*	*-19.3*

Source: World Tourism Organization (UNWTO) ©   (Data as collected by UNWTO for TMT 2006 Edition)

III.4.9   Mauritius   East Africa

Promotional: www.mauritius.net
Institutional/corporate: http://tourism.gov.mu
Research and data: http://statsmauritius.gov.mu

Profile

Mauritius

Capital	Port Louis
Year of entry in UNWTO	1975
Area (10 km²)	204
Population (2005, million)	1.2
Gross Domestic Product (GDP) (2005, US$ million)	6,231
GDP per capita (2005, US$)	5,029

Africa
East Africa

GDP growth (real, %)
'-> 2004: 4.5;   2005: 3.4;   2006*: 3.4;   2007*: 3.4

	2003	2004	2005*	2004/2003	2005*/2004
International Arrivals					
Visitors (1000)	722	739	782	2.4	5.8
Tourists (overnight visitors) (1000)	702	719	761	2.4	5.9
- per 100 of inhabitants	58	59	62		
Same-day visitors (1000)	11	11	11		
Cruise passengers (1000)	9	9	9		
Tourism accommodation					
Number of rooms	9,647	10,640	10,497	10.3	-1.3
Nights spent in hotels and similar establishments (1000)					
by non-residents (inbound tourism)	6,952	7,119	7,498	2.4	5.3
Outbound Tourism					
Trips abroad (1000)	161	180	183	11.8	1.7
- per 100 of inhabitants	13	15	15		
Receipts and Expenditure for International Tourism					
International Tourism Receipts (US$ million)	696	853	871	22.5	2.2
- per Tourist Arrival (US$)	991	1,186	1,145	19.7	-3.5
- per Visitor Arrival (US$)	964	1,154	1,114	19.7	-3.4
- per capita (US$)	575	699	708		
International Fare Receipts (US$ million)	263	300	318	14.1	5.9
International Tourism Expenditure (US$ million)	216	255	275	17.9	8.0
- per trip (US$)	1,342	1,414	1,502	5.4	6.2
- per capita (US$)	178	209	223		
International Fare Expenditure (US$ million)	20	22	20	10.0	-7.1
Δ International Tourism Balance (US$ million)	480	598	596		
Δ International Fare Balance (US$ million)	243	278	297		

Source: World Tourism Organization (UNWTO)   (Data as collected by UNWTO for TMT 2006 Edition)

See annex for methodological notes and reference of external sources used.

International Tourism by Origin

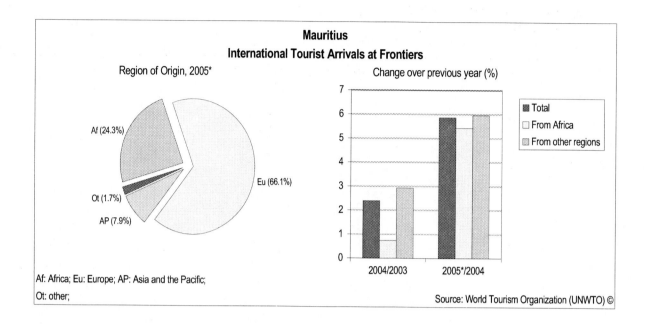

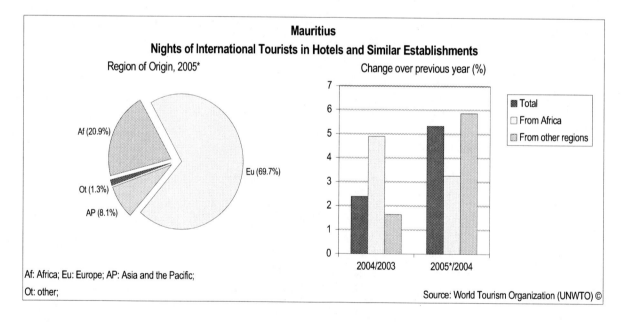

Mauritius

International Tourist Arrivals at Frontiers (by residence)

	1995	2000	2003	2004	2005*	Market share (%) 2000	Market share (%) 2005*	Growth rate (%) 04/03	Growth rate (%) 05*/04	Average per year (%) 2000-2005*
Total	**422,463**	**656,453**	**702,018**	**718,861**	**761,063**	**100**	**100**	**2.4**	**5.9**	**3.0**
From Africa	*143,586*	*163,763*	*173,996*	*175,295*	*184,821*	*24.9*	*24.3*	*0.7*	*5.4*	*2.4*
Reunion	78,431	86,945	95,679	96,510	99,036	13.2	13.0	0.9	2.6	2.6
South Africa	42,653	48,683	45,756	52,609	58,446	7.4	7.7	15.0	11.1	3.7
Seychelles	7,116	9,229	9,869	7,456	10,084	1.4	1.3	-24.5	35.2	1.8
Madagascar	6,885	7,057	11,044	8,256	7,397	1.1	1.0	-25.2	-10.4	0.9
Zimbabwe	2,965	3,435	2,343	2,345	2,419	0.5	0.3	0.1	3.2	-6.8
Kenya	1,158	1,801	1,510	1,506	1,358	0.3	0.2	-0.3	-9.8	-5.5
Comoros	1,348	945	1,437	949	1,166	0.1	0.2	-34.0	22.9	4.3
Namibia	..	503	550	578	506	0.1	0.1	5.1	-12.5	0.1
Botswana	..	400	445	449	375	0.1	0.0	0.9	-16.5	-1.3
Tanzania	..	1,032	342	422	317	0.2	0.0	23.4	-24.9	-21.0
Zambia	443	445	456	395	305	0.1	0.0	-13.4	-22.8	-7.3
Mozambique	..	434	394	336	275	0.1	0.0	-14.7	-18.2	-8.7
Morocco	..	91	149	183	191	0.0	0.0	22.8	4.4	16.0
Nigeria	..	131	231	221	180	0.0	0.0	-4.3	-18.6	6.6
Tunisia	..	104	181	144	180	0.0	0.0	-20.4	25.0	11.6
Angola	..	111	119	230	139	0.0	0.0	93.3	-39.6	4.6
Other intraregional	2,587	2,417	3,491	2,706	2,447	0.4	0.3	-22.5	-9.6	0.2
From other regions	*277,975*	*492,194*	*527,737*	*543,194*	*575,576*	*75.0*	*75.6*	*2.9*	*6.0*	*3.2*
France	116,701	198,423	200,229	210,411	220,421	30.2	29.0	5.1	4.8	2.1
United Kingdom	31,324	74,488	91,210	92,652	95,407	11.3	12.5	1.6	3.0	5.1
Germany	41,637	52,869	53,970	52,277	55,983	8.1	7.4	-3.1	7.1	1.2
Italy	17,384	39,000	39,774	41,277	43,458	5.9	5.7	3.8	5.3	2.2
India	11,225	17,241	25,367	24,716	29,755	2.6	3.9	-2.6	20.4	11.5
Switzerland	13,815	20,473	17,929	16,110	15,773	3.1	2.1	-10.1	-2.1	-5.1
Australia	5,558	8,771	9,103	11,373	13,486	1.3	1.8	24.9	18.6	9.0
Austria	4,841	8,874	8,893	10,304	10,440	1.4	1.4	15.9	1.3	3.3
Spain	3,019	7,226	9,081	8,475	9,682	1.1	1.3	-6.7	14.2	6.0
Belgium	5,802	10,998	10,170	8,524	8,973	1.7	1.2	-16.2	5.3	-4.0
China	1,918	2,459	3,738	5,291	5,526	0.4	0.7	41.5	4.4	17.6
Netherlands	1,513	4,925	4,403	4,867	5,111	0.8	0.7	10.5	5.0	0.7
United States	2,093	3,704	4,505	4,305	4,890	0.6	0.6	-4.4	13.6	5.7
Sweden	1,709	5,694	4,857	4,609	4,224	0.9	0.6	-5.1	-8.4	-5.8
Russian Federation	..	1,400	2,908	3,209	4,000	0.2	0.5	10.4	24.6	23.4
Ireland	..	1,979	3,414	3,492	3,964	0.3	0.5	2.3	13.5	14.9
Norway	..	3,275	2,641	3,027	2,971	0.5	0.4	14.6	-1.9	-1.9
Denmark	..	1,225	1,836	2,239	2,570	0.2	0.3	21.9	14.8	16.0
Finland	..	1,413	1,914	2,353	2,430	0.2	0.3	22.9	3.3	11.5
Hungary	..	631	932	907	2,393	0.1	0.3	-2.7	163.8	30.6
Greece	..	506	1,910	1,864	2,328	0.1	0.3	-2.4	24.9	35.7
Canada	1,157	1,812	1,845	2,341	2,119	0.3	0.3	26.9	-9.5	3.2
Czech Rep	..	894	1,359	1,846	1,927	0.1	0.3	35.8	4.4	16.6
Poland	..	1,308	1,329	1,504	1,862	0.2	0.2	13.2	23.8	7.3
Portugal	..	1,333	1,616	1,599	1,851	0.2	0.2	-1.1	15.8	6.8
Other interregional	18,279	21,273	22,804	23,622	24,032	3.2	3.2	3.6	1.7	2.5
Other World/Not specified	*902*	*496*	*285*	*372*	*666*	*0.1*	*0.1*	*30.5*	*79.0*	*6.1*

Source: World Tourism Organization (UNWTO) ©   (Data as collected by UNWTO for TMT 2006 Edition)

Mauritius

Nights of International Tourists in Hotels and Similar Establishments (by residence)

	1995	2000	2003	2004	2005*	Market share (%) 2000	Market share (%) 2005*	Growth rate (%) 04/03	Growth rate (%) 05*/04	Average per year (%) 2000-2005*
Total	4,434,891	6,412,876	6,952,313	7,118,603	7,498,251	100	100	2.4	5.3	3.2
From Africa	*1,159,776*	*1,278,549*	*1,446,983*	*1,517,745*	*1,567,206*	*19.9*	*20.9*	*4.9*	*3.3*	*4.2*
Reunion	573,206	596,449	738,968	832,879	828,889	9.3	11.1	12.7	-0.5	6.8
South Africa	378,812	422,300	379,561	425,680	467,603	6.6	6.2	12.2	9.8	2.1
Seychelles	65,577	82,577	92,493	75,277	93,951	1.3	1.3	-18.6	24.8	2.6
Madagascar	54,783	65,526	128,437	83,961	73,964	1.0	1.0	-34.6	-11.9	2.5
Zimbabwe	29,306	37,555	26,469	28,831	31,233	0.6	0.4	8.9	8.3	-3.6
Comoros	18,972	12,394	15,971	12,270	12,434	0.2	0.2	-23.2	1.3	0.1
Kenya	9,242	12,585	11,347	11,069	12,258	0.2	0.2	-2.4	10.7	-0.5
Zambia	3,344	..	..	..	..					
Other Africa	26,534	49,163	53,737	47,778	46,874	0.8	0.6	-11.1	-1.9	-0.9
From other regions	*3,266,844*	*5,131,398*	*5,502,720*	*5,593,345*	*5,921,189*	*80.0*	*79.0*	*1.6*	*5.9*	*2.9*
France	1,232,159	1,934,683	1,996,305	2,101,125	2,208,575	30.2	29.5	5.3	5.1	2.7
United Kingdom	470,448	884,799	1,043,113	1,053,881	1,070,185	13.8	14.3	1.0	1.5	3.9
Germany	521,984	635,600	636,435	608,031	655,283	9.9	8.7	-4.5	7.8	0.6
Italy	180,214	349,267	346,865	362,758	397,160	5.4	5.3	4.6	9.5	2.6
India	143,884	188,008	287,741	265,174	295,698	2.9	3.9	-7.8	11.5	9.5
Switzerland	179,118	248,345	220,382	189,115	185,482	3.9	2.5	-14.2	-1.9	-5.7
Belgium	85,274	132,571	121,687	105,445	117,210	2.1	1.6	-13.3	11.2	-2.4
Australia	85,473	96,932	100,332	111,546	115,851	1.5	1.5	11.2	3.9	3.6
Austria	60,073	96,998	96,299	108,429	111,840	1.5	1.5	12.6	3.1	2.9
Spain	23,483	55,869	64,485	60,739	67,724	0.9	0.9	-5.8	11.5	3.9
China	28,163	30,110	44,106	50,202	64,707	0.5	0.9	13.8	28.9	16.5
Netherlands	16,990	52,137	48,417	52,009	53,743	0.8	0.7	7.4	3.3	0.6
Sweden	17,189	55,381	47,100	43,963	45,612	0.9	0.6	-6.7	3.8	-3.8
United States	21,170	32,719	38,795	39,039	41,298	0.5	0.6	0.6	5.8	4.8
Canada	24,563	28,920	27,268	33,084	29,821	0.5	0.4	21.3	-9.9	0.6
Singapore	18,323	21,998	14,871	16,094	12,106	0.3	0.2	8.2	-24.8	-11.3
Malaysia	15,327	12,750	12,258	16,160	11,868	0.2	0.2	31.8	-26.6	-1.4
Japan	19,007	14,054	9,302	9,881	10,538	0.2	0.1	6.2	6.6	-5.6
Taiwan (pr. of China)	10,386	..	..	..	..					
Hong Kong (China)	14,387	9,601	6,767	7,984	4,694	0.1	0.1	18.0	-41.2	-13.3
Other Americas	2,981	17,110	17,531	12,619	15,884	0.3	0.2	-28.0	25.9	-1.5
Other Asia	22,105	54,850	79,386	78,389	83,001	0.9	1.1	-1.3	5.9	8.6
Other Europe	70,162	171,863	237,281	262,409	313,908	2.7	4.2	10.6	19.6	12.8
Other Oceania	3,981	6,833	5,994	5,269	9,001	0.1	0.1	-12.1	70.8	5.7
Other World/Not specified	*8,271*	*2,929*	*2,610*	*7,513*	*9,856*	*0.0*	*0.1*	*187.9*	*31.2*	*27.5*

Source: World Tourism Organization (UNWTO) ©   (Data as collected by UNWTO for TMT 2006 Edition)

III.4.10 Mozambique — East Africa

Profile

Mozambique

Africa
East Africa

Capital	Maputo
Year of entry in UNWTO	1995
Area (1000 km²)	802
Population (2005, million)	20.2
Gross Domestic Product (GDP) (2005, US$ million)	6,491
GDP per capita (2005, US$)	331
GDP growth (real, %)	
'-> 2004: 7.5; 2005: 7.7; 2006*: 7.9; 2007*: 7.0	

	2003	2004	2005*	2004/2003	2005*/2004
International Arrivals					
Visitors (1000)	726	711	954	-2.1	34.2
Tourists (overnight visitors) (1000)	441	470	578	6.6	23.0
- per 100 of inhabitants	2	2	3		
Same-day visitors (1000)	285	241	376	-15.4	56.0
Tourism accommodation					
Number of bed-places	13,601	13,807	14,827	1.5	7.4
Nights spent in hotels and similar establishments (1000)		705	706		0.1
by non-residents (inbound tourism)	..	408	389		-4.7
by residents (domestic tourism)	..	297	317		6.7
Receipts and Expenditure for International Tourism					
International Tourism Receipts (US$ million)	98	95	130	-2.4	36.0
- per Tourist Arrival (US$)	221	203	224	-8.4	10.6
- per Visitor Arrival (US$)	134	134	136	-0.3	1.4
- per capita (US$)	5	5	6		
International Fare Receipts (US$ million)	8	1	8	-87.5	700.0
International Tourism Expenditure (US$ million)	140	134	176	-4.0	31.2
- per capita (US$)	7	7	9		
International Fare Expenditure (US$ million)	1	6	11	500.0	83.3
Δ International Tourism Balance (US$ million)	-42	-39	-47		
Δ International Fare Balance (US$ million)	7	-5	-3		

Source: World Tourism Organization (UNWTO) (Data as collected by UNWTO for TMT 2006 Edition)

See annex for methodological notes and reference of external sources used.

International Tourism by Origin

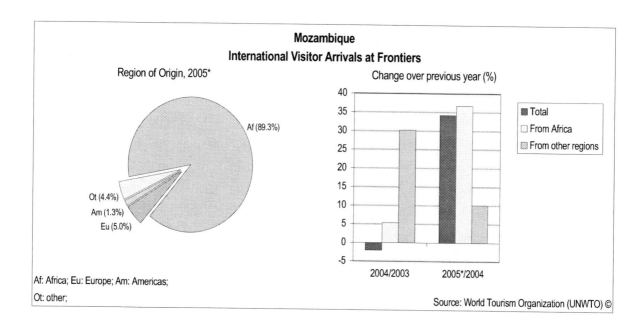

Mozambique
International Visitor Arrivals at Frontiers (by residence)

	1995	2000	2003	2004	2005*	Market share (%) 2000	Market share (%) 2005*	Growth rate (%) 04/03	Growth rate (%) 05*/04	Average per year (%) 2000-2005*
Total	..	..	**726,099**	**711,060**	**954,433**		100	-2.1	34.2	
From Africa	..	..	*591,647*	*623,240*	*851,999*		*89.3*	*5.3*	*36.7*	
South Africa	..	..	335,426	228,104	306,177		32.1	-32.0	34.2	
Malawi	..	..	121,267	74,933	100,580		10.5	-38.2	34.2	
Zimbabwe	..	..	114,936	65,896	88,450		9.3	-42.7	34.2	
Swaziland	..	..	20,018	17,773	23,856		2.5	-11.2	34.2	
Other Africa	..	..	..	236,534	332,936		34.9		40.8	
From other regions	..	..	*47,733*	*62,155*	*68,434*		*7.2*	*30.2*	*10.1*	
Portugal	..	..	25,392	11,898	15,970		1.7	-53.1	34.2	
United Kingdom	..	..	5,798	6,700	8,993		0.9	15.6	34.2	
All Asia	..	..	..	..	8,036		0.8			
United States	..	..	5,035	5,647	7,878		0.8	12.2	39.5	
Other Americas	..	..	..	..	4,521		0.5			
Other Europe	..	..	11,508	37,910	23,036		2.4	229.4	-39.2	
Other World/Not specified	..	..	*86,719*	*25,665*	*34,000*		*3.6*	*-70.4*	*32.5*	

Source: World Tourism Organization (UNWTO) ©

(Data as collected by UNWTO for TMT 2006 Edition)

III.4.11 Reunion   East Africa

Promotional: www.la-reunion-tourisme.com
Institutional/corporate: www.la-reunion-tourisme.com
Research and data: www.la-reunion-tourisme.com

Profile

Reunion

	Capital	Saint-Denis
	Area (100 km²)	25
	Population (2005, 1000)	777

Africa
East Africa

	2003	2004	2005*	2004/2003	2005*/2004
International Arrivals					
Tourists (overnight visitors) (1000)	432	430	409	-0.5	-4.9
- per 100 of inhabitants	57	56	53		
Tourism accommodation					
Number of rooms	2,910	2,904	2,930	-0.2	0.9
Nights spent in hotels and similar establishments (1000)					
by non-residents (inbound tourism)	..	1,154	1,112		-3.6
Outbound Tourism					
Trips abroad (1000)	333	385	395	15.6	2.6
- per 100 of inhabitants	44	50	51		
Receipts and Expenditure for International Tourism					
International Tourism Receipts (US$ million)	413	448	384	8.5	-14.3
- per Tourist Arrival (US$)	956	1,042	939	9.0	-9.9
- per capita (US$)	547	585	494		

Source: World Tourism Organization (UNWTO)   (Data as collected by UNWTO for TMT 2006 Edition)

See annex for methodological notes and reference of external sources used.

International Tourism by Origin

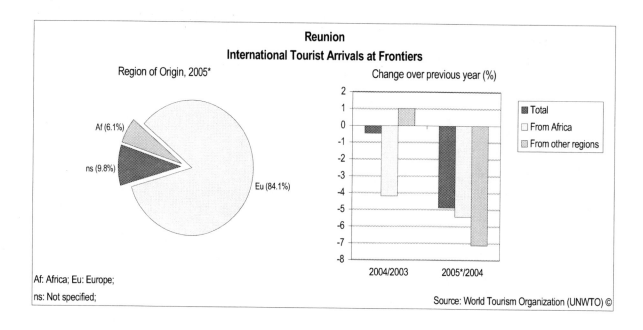

Reunion
International Tourist Arrivals at Frontiers

Region of Origin, 2005*

Af (6.1%)
ns (9.8%)
Eu (84.1%)

Change over previous year (%)

Total
From Africa
From other regions

2004/2003   2005*/2004

Af: Africa; Eu: Europe;
ns: Not specified;

Source: World Tourism Organization (UNWTO) ©

Reunion
International Tourist Arrivals at Frontiers (by residence)

	1995	2000	2003	2004	2005*	Market share (%)		Growth rate (%)		Average per year (%)
						2000	2005*	04/03	05*/04	2000-2005*
Total	**304,000**	**430,000**	**432,000**	**430,000**	**409,000**	**100**	**100**	**-0.5**	**-4.9**	**-1.0**
From Africa	*40,119*	*44,240*	*27,367*	*26,222*	*24,800*	*10.3*	*6.1*	*-4.2*	*-5.4*	*-10.9*
Mauritius	28,077	36,988	27,367	26,222	24,800	8.6	6.1	-4.2	-5.4	-7.7
Madagascar	7,711	7,252	..	..	..	1.7				
South Africa	1,214	..	..	..	..					
Seychelles	914	..	..	..	..					
Comoros	827	..	..	..	..					
Other Africa	1,376	..	..	..	..					
From other regions	*262,682*	*364,548*	*366,725*	*370,474*	*344,100*	*84.8*	*84.1*	*1.0*	*-7.1*	*-1.1*
France	249,200	345,230	347,219	343,171	330,000	80.3	80.7	-1.2	-3.8	-0.9
Germany	..	..	..	8,491	..					
Switzerland	1,374	..	..	4,717	..					
Italy	..	..	..	3,176	..					
United States	837	..	..	..	..					
India	608	..	..	..	..					
Australia	401	..	..	..	..					
Canada	382	..	..	..	..					
Japan	356	..	..	..	..					
China	243	..	..	..	..					
Singapore	96	..	..	..	..					
Other Asia	191	..	..	..	..					
Other Europe	8,994	19,318	19,506	10,919	14,100	4.5	3.4	-44.0	29.1	-6.1
Other World/Not specified	*1,199*	*21,212*	*37,908*	*33,304*	*40,100*	*4.9*	*9.8*	*-12.1*	*20.4*	*13.6*

Source: World Tourism Organization (UNWTO) ©   (Data as collected by UNWTO for TMT 2006 Edition)

World Tourism Organization ©

III.4.12 Rwanda   East Africa

Promotional: www.rwandatourism.com
Institutional/corporate: www.minicom.gov.rw
Research and data: www.rwandatourism.com

Profile

Rwanda

Africa
East Africa

Capital	Kigali
Year of entry in UNWTO	1975
Area (1000 km²)	26
Population (2005, million)	9.4
Gross Domestic Product (GDP) (2005, US$ million)	2,137
GDP per capita (2005, US$)	242

GDP growth (real, %)
'-> 2004: 4.0;   2005: 6.0;   2006*: 3.0;   2007*: 4.3

	2003	2004	2005*	2004/2003	2005*/2004
Receipts and Expenditure for International Tourism					
International Tourism Receipts (US$ million)	26	44	49	69.1	11.4
- per capita (US$)	3	5	5		
International Tourism Expenditure (US$ million)	27	31	37	13.8	19.4
- per capita (US$)	3	3	4		
Δ International Tourism Balance (US$ million)	-1	13	12		

Source: World Tourism Organization (UNWTO)   (Data as collected by UNWTO for TMT 2006 Edition)
See annex for methodological notes and reference of external sources used.

International Tourism by Origin

Rwanda
International Tourist Arrivals at Frontiers (by residence)

	1995	2000	2002	2003	2004	Market share (%) 2000	Market share (%) 2004	Growth rate (%) 03/02	Growth rate (%) 04/03	Average per year (%) 2000-2004
Total	..	104,216	..	..	..	100				
From Africa	..	*93,058*	..	..	..	*89.3*				
Uganda	..	38,897	..	..	..	37.3				
Dem.R.Congo	..	10,450	..	..	..	10.0				
Tanzania	..	18,320	..	..	..	17.6				
Burundi	..	20,972	..	..	..	20.1				
Kenya	..	2,050	..	..	..	2.0				
South Africa	..	431	..	..	..	0.4				
Cameroon	..	223	..	..	..	0.2				
Ethiopia	..	224	..	..	..	0.2				
Mali	..	122	..	..	..	0.1				
Senegal	..	164	..	..	..	0.2				
Nigeria	..	71	..	..	..	0.1				
Ghana	..	89	..	..	..	0.1				
Côte d'Ivoire	..	87	..	..	..	0.1				
Burkina Faso	..	245	..	..	..	0.2				
Other intraregional	..	713	..	..	..	0.7				
From other regions	..	*11,158*	..	..	..	*10.7*				
Belgium	..	1,866	..	..	..	1.8				
United States	..	1,586	..	..	..	1.5				
United Kingdom	..	150	..	..	..	0.1				
France	..	848	..	..	..	0.8				
India	..	1,021	..	..	..	1.0				
Germany	..	853	..	..	..	0.8				
Canada	..	601	..	..	..	0.6				
Netherlands	..	218	..	..	..	0.2				
Italy	..	485	..	..	..	0.5				
Switzerland	..	286	..	..	..	0.3				
China	..	354	..	..	..	0.3				
Russian Federation	..	111	..	..	..	0.1				
Spain	..	168	..	..	..	0.2				
Australia	..	142	..	..	..	0.1				
Oman	..	307	..	..	..	0.3				
Sweden	..	169	..	..	..	0.2				
Norway	..	119	..	..	..	0.1				
Denmark	..	64	..	..	..	0.1				
Japan	..	105	..	..	..	0.1				
Poland	..	73	..	..	..	0.1				
Pakistan	..	138	..	..	..	0.1				
Israel	..	65	..	..	..	0.1				
Egypt	..	86	..	..	..	0.1				
New Zealand	..	66	..	..	..	0.1				
Korea, Republic of	..	39	..	..	..	0.0				
Other interregional	..	1,238	..	..	..	1.2				

Source: World Tourism Organization (UNWTO) ©

(Data as collected by UNWTO for TMT 2006 Edition)

III.4.13 Seychelles   East Africa

Promotional: www.seychelles.com ; www.aspureasitgets.com ; www.resa.seycheles.com
Institutional/corporate: www.tourism.gov.sc ; www.pps.gov.sc
Research and data: www.envi.gov.sc ; www.misd.gov.sc

Profile

Seychelles

Africa
East Africa

Capital	Victoria
Year of entry in UNWTO	1991
Area (10 km²)	45
Population (2005, 1000)	81
Gross Domestic Product (GDP) (2005, US$ million)	695
GDP per capita (2005, US$)	8,556
GDP growth (real, %)	
2004: -2.0; 2005: -2.2; 2006*: -1.4; 2007*: -1.6	

	2003	2004	2005*	2004/2003	2005*/2004
International Arrivals					
Visitors (1000)	127	126	135	-0.8	7.1
Tourists (overnight visitors) (1000)	122	121	129	-1.0	6.5
- per 100 of inhabitants	152	149	158		
Cruise passengers (1000)	5	5	6		20.0
Tourism accommodation					
Number of bed-places	4,930	5,030	4,920	2.0	-2.2
Nights spent in hotels and similar establishments (1000)	833	808		-3.0	
by non-residents (inbound tourism)	825	798	..	-3.3	
by residents (domestic tourism)	8	10	..	25.0	
Outbound Tourism					
Trips abroad (1000)	50	48	52	-4.0	8.3
- per 100 of inhabitants	62	59	64		
Receipts and Expenditure for International Tourism					
International Tourism Receipts (US$ million)	171	172	192	0.3	11.9
- per Tourist Arrival (US$)	1,402	1,422	1,493	1.4	5.0
- per Visitor Arrival (US$)	1,347	1,363	1,423	1.1	4.4
- per capita (US$)	2,127	2,124	2,366		
International Fare Receipts (US$ million)	87	84	77	-3.7	-8.6
International Tourism Expenditure (US$ million)	36	34	39	-7.6	15.3
- per trip (US$)	726	698	744	-3.8	6.5
- per capita (US$)	451	415	476		
International Fare Expenditure (US$ million)	18	21	20	12.7	-2.9
Δ International Tourism Balance (US$ million)	135	138	153		
Δ International Fare Balance (US$ million)	69	64	57		

Source: World Tourism Organization (UNWTO)   (Data as collected by UNWTO for TMT 2006 Edition)

See annex for methodological notes and reference of external sources used.

International Tourism by Origin

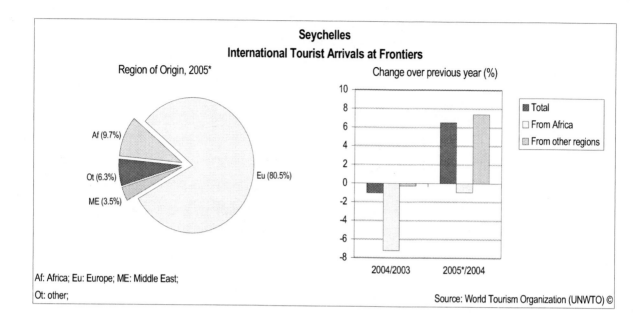

Seychelles
International Tourist Arrivals at Frontiers

Region of Origin, 2005*

Af (9.7%)
Ot (6.3%)
ME (3.5%)
Eu (80.5%)

Change over previous year (%)

- Total
- From Africa
- From other regions

2004/2003   2005*/2004

Af: Africa; Eu: Europe; ME: Middle East;
Ot: other;

Source: World Tourism Organization (UNWTO) ©

World Tourism Organization ©

Seychelles

International Tourist Arrivals at Frontiers (by residence)

	1995	2000	2003	2004	2005*	Market share (%) 2000	Market share (%) 2005*	Growth rate (%) 04/03	Growth rate (%) 05*/04	Average per year (%) 2000-2005*
Total	**120,716**	**130,046**	**122,038**	**120,765**	**128,654**	**100**	**100**	**-1.0**	**6.5**	**-0.2**
From Africa	*14,202*	*13,746*	*13,578*	*12,598*	*12,478*	*10.6*	*9.7*	*-7.2*	*-1.0*	*-1.9*
South Africa	6,531	4,260	5,003	5,130	5,395	3.3	4.2	2.5	5.2	4.8
Mauritius	2,027	3,068	2,351	2,345	2,626	2.4	2.0	-0.3	12.0	-3.1
Reunion	3,540	2,842	2,816	2,458	2,167	2.2	1.7	-12.7	-11.8	-5.3
Kenya	738	1,333	1,038	954	801	1.0	0.6	-8.1	-16.0	-9.7
Madagascar	256	342	329	174	226	0.3	0.2	-47.1	29.9	-8.0
Uganda	106	154	103	131	121	0.1	0.1	27.2	-7.6	-4.7
Nigeria	26	99	104	105	115	0.1	0.1	1.0	9.5	3.0
Tanzania	104	150	97	137	105	0.1	0.1	41.2	-23.4	-6.9
Zimbabwe	139	264	143	91	94	0.2	0.1	-36.4	3.3	-18.7
Ethiopia	118	77	104	90	67	0.1	0.1	-13.5	-25.6	-2.7
Sudan	19	18	44	74	66	0.0	0.1	68.2	-10.8	29.7
Zambia	20	109	102	73	55	0.1	0.0	-28.4	-24.7	-12.8
Botswana	49	82	67	57	46	0.1	0.0	-14.9	-19.3	-10.9
Mozambique	49	57	56	29	36	0.0	0.0	-48.2	24.1	-8.8
Algeria	16	17	7	22	23	0.0	0.0	214.3	4.5	6.2
Ghana	7	61	34	33	21	0.0	0.0	-2.9	-36.4	-19.2
Other Africa	344	696	1,066	580	437	0.5	0.3	-45.6	-24.7	-8.9
Other intraregional	113	117	114	115	77	0.1	0.1	0.9	-33.0	-8.0
From other regions	*106,514*	*116,300*	*108,460*	*108,167*	*116,176*	*89.4*	*90.3*	*-0.3*	*7.4*	*0.0*
France	24,903	28,282	25,990	26,049	27,592	21.7	21.4	0.2	5.9	-0.5
Italy	11,477	19,951	17,778	17,099	18,377	15.3	14.3	-3.8	7.5	-1.6
Germany	19,258	17,720	15,903	15,509	17,011	13.6	13.2	-2.5	9.7	-0.8
United Kingdom	17,330	16,117	18,765	17,629	16,497	12.4	12.8	-6.1	-6.4	0.5
Switzerland	5,104	5,001	4,737	4,503	4,473	3.8	3.5	-4.9	-0.7	-2.2
Commonwealth Indep. States	..	2,132	3,384	4,260	4,248	1.6	3.3	25.9	-0.3	14.8
United States	5,235	4,746	2,793	3,146	2,878	3.6	2.2	12.6	-8.5	-9.5
Untd Arab Emirates	450	679	888	924	2,767	0.5	2.2	4.1	199.5	32.4
Spain	4,370	1,989	2,062	2,449	2,686	1.5	2.1	18.8	9.7	6.2
Austria	1,311	1,929	1,889	2,221	2,438	1.5	1.9	17.6	9.8	4.8
Former U.S.S.R.	2,427	..	..	..	..					
Belgium	1,136	1,529	1,392	1,283	1,461	1.2	1.1	-7.8	13.9	-0.9
Netherlands	756	1,267	978	1,035	1,039	1.0	0.8	5.8	0.4	-3.9
India	758	941	893	1,012	981	0.7	0.8	13.3	-3.1	0.8
Denmark	522	1,454	882	752	837	1.1	0.7	-14.7	11.3	-10.5
Australia	803	430	432	611	777	0.3	0.6	41.4	27.2	12.6
Sweden	1,136	1,671	1,031	996	677	1.3	0.5	-3.4	-32.0	-16.5
Greece	117	137	144	174	654	0.1	0.5	20.8	275.9	36.7
Canada	514	334	331	428	597	0.3	0.5	29.3	39.5	12.3
Saudi Arabia	299	344	247	341	585	0.3	0.5	38.1	71.6	11.2
Norway	530	683	717	717	533	0.5	0.4	0.0	-25.7	-4.8
China	431	472	407	400	505	0.4	0.4	-1.7	26.3	1.4
Portugal	843	1,047	522	575	405	0.8	0.3	10.2	-29.6	-17.3
Qatar	22	31	24	105	403	0.0	0.3	337.5	283.8	67.0
Japan	1,423	414	306	300	368	0.3	0.3	-2.0	22.7	-2.3
Other interregional	5,359	7,000	5,965	5,649	7,387	5.4	5.7	-5.3	30.8	1.1

Source: World Tourism Organization (UNWTO) ©   (Data as collected by UNWTO for TMT 2006 Edition)

III.4.14 Somalia   East Africa

Profile

Somalia

Capital	Mogadiscio
Area (1000 km²)	638
Population (2005, million)	8.6

Africa
East Africa

Source: World Tourism Organization (UNWTO)   (Data as collected by UNWTO for TMT 2006 Edition)

See annex for methodological notes and reference of external sources used.

III.4.15 Tanzania   East Africa

Promotional: www.tanzania-web.com/home2.htm

Profile

Tanzania

Capital	Dodoma
Year of entry in UNWTO	1975
Area (1000 km²)	945
Population (2005, million)	36.8
Gross Domestic Product (GDP) (2005, US$ million)	12,607
GDP per capita (2005, US$)	336

Africa
East Africa

GDP growth (real, %)
'-> 2004: 6.7;   2005: 6.8;   2006*: 5.9;   2007*: 7.3

	2003	2004	2005*	2004/2003	2005*/2004
International Arrivals					
Visitors (1000)	576	583	613	1.1	5.1
Tourists (overnight visitors) (1000)	552	566	590	2.5	4.2
- per 100 of inhabitants	2	2	2		
Same-day visitors (1000)	24	17	23	-29.2	35.3
Tourism accommodation					
Number of rooms	30,600	30,840	31,365	0.8	1.7
Nights spent in collective establishments (1000)	9,600	9,625	10,630	0.3	10.4
by non-residents (inbound tourism)	5,500	5,525	6,130	0.5	11.0
by residents (domestic tourism)	4,100	4,100	4,500		9.8
Receipts and Expenditure for International Tourism					
International Tourism Receipts (US$ million)	647	746	796	15.4	6.7
- per Tourist Arrival (US$)	1,171	1,318	1,350	12.5	2.4
- per Visitor Arrival (US$)	1,122	1,280	1,300	14.1	1.5
- per capita (US$)	18	21	22		
International Fare Receipts (US$ million)	7	16	12	128.6	-25.0
International Tourism Expenditure (US$ million)	353	445	554	26.1	24.4
- per capita (US$)	10	12	15		
International Fare Expenditure (US$ million)	22	25	23	13.6	-8.0
Δ International Tourism Balance (US$ million)	293	301	243		
Δ International Fare Balance (US$ million)	-15	-9	-11		

Source: World Tourism Organization (UNWTO)   (Data as collected by UNWTO for TMT 2006 Edition)

See annex for methodological notes and reference of external sources used.

International Tourism by Origin

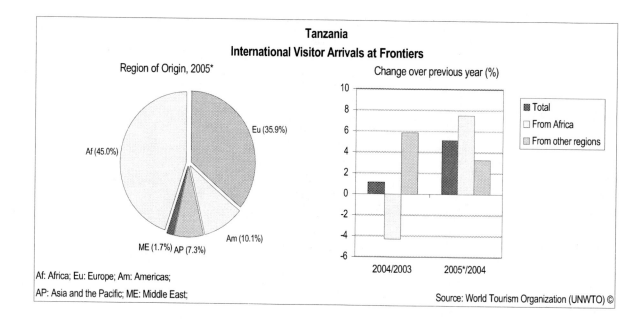

Tanzania
International Visitor Arrivals at Frontiers

Region of Origin, 2005*

Af (45.0%)
Eu (35.9%)
Am (10.1%)
AP (7.3%)
ME (1.7%)

Change over previous year (%)

- Total
- From Africa
- From other regions

2004/2003   2005*/2004

Af: Africa; Eu: Europe; Am: Americas;

AP: Asia and the Pacific; ME: Middle East;

Source: World Tourism Organization (UNWTO) ©

Tanzania
International Visitor Arrivals at Frontiers (by residence)

	1995	2000	2003	2004	2005*	Market share (%) 2000	Market share (%) 2005*	Growth rate (%) 04/03	Growth rate (%) 05*/04	Average per year (%) 2000-2005*
Total	295,311	501,669	576,198	582,807	612,754	100	100	1.1	5.1	4.1
From Africa	123,581	201,934	267,940	256,455	275,718	40.3	45.0	-4.3	7.5	6.4
Kenya	50,032	84,993	119,406	124,967	112,766	16.9	18.4	4.7	-9.8	5.8
Zambia	3,737	6,349	10,670	25,405	29,120	1.3	4.8	138.1	14.6	35.6
South Africa	8,817	14,977	35,071	25,849	28,922	3.0	4.7	-26.3	11.9	14.1
Uganda	12,382	21,035	34,664	24,253	25,373	4.2	4.1	-30.0	4.6	3.8
Malawi	6,788	11,531	14,267	16,868	19,999	2.3	3.3	18.2	18.6	11.6
Rwanda	5,740	9,752	12,061	6,089	17,037	1.9	2.8	-49.5	179.8	11.8
Dem.R.Congo	9	16	6,850	8,030	9,479	0.0	1.5	17.2	18.0	258.5
Zimbabwe	1,976	3,356	3,795	5,319	8,884	0.7	1.4	40.2	67.0	21.5
Burundi	13,332	14,651	11,907	3,157	5,767	2.9	0.9	-73.5	82.7	-17.0
Comoros	526	894	1,346	5,740	4,467	0.2	0.7	326.4	-22.2	38.0
Mozambique	3,660	6,215	3,340	1,562	1,530	1.2	0.2	-53.2	-2.0	-24.4
Botswana	1,025	1,741	632	773	1,299	0.3	0.2	22.3	68.0	-5.7
Ethiopia	1,457	2,474	1,465	877	1,234	0.5	0.2	-40.1	40.7	-13.0
Ghana	1,374	2,335	1,303	603	832	0.5	0.1	-53.7	38.0	-18.6
Cameroon	1,091	1,856	806	315	810	0.4	0.1	-60.9	157.1	-15.3
Nigeria	491	835	1,214	763	803	0.2	0.1	-37.1	5.2	-0.8
Namibia	395	670	598	615	780	0.1	0.1	2.8	26.8	3.1
Other intraregional	10,749	18,254	8,545	5,270	6,616	3.6	1.1	-38.3	25.5	-18.4
From other regions	171,730	299,735	308,258	326,352	337,036	59.7	55.0	5.9	3.3	2.4
United Kingdom	20,315	34,511	43,656	59,547	52,442	6.9	8.6	36.4	-11.9	8.7
Italy	3,395	5,768	24,675	44,045	49,829	1.1	8.1	78.5	13.1	53.9
United States	19,461	33,060	36,419	40,248	47,621	6.6	7.8	10.5	18.3	7.6
France	10,116	17,186	22,103	21,849	23,547	3.4	3.8	-1.1	7.8	6.5
Germany	13,307	22,606	19,222	20,209	18,170	4.5	3.0	5.1	-10.1	-4.3
India	11,093	18,844	22,215	14,804	17,598	3.8	2.9	-33.4	18.9	-1.4
Netherlands	265	8,451	15,272	14,594	15,805	1.7	2.6	-4.4	8.3	13.3
Spain	4,733	8,040	9,565	11,168	11,709	1.6	1.9	16.8	4.8	7.8
Canada	5,508	9,357	10,354	10,613	10,922	1.9	1.8	2.5	2.9	3.1
Australia	4,928	8,372	9,698	8,161	8,270	1.7	1.3	-15.8	1.3	-0.2
Sweden	9,447	16,049	8,427	7,212	7,964	3.2	1.3	-14.4	10.4	-13.1
Belgium	5,070	8,613	6,497	8,378	5,466	1.7	0.9	29.0	-34.8	-8.7
Norway	4,831	8,205	5,590	4,674	5,172	1.6	0.8	-16.4	10.7	-8.8
Switzerland	5,011	8,513	6,983	6,360	5,141	1.7	0.8	-8.9	-19.2	-9.6
Denmark	4	506	5,210	4,813	4,848	0.1	0.8	-7.6	0.7	57.1
Japan	3,544	6,020	5,936	4,504	4,534	1.2	0.7	-24.1	0.7	-5.5
Oman	5,131	8,717	5,225	7,601	4,488	1.7	0.7	45.5	-41.0	-12.4
China	3,334	5,664	4,007	3,602	4,289	1.1	0.7	-10.1	19.1	-5.4
Ireland	3,725	6,328	4,145	3,484	3,295	1.3	0.5	-15.9	-5.4	-12.2
Bahrain	..	..	118	60	2,951		0.5	-49.2	4818.3	
Finland	2,665	4,527	4,163	2,104	2,649	0.9	0.4	-49.5	25.9	-10.2
Austria	1,423	2,418	2,908	4,025	2,405	0.5	0.4	38.4	-40.2	-0.1
Korea, Republic of	1,856	3,152	2,690	2,210	2,304	0.6	0.4	-17.8	4.3	-6.1
New Zealand	4,765	8,095	2,291	2,001	2,190	1.6	0.4	-12.7	9.4	-23.0
Israel	470	799	1,188	1,512	1,835	0.2	0.3	27.3	21.4	18.1
Other interregional	27,333	45,934	29,701	18,574	21,592	9.2	3.5	-37.5	16.2	-14.0

Source: World Tourism Organization (UNWTO) ©

(Data as collected by UNWTO for TMT 2006 Edition)

III.4.16 Uganda   East Africa

Promotional: www.visituganda.com ; www.ugandawildlifecentre.org ; www.ucota.com ;
                          www.traveluganda.com ; www.giftedbynature.org
Institutional/corporate: www.mttitourism.co.ug ; www.visituganda.com ; www.mtti.go.ug
Research and data: www.mttitourism.co.ug ; www.ubos.org ; www.bou.or.ug ; www.mtti.go.ug

Profile

Uganda

		Kampala
Capital		Kampala
Year of entry in UNWTO		1975
Area (1000 km²)		241
Population (2005, million)		28.2
Gross Domestic Product (GDP) (2005, US$ million)		8,729
GDP per capita (2005, US$)		303

Africa
East Africa

GDP growth (real, %)
'-> 2004: 5.7;   2005: 6.0;   2006*: 5.5;   2007*: 6.0

	2003	2004	2005*	2004/2003	2005*/2004
International Arrivals					
Tourists (overnight visitors) (1000)	305	512	468	68.2	-8.7
- per 100 of inhabitants	1	2	2		
Outbound Tourism					
Trips abroad (1000)	189	231	189	22.2	-18.2
- per 100 of inhabitants	1	1	1		
Receipts and Expenditure for International Tourism					
International Tourism Receipts (US$ million)	184	256	355	39.1	38.7
- per Tourist Arrival (US$)	604	500	759	-17.3	51.9
- per capita (US$)	7	9	13		
International Fare Receipts (US$ million)	1	1	2		100.0
International Tourism Expenditure (US$ million)	..	133	133		
- per trip (US$)	..	576	704		22.2
- per capita (US$)	..	5	5		
International Fare Expenditure (US$ million)	..	3	4		33.3
Δ International Tourism Balance (US$ million)	..	123	222		
Δ International Fare Balance (US$ million)	..	-2	-2		

Source: World Tourism Organization (UNWTO)   (Data as collected by UNWTO for TMT 2006 Edition)

See annex for methodological notes and reference of external sources used.

International Tourism by Origin

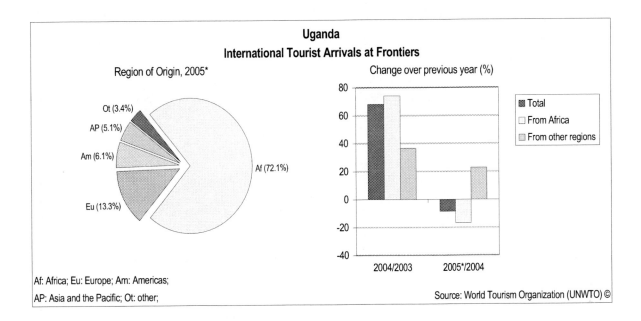

Uganda
International Tourist Arrivals at Frontiers

Region of Origin, 2005*

Change over previous year (%)

Total
From Africa
From other regions

2004/2003   2005*/2004

Ot (3.4%)
AP (5.1%)
Am (6.1%)
Af (72.1%)
Eu (13.3%)

Af: Africa; Eu: Europe; Am: Americas;
AP: Asia and the Pacific; Ot: other;

Source: World Tourism Organization (UNWTO) ©

Uganda
International Tourist Arrivals at Frontiers (by residence)

	1995	2000	2003	2004	2005*	Market share (%) 2000	Market share (%) 2005*	Growth rate (%) 04/03	Growth rate (%) 05*/04	Average per year (%) 2000-2005*
Total	**159,899**	**192,755**	**304,656**	**512,379**	**467,728**	**100**	**100**	**68.2**	**-8.7**	**19.4**
From Africa	*102,129*	*131,687*	*233,043*	*405,706*	*337,188*	*68.3*	*72.1*	*74.1*	*-16.9*	*20.7*
Kenya	57,612	60,900	113,681	220,062	138,346	31.6	29.6	93.6	-37.1	17.8
Rwanda	8,705	36,041	50,107	65,298	80,522	18.7	17.2	30.3	23.3	17.4
Tanzania	12,590	14,375	30,407	67,885	50,723	7.5	10.8	123.3	-25.3	28.7
South Africa	..	..	..	..	10,423		2.2			
Dem.R.Congo	9,487	7,957	5,890	3,998	6,277	4.1	1.3	-32.1	57.0	-4.6
Ethiopia	1,378	1,300	1,811	2,482	2,954	0.7	0.6	37.1	19.0	17.8
Sudan	851	760	5,606	5,535	2,819	0.4	0.6	-1.3	-49.1	30.0
Other Africa	11,506	10,354	25,541	40,446	45,124	5.4	9.6	58.4	11.6	34.2
From other regions	*56,819*	*60,466*	*70,084*	*95,707*	*117,525*	*31.4*	*25.1*	*36.6*	*22.8*	*14.2*
United Kingdom	14,124	13,954	17,176	22,402	28,227	7.2	6.0	30.4	26.0	15.1
United States	7,598	9,593	13,176	18,898	21,968	5.0	4.7	43.4	16.2	18.0
India	5,209	4,810	6,623	9,366	10,691	2.5	2.3	41.4	14.1	17.3
Canada	2,801	2,053	2,507	3,669	5,195	1.1	1.1	46.4	41.6	20.4
Germany	3,269	2,497	3,519	4,241	4,972	1.3	1.1	20.5	17.2	14.8
Netherlands	1,808	2,203	2,474	3,313	4,751	1.1	1.0	33.9	43.4	16.6
Italy	1,536	1,560	1,924	2,406	3,301	0.8	0.7	25.1	37.2	16.2
Australia	1,737	1,550	1,349	2,132	3,190	0.8	0.7	58.0	49.6	15.5
Pakistan	1,265	728	1,024	2,773	3,188	0.4	0.7	170.8	15.0	34.4
All Middle East	..	..	..	..	2,731		0.6			
Belgium	1,569	1,446	1,748	1,914	2,675	0.8	0.6	9.5	39.8	13.1
Denmark	1,627	1,654	1,642	1,891	2,509	0.9	0.5	15.2	32.7	8.7
Sweden	1,473	1,496	1,844	2,471	2,458	0.8	0.5	34.0	-0.5	10.4
France	1,737	1,320	3,022	2,079	2,351	0.7	0.5	-31.2	13.1	12.2
Norway	665	6,717	1,528	1,749	2,262	3.5	0.5	14.5	29.3	-19.6
China	1,149	945	1,181	1,798	2,177	0.5	0.5	52.2	21.1	18.2
Switzerland	1,098	891	1,134	1,568	1,966	0.5	0.4	38.3	25.4	17.1
Japan	682	773	661	897	1,514	0.4	0.3	35.7	68.8	14.4
Ireland	747	707	863	1,139	1,422	0.4	0.3	32.0	24.8	15.0
Egypt	455	553	583	1,038	..	0.3		78.0		
Russian Federation	134	139	286	486	623	0.1	0.1	69.9	28.2	35.0
Finland	154	178	224	354	411	0.1	0.1	58.0	16.1	18.2
Austria	754	249	349	500	396	0.1	0.1	43.3	-20.8	9.7
New Zealand	735	519	206	273	312	0.3	0.1	32.5	14.3	-9.7
Former Czechoslovakia	47	28	63	135	236	0.0	0.1	114.3	74.8	53.2
Other interregional	4,446	3,903	4,978	8,215	7,999	2.0	1.7	65.0	-2.6	15.4
Other World/Not specified	*951*	*602*	*1,529*	*10,966*	*13,015*	*0.3*	*2.8*	*617.2*	*18.7*	*84.9*

Source: World Tourism Organization (UNWTO) ©   (Data as collected by UNWTO for TMT 2006 Edition)

III.4.17 Zambia   East Africa

Promotional: www.zambiatourism.com
Institutional/corporate: www.zambiatourism.com ; www.zambiatourism.com/zntb

Profile

Zambia

Capital	Lusaka
Year of entry in UNWTO	1975
Area (1000 km²)	753
Population (2005, million)	11.1
Gross Domestic Product (GDP) (2005, US$ million)	7,269
GDP per capita (2005, US$)	627

Africa

East Africa

GDP growth (real, %)

'-> 2004: 5.4; 2005: 5.1; 2006*: 6.0; 2007*: 6.0

	2003	2004	2005*	2004/2003	2005*/2004
International Arrivals					
Tourists (overnight visitors) (1000)	413	515	669	24.8	29.9
- per 100 of inhabitants	4	5	6		
Tourism accommodation					
Number of rooms	5,202	5,360	5,521	3.0	3.0
Nights spent in hotels and similar establishments (1000)					
by residents (domestic tourism)	241	267	289	10.8	8.2
Receipts and Expenditure for International Tourism					
International Tourism Receipts (US$ million)	149	161	164	8.1	1.9
- per Tourist Arrival (US$)	361	313	245	-13.4	-21.6
- per capita (US$)	14	15	15		
International Tourism Expenditure (US$ million)	77	89	94	15.6	5.6
- per capita (US$)	7	8	8		
Δ International Tourism Balance (US$ million)	72	72	70		

Source: World Tourism Organization (UNWTO)   (Data as collected by UNWTO for TMT 2006 Edition)

See annex for methodological notes and reference of external sources used.

International Tourism by Origin

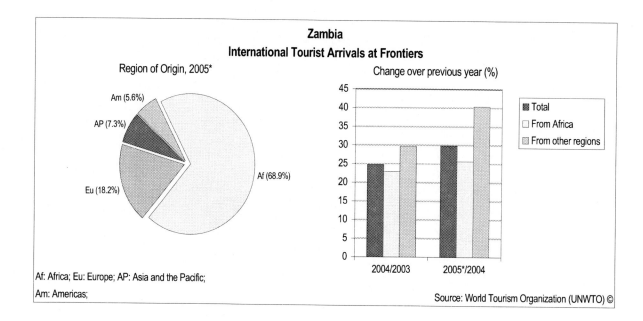

Zambia
International Tourist Arrivals at Frontiers

Region of Origin, 2005*

Am (5.6%)
AP (7.3%)
Eu (18.2%)
Af (68.9%)

Change over previous year (%)

- Total
- From Africa
- From other regions

2004/2003   2005*/2004

Af: Africa; Eu: Europe; AP: Asia and the Pacific;
Am: Americas;

Source: World Tourism Organization (UNWTO) ©

Zambia
International Tourist Arrivals at Frontiers (by residence)

	1995	2000	2003	2004	2005*	Market share (%) 2000	Market share (%) 2005*	Growth rate (%) 04/03	Growth rate (%) 05*/04	Average per year (%) 2000-2005*
Total	**159,217**	**457,419**	**412,675**	**515,000**	**668,862**	**100**	**100**	**24.8**	**29.9**	**7.9**
From Africa	*120,092*	*294,479*	*298,485*	*366,918*	*461,000*	*64.4*	*68.9*	*22.9*	*25.6*	*9.4*
Zimbabwe	48,350	116,461	138,288	123,573	148,436	25.5	22.2	-10.6	20.1	5.0
South Africa	7,110	70,899	62,604	110,710	110,272	15.5	16.5	76.8	-0.4	9.2
Tanzania	10,041	27,308	30,776	33,502	65,881	6.0	9.8	8.9	96.6	19.3
All Central Africa	..	43,056	24,736	23,087	47,780	9.4	7.1	-6.7	107.0	2.1
Kenya	1,405	2,113	9,064	7,087	11,738	0.5	1.8	-21.8	65.6	40.9
Dem.R.Congo	10,715	..	..	..	..					
Malawi	8,140	..	..	..	..					
All West Africa	..	1,131	3,905	3,757	5,807	0.2	0.9	-3.8	54.6	38.7
All North Africa	..	529	2,806	2,533	2,752	0.1	0.4	-9.7	8.6	39.1
Botswana	1,654	..	..	..	..					
Angola	821	..	..	..	..					
Uganda	600	..	..	..	..					
Nigeria	570	..	..	..	..					
Mozambique	560	..	..	..	..					
Ghana	360	..	..	..	..					
Other East Africa	..	2,770	6,027	14,218	17,449	0.6	2.6	135.9	22.7	44.5
Other Southern Africa	..	30,212	20,279	48,451	50,885	6.6	7.6	138.9	5.0	11.0
Other Africa	29,528	..	..	..	..					
Other intraregional	238	..	..	..	..					
From other regions	*39,125*	*162,940*	*114,190*	*148,082*	*207,862*	*35.6*	*31.1*	*29.7*	*40.4*	*5.0*
United Kingdom	12,000	51,459	31,072	37,520	44,369	11.2	6.6	20.8	18.3	-2.9
United States	238	17,512	15,879	20,547	23,895	3.8	3.6	29.4	16.3	6.4
Germany	2,013	4,457	6,679	9,385	17,760	1.0	2.7	40.5	89.2	31.8
Australia	1,381	15,791	5,957	7,490	16,336	3.5	2.4	25.7	118.1	0.7
Canada	1,027	7,524	4,687	6,181	11,230	1.6	1.7	31.9	81.7	8.3
India	2,864	2,353	2,863	4,059	8,658	0.5	1.3	41.8	113.3	29.8
Scandinavia	..	7,810	4,691	4,915	8,110	1.7	1.2	4.8	65.0	0.8
France	620	3,208	8,380	9,123	8,024	0.7	1.2	8.9	-12.0	20.1
Italy	1,186	2,396	6,659	5,460	7,698	0.5	1.2	-18.0	41.0	26.3
New Zealand	439	3,957	3,660	4,397	7,635	0.9	1.1	20.1	73.6	14.0
Sweden	477	3,667	2,941	4,395	5,738	0.8	0.9	49.4	30.6	9.4
Japan	780	2,266	1,703	1,683	5,204	0.5	0.8	-1.2	209.2	18.1
Denmark	830	4,077	3,256	4,256	4,142	0.9	0.6	30.7	-2.7	0.3
Netherlands	1,240	..	..	..	..					
Belgium	747	..	..	..	..					
Ireland	730	..	..	..	..					
Pakistan	480	..	..	..	..					
Sri Lanka	407	..	..	..	..					
Austria	360	..	..	..	..					
Norway	360	..	..	..	..					
China	334	..	..	..	..					
Switzerland	260	..	..	..	..					
Greece	245	..	..	..	..					
Portugal	208	..	..	..	..					
Other interregional	9,899	36,463	15,763	28,671	39,063	8.0	5.8	81.9	36.2	1.4

Source: World Tourism Organization (UNWTO) ©   (Data as collected by UNWTO for TMT 2006 Edition)

III.4.18 Zimbabwe   East Africa

Promotional: www.zimbabwetourism.co.zw
Institutional/corporate: www.zimbabwetourism.co.zw
Research and data: www.zimbabwetourism.co.zw

Profile

Zimbabwe

Capital	Harare
Year of entry in UNWTO	1981
Area (1000 km²)	391
Population (2005, million)	12.2
Gross Domestic Product (GDP) (2005, US$ million)	4,491
GDP per capita (2005, US$)	383

Africa
East Africa

GDP growth (real, %)
2004: -3.8;   2005: -6.5;   2006*: -5.1;   2007*: -4.7

	2003	2004	2005*	2004/2003	2005*/2004
International Arrivals					
Visitors (1000)	2,256	1,854	1,559	-17.8	-15.9
- per 100 of inhabitants	19	15	13		
Tourism accommodation					
Number of rooms	5,766	5,766	5,657		-1.9
Receipts and Expenditure for International Tourism					
International Tourism Receipts (US$ million)	61	194	99	217.5	-48.9
- per Visitor Arrival (US$)	27	104	64	286.4	-39.2
- per capita (US$)	5	16	8		

Source: World Tourism Organization (UNWTO)   (Data as collected by UNWTO for TMT 2006 Edition)

See annex for methodological notes and reference of external sources used.

World Tourism Organization ©

International Tourism by Origin

Zimbabwe
International Tourist Arrivals at Frontiers (by residence)

	1995	2000	2002	2003	2004	Market share (%)		Growth rate (%)		Average per year (%)
						2000	2004	03/02	04/03	2000-2004
Total	**1,363,412**	**1,868,412**	..	..	..	100				
From Africa	*1,137,072*	*1,403,774*	..	..	..	75.1				
Zambia	518,795	365,695	..	..	..	19.6				
All Southern Africa	475,653	812,370	..	..	..	43.5				
Mozambique	98,331	111,970	..	..	..	6.0				
Other East Africa	10,198	30,440	..	..	..	1.6				
Other Africa	34,095	83,299	..	..	..	4.5				
From other regions	*226,340*	*464,638*	..	..	..	24.9				
United Kingdom/Ireland	66,346	135,643	..	..	..	7.3				
Canada, USA	36,081	78,592	..	..	..	4.2				
Australia, New Zealand	22,609	56,053	..	..	..	3.0				
Germany	31,165	32,971	..	..	..	1.8				
All Asia	11,693	23,477	..	..	..	1.3				
Netherlands	16,025	23,311	..	..	..	1.2				
Switzerland	14,511	11,798	..	..	..	0.6				
Other Americas	4,228	37,536	..	..	..	2.0				
Other Europe	23,682	65,257	..	..	..	3.5				

Source: World Tourism Organization (UNWTO) ©   (Data as collected by UNWTO for TMT 2006 Edition)

World Tourism Organization ©

III.5 Southern Africa

III.5.1 Botswana

Southern Africa

Promotional: www.botswanatourism.org
Institutional/corporate: www.botswanatourism.org
Research and data: www.botswanatourism.org

Profile

Botswana

Capital	Gaborone
Year of entry in UNWTO	1995
Area (1000 km²)	582
Population (2005, million)	1.6
Gross Domestic Product (GDP) (2005, US$ million)	10,196
GDP per capita (2005, US$)	6,439

Africa
Southern Africa

GDP growth (real, %)
'-> 2004: 6.0; 2005: 6.2; 2006*: 4.2; 2007*: 4.3

	2003	2004	2005*	2004/2003	2005*/2004
International Arrivals					
Visitors (1000)	1,592	1,727	1,885	8.5	9.1
Tourists (overnight visitors) (1000)	1,406	1,523	1,675	8.3	10.0
- per 100 of inhabitants	86	93	102		
Same-day visitors (1000)	187	204	210	9.1	2.9
Tourism accommodation					
Number of rooms	3,589	4,050	..	12.8	
Receipts and Expenditure for International Tourism					
International Tourism Receipts (US$ million)	457	549	562	20.2	2.3
- per Tourist Arrival (US$)	325	361	335	11.0	-7.0
- per Visitor Arrival (US$)	287	318	298	10.8	-6.3
- per capita (US$)	279	335	343		
International Fare Receipts (US$ million)	2	1	1	-50.0	
International Tourism Expenditure (US$ million)	230	276	282	20.2	2.3
- per capita (US$)	140	168	172		
International Fare Expenditure (US$ million)	5	4	19	-20.0	375.0
Δ International Tourism Balance (US$ million)	227	273	279		
Δ International Fare Balance (US$ million)	-3	-3	-18		

Source: World Tourism Organization (UNWTO)   (Data as collected by UNWTO for TMT 2006 Edition)

See annex for methodological notes and reference of external sources used.

International Tourism by Origin

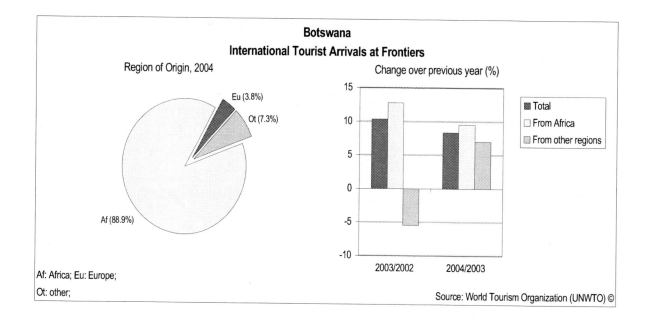

Botswana
International Tourist Arrivals at Frontiers

Region of Origin, 2004

Eu (3.8%)
Ot (7.3%)
Af (88.9%)

Change over previous year (%)

Total
From Africa
From other regions

2003/2002   2004/2003

Af: Africa; Eu: Europe;
Ot: other;

Source: World Tourism Organization (UNWTO) ©

World Tourism Organization ©

Botswana

International Tourist Arrivals at Frontiers (by residence)

	1995	2000	2002	2003	2004	Market share (%) 2000	Market share (%) 2004	Growth rate (%) 03/02	Growth rate (%) 04/03	Average per year (%) 2000-2004
Total	**521,041**	**1,103,795**	**1,273,784**	**1,405,535**	**1,522,807**	**100**	**100**	**10.3**	**8.3**	**8.4**
From Africa	*462,591*	*913,641*	*1,095,572*	*1,235,404*	*1,353,125*	*82.8*	*88.9*	*12.8*	*9.5*	*10.3*
South Africa	242,600	507,610	527,505	514,708	626,207	46.0	41.1	-2.4	21.7	5.4
Zimbabwe	171,671	311,451	454,847	550,994	576,328	28.2	37.8	21.1	4.6	16.6
Zambia	20,772	40,343	25,637	83,588	72,492	3.7	4.8	226.0	-13.3	15.8
Namibia	14,666	40,429	64,001	69,587	57,542	3.7	3.8	8.7	-17.3	9.2
Lesotho	2,379	3,036	5,053	3,193	5,474	0.3	0.4	-36.8	71.4	15.9
Swaziland	2,651	2,273	5,045	2,514	4,911	0.2	0.3	-50.2	95.3	21.2
Malawi	4,850	2,975	3,942	3,142	3,109	0.3	0.2	-20.3	-1.1	1.1
Kenya	844	1,775	2,832	2,107	1,910	0.2	0.1	-25.6	-9.3	1.8
Tanzania	520	942	1,380	1,508	1,587	0.1	0.1	9.3	5.2	13.9
Uganda	182	320	740	673	650	0.0	0.0	-9.1	-3.4	19.4
Mozambique	461	479	790	713	615	0.0	0.0	-9.7	-13.7	6.4
Mauritius	80	497	930	480	481	0.0	0.0	-48.4	0.2	-0.8
Ghana	130	210	480	300	410	0.0	0.0	-37.5	36.7	18.2
Angola	110	206	810	420	350	0.0	0.0	-48.1	-16.7	14.2
Ethiopia	110	210	240	210	245	0.0	0.0	-12.5	16.7	3.9
Other intraregional	565	885	1,340	1,267	814	0.1	0.1	-5.4	-35.8	-2.1
From other regions	*42,966*	*110,312*	*92,465*	*87,410*	*93,526*	*10.0*	*6.1*	*-5.5*	*7.0*	*-4.0*
United Kingdom	10,213	22,868	20,548	18,518	24,069	2.1	1.6	-9.9	30.0	1.3
United States	5,493	23,967	16,322	15,087	17,670	2.2	1.2	-7.6	17.1	-7.3
Germany	7,237	13,317	9,985	10,444	9,685	1.2	0.6	4.6	-7.3	-7.7
Australia	4,003	8,217	5,728	5,708	5,595	0.7	0.4	-0.3	-2.0	-9.2
Netherlands	2,010	7,038	6,377	6,146	4,929	0.6	0.3	-3.6	-19.8	-8.5
France	2,081	4,562	3,596	3,732	3,989	0.4	0.3	3.8	6.9	-3.3
Italy	1,220	2,350	2,323	2,782	3,196	0.2	0.2	19.8	14.9	8.0
Canada	1,021	2,432	1,932	2,065	2,811	0.2	0.2	6.9	36.1	3.7
Japan	847	2,959	2,281	2,492	2,518	0.3	0.2	9.3	1.0	-4.0
Spain	474	1,665	2,546	3,210	1,956	0.2	0.1	26.1	-39.1	4.1
Switzerland	1,130	2,628	2,070	1,856	1,846	0.2	0.1	-10.3	-0.5	-8.5
Belgium/Luxembourg	909	3,133	2,073	2,102	1,786	0.3	0.1	1.4	-15.0	-13.1
India	350	1,754	3,421	1,476	1,691	0.2	0.1	-56.9	14.6	-0.9
New Zealand	1,105	1,971	1,330	1,835	1,381	0.2	0.1	38.0	-24.7	-8.5
China	411	586	1,203	934	1,062	0.1	0.1	-22.4	13.7	16.0
Sweden	563	1,163	727	645	1,044	0.1	0.1	-11.3	61.9	-2.7
Ireland	468	1,563	1,136	940	945	0.1	0.1	-17.3	0.5	-11.8
Austria	603	1,256	463	1,000	930	0.1	0.1	116.0	-7.0	-7.2
Denmark	341	1,013	642	832	905	0.1	0.1	29.6	8.8	-2.8
Norway	..	..	1,195	704	671		0.0	-41.1	-4.7	
Czech Rep	100	512	361	284	568	0.0	0.0	-21.3	100.0	2.6
Portugal	132	540	430	255	440	0.0	0.0	-40.7	72.5	-5.0
Russian Federation	143	180	160	..	385	0.0	0.0			20.9
Pakistan	50	360	300	190	320	0.0	0.0	-36.7	68.4	-2.9
Finland	24	326	252	197	263	0.0	0.0	-21.8	33.5	-5.2
Other interregional	2,038	3,952	5,064	3,976	2,871	0.4	0.2	-21.5	-27.8	-7.7
Nationals residing abroad	*..*	*6,651*	*..*	*..*	*..*	*0.6*				
Other World/Not specified	*15,484*	*73,191*	*85,747*	*82,721*	*76,156*	*6.6*	*5.0*	*-3.5*	*-7.9*	*1.0*

Source: World Tourism Organization (UNWTO) ©　　　　　　　　(Data as collected by UNWTO for TMT 2006 Edition)

III.5.2   Lesotho   Southern Africa

Promotional: www.ltdc.org.ls
Research and data: www.ltdc.org.ls

Profile

Lesotho

Africa
Southern Africa

Capital	Maseru
Year of entry in UNWTO	1981
Area (1000 km²)	30
Population (2005, million)	2.0
Gross Domestic Product (GDP) (2005, US$ million)	1,467
GDP per capita (2005, US$)	621

GDP growth (real, %)
'-> 2004: 2.7;   2005: 1.3;   2006*: 1.6;   2007*: 1.4

	2003	2004	2005*	2004/2003	2005*/2004
International Arrivals					
Visitors (1000)	329	304	304	-7.8	0.0
- per 100 of inhabitants	16	15	15		
Tourism accommodation					
Number of rooms	..	1,492	..		
Receipts and Expenditure for International Tourism					
International Tourism Receipts (US$ million)	28	34	30	21.4	-11.8
- per Visitor Arrival (US$)	85	112	99	31.7	-11.8
- per capita (US$)	14	17	15		
International Tourism Expenditure (US$ million)	26	30	27	15.4	-10.0
- per capita (US$)	13	15	13		
International Fare Expenditure (US$ million)	4	7	9	75.0	28.6
Δ International Tourism Balance (US$ million)	2	4	3		

Source: World Tourism Organization (UNWTO)   (Data as collected by UNWTO for TMT 2006 Edition)

See annex for methodological notes and reference of external sources used.

World Tourism Organization ©

International Tourism by Origin

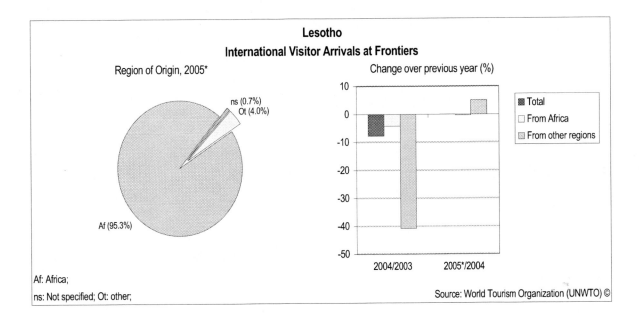

Lesotho
International Visitor Arrivals at Frontiers

Region of Origin, 2005*

Change over previous year (%)

- Total
- From Africa
- From other regions

ns (0.7%)
Ot (4.0%)
Af (95.3%)

2004/2003   2005*/2004

Af: Africa;
ns: Not specified; Ot: other;

Source: World Tourism Organization (UNWTO) ©

Lesotho
International Visitor Arrivals at Frontiers (by residence)

	1995	2000	2003	2004	2005*	Market share (%)		Growth rate (%)		Average per year (%)
						2000	2005*	04/03	05*/04	2000-2005*
Total	208,906	301,759	329,301	303,530	303,578	100	100	-7.8	0.0	0.1
From Africa	202,007	292,704	302,924	290,295	289,342	97.0	95.3	-4.2	-0.3	-0.2
South Africa	196,674	287,141	286,349	282,070	280,399	95.2	92.4	-1.5	-0.6	-0.5
Botswana	1,243	1,336	3,970	1,973	2,129	0.4	0.7	-50.3	7.9	9.8
Zimbabwe	1,192	1,454	3,590	1,963	2,088	0.5	0.7	-45.3	6.4	7.5
Swaziland	1,152	1,109	2,380	1,408	1,481	0.4	0.5	-40.8	5.2	6.0
Zambia	257	253	451	298	309	0.1	0.1	-33.9	3.7	4.1
Malawi	216	..	..	..	..					
Mozambique	..	176	298	204	211	0.1	0.1	-31.5	3.4	3.7
Kenya	157	151	231	169	173	0.1	0.1	-26.8	2.4	2.8
Tanzania	126	..	..	..	..					
Nigeria	58	..	..	..	..					
Other Africa	932	1,084	5,655	2,210	2,552	0.4	0.8	-60.9	15.5	18.7
From other regions	6,899	9,055	19,420	11,494	12,077	3.0	4.0	-40.8	5.1	5.9
All Asia	1,073	2,113	3,620	2,011	2,134	0.7	0.7	-44.4	6.1	0.2
United Kingdom	1,948	2,004	2,005	1,970	1,950	0.7	0.6	-1.7	-1.0	-0.5
Germany	857	1,320	2,878	1,687	1,775	0.4	0.6	-41.4	5.2	6.1
Netherlands	263	188	..	..	..	0.1				
United States	719	554	2,196	955	1,054	0.2	0.3	-56.5	10.4	13.7
Australia	..	..	389	540	523		0.2	38.8	-3.1	
Ireland	526	517	198	428	406	0.2	0.1	116.2	-5.1	-4.7
France	297	..	..	..	..					
Canada	201	214	392	255	265	0.1	0.1	-34.9	3.9	4.4
Sweden	156	197	221	200	200	0.1	0.1	-9.5	0.0	0.3
Italy	153	..	..	..	..					
Denmark	147	..	..	..	..					
Other Americas	200	138	254	165	171	0.0	0.1	-35.0	3.6	4.4
Other Europe	359	1,810	7,267	3,283	3,599	0.6	1.2	-54.8	9.6	14.7
Other World/Not specified	..	..	6,957	1,741	2,159		0.7	-75.0	24.0	

Source: World Tourism Organization (UNWTO) ©

(Data as collected by UNWTO for TMT 2006 Edition)

III.5.3 Namibia   Southern Africa

Promotional: www.namibiatourism.com.na
Institutional/corporate: www.namibiatourism.com.na
Research and data: www.namibiatourism.com.na

Profile

Namibia

Capital	Windhoek
Year of entry in UNWTO	1997
Area (1000 km²)	824
Population (2005, million)	2.0
Gross Domestic Product (GDP) (2005, US$ million)	6,121
GDP per capita (2005, US$)	3,022

Africa
Southern Africa

GDP growth (real, %)
'-> 2004: 5.9; 2005: 3.5; 2006*: 4.5; 2007*: 4.5

	2003	2004	2005*	2004/2003	2005*/2004
International Arrivals					
Visitors (1000)	917	986	972	7.5	-1.4
Tourists (overnight visitors) (1000)	695	..	778		
- per 100 of inhabitants	35	..	38		
Same-day visitors (1000)	44	..	78		
Tourism accommodation					
Number of rooms	2,749	..	2,900		
Nights spent in collective establishments (1000)	547				
by non-residents (inbound tourism)	424	..	1,409		
by residents (domestic tourism)	123	..	..		
Nights spent in hotels and similar establishments (1000)	381				
by non-residents (inbound tourism)	299	..	606		
by residents (domestic tourism)	82	..	..		
Receipts and Expenditure for International Tourism					
International Tourism Receipts (US$ million)	330	403	348	22.1	-13.8
- per Tourist Arrival (US$)	475	..	447		
- per Visitor Arrival (US$)	360	409	358	13.6	-12.5
- per capita (US$)	166	200	171		
International Fare Receipts (US$ million)	50	21	..	-58.0	
International Tourism Expenditure (US$ million)	73	122	108	66.4	-11.8
- per capita (US$)	37	61	53		
Δ International Tourism Balance (US$ million)	257	281	240		

Source: World Tourism Organization (UNWTO)   (Data as collected by UNWTO for TMT 2006 Edition)
See annex for methodological notes and reference of external sources used.

International Tourism by Origin

Namibia
International Tourist Arrivals at Frontiers

Region of Origin, 2005*

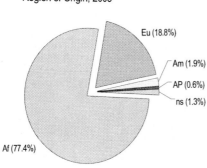

Eu (18.8%)

Am (1.9%)

AP (0.6%)

ns (1.3%)

Af (77.4%)

Af: Africa; Eu: Europe; Am: Americas;
AP: Asia and the Pacific; ns: Not specified;

Source: World Tourism Organization (UNWTO) ©

Namibia

International Tourist Arrivals at Frontiers (by residence)

	1995	2000	2003	2004	2005*	Market share (%) 2000	Market share (%) 2005*	Growth rate (%) 04/03	Growth rate (%) 05*/04	Average per year (%) 2000-2005*
Total	..	..	**695,221**	..	**777,890**		100			
From Africa	..	..	*525,885*	..	*601,737*		77.4			
Angola	..	..	222,752	..	281,365		36.2			
South Africa	..	..	222,009	..	230,949		29.7			
Zambia	..	..	33,634	..	35,782		4.6			
Zimbabwe	..	..	17,795	..	22,765		2.9			
Botswana	..	..	22,679	..	22,333		2.9			
Other Africa	..	..	7,016	..	8,543		1.1			
From other regions	..	..	*157,889*	..	*165,654*		21.3			
Germany	..	..	58,036	..	61,222		7.9			
United Kingdom	..	..	19,291	..	20,978		2.7			
United States	..	..	11,775	..	14,685		1.9			
Netherlands	..	..	11,778	..	11,570		1.5			
France	..	..	9,364	..	9,959		1.3			
Italy	..	..	8,809	..	8,557		1.1			
Switzerland	..	..	7,319	..	8,363		1.1			
Scandinavia	..	..	5,316	..	6,327		0.8			
Austria	..	..	5,023	..	5,160		0.7			
Australia	..	..	4,280	..	4,607		0.6			
Spain	..	..	4,448	..	3,492		0.4			
Belgium	..	..	4,197	..	3,240		0.4			
Portugal	..	..	3,535	..	2,753		0.4			
Other Europe	..	..	4,718	..	4,741		0.6			
Other World/Not specified	..	..	*11,447*	..	*10,499*		1.3			

Source: World Tourism Organization (UNWTO) ©

(Data as collected by UNWTO for TMT 2006 Edition)

III.5.4   South Africa   Southern Africa

Promotional: www.zulu.org.za
Institutional/corporate: www.zulu.org.za
Research and data: www.zulu.org.za

Profile

South Africa

Capital	Pretoria
Year of entry in UNWTO	1994
Area (1000 km²)	1,221
Population (2005, million)	44.3
Gross Domestic Product (GDP) (2005, US$ million)	239,419
GDP per capita (2005, US$)	5,106

Africa
Southern Africa

GDP growth (real, %)
'-> 2004: 4.5;   2005: 4.9;   2006*: 4.2;   2007*: 4.0

	2003	2004	2005*	2004/2003	2005*/2004
International Arrivals					
Visitors (1000)	6,640	6,815	7,518	2.6	10.3
Tourists (overnight visitors) (1000)	6,505	6,678	7,369	2.7	10.3
- per 100 of inhabitants	15	15	17		
Tourism accommodation					
Number of rooms	52,329	52,728	54,853	0.8	4.0
Receipts and Expenditure for International Tourism					
International Tourism Receipts (US$ million)	5,523	6,282	7,327	13.7	16.6
- per Tourist Arrival (US$)	849	941	994	10.8	5.7
- per Visitor Arrival (US$)	832	922	975	10.8	5.7
- per capita (US$)	124	141	165		
International Fare Receipts (US$ million)	956	1,054	1,112	10.2	5.5
International Tourism Expenditure (US$ million)	2,846	3,144	3,375	10.5	7.3
- per capita (US$)	64	71	76		
International Fare Expenditure (US$ million)	762	1,078	1,442	41.4	33.7
Δ International Tourism Balance (US$ million)	2,677	3,138	3,952		
Δ International Fare Balance (US$ million)	194	-24	-330		

Source: World Tourism Organization (UNWTO)   (Data as collected by UNWTO for TMT 2006 Edition)

See annex for methodological notes and reference of external sources used.

International Tourism by Origin

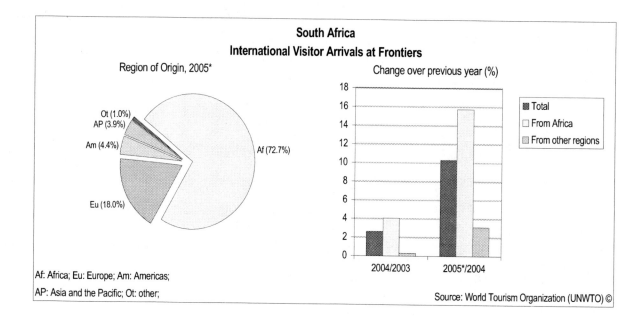

South Africa
International Visitor Arrivals at Frontiers

Region of Origin, 2005*

Change over previous year (%)

Ot (1.0%)
AP (3.9%)
Am (4.4%)
Af (72.7%)
Eu (18.0%)

Total
From Africa
From other regions

2004/2003   2005*/2004

Af: Africa; Eu: Europe; Am: Americas;
AP: Asia and the Pacific; Ot: other;

Source: World Tourism Organization (UNWTO) ©

South Africa
International Visitor Arrivals at Frontiers (by residence)

	1995	2000	2003	2004	2005*	Market share (%) 2000	Market share (%) 2005*	Growth rate (%) 04/03	Growth rate (%) 05*/04	Average per year (%) 2000-2005*
Total	4,684,064	6,000,538	6,640,095	6,815,202	7,517,258	100	100	2.6	10.3	4.6
From Africa	*3,449,460*	*4,309,893*	*4,536,397*	*4,720,457*	*5,463,441*	*71.8*	*72.7*	*4.1*	*15.7*	*4.9*
Lesotho	1,097,351	1,559,422	1,291,242	1,479,802	1,668,826	26.0	22.2	14.6	12.8	1.4
Swaziland	664,863	742,621	809,049	852,636	911,990	12.4	12.1	5.4	7.0	4.2
Botswana	363,890	563,365	797,315	806,820	798,455	9.4	10.6	1.2	-1.0	7.2
Zimbabwe	729,971	477,380	568,626	558,093	783,100	8.0	10.4	-1.9	40.3	10.4
Mozambique	192,987	491,526	474,790	405,579	648,526	8.2	8.6	-14.6	59.9	5.7
Namibia	213,063	206,022	216,978	226,525	220,045	3.4	2.9	4.4	-2.9	1.3
Zambia	48,323	75,882	115,650	122,512	128,390	1.3	1.7	5.9	4.8	11.1
Malawi	45,040	70,732	89,469	89,743	107,258	1.2	1.4	0.3	19.5	8.7
Nigeria	4,758	13,451	23,477	24,627	30,248	0.2	0.4	4.9	22.8	17.6
Angola	17,865	28,281	29,511	29,058	28,515	0.5	0.4	-1.5	-1.9	0.2
Kenya	12,854	14,646	18,780	20,825	22,389	0.2	0.3	10.9	7.5	8.9
Dem.R.Congo	9,575	2,437	6,042	11,391	16,079	0.0	0.2	88.5	41.2	45.8
Mauritius	8,855	12,042	15,468	14,009	14,103	0.2	0.2	-9.4	0.7	3.2
Tanzania	4,347	7,529	11,173	11,399	11,995	0.1	0.2	2.0	5.2	9.8
Uganda	4,430	6,294	9,889	10,314	10,237	0.1	0.1	4.3	-0.7	10.2
Ghana	4,191	6,193	8,700	8,887	8,970	0.1	0.1	2.1	0.9	7.7
Other intraregional	27,097	32,070	50,238	48,237	54,315	0.5	0.7	-4.0	12.6	11.1
From other regions	*1,104,675*	*1,566,747*	*1,926,631*	*1,932,554*	*1,992,580*	*26.1*	*26.5*	*0.3*	*3.1*	*4.9*
United Kingdom	252,437	358,072	463,021	463,176	476,627	6.0	6.3	0.0	2.9	5.9
Germany	172,502	215,011	261,194	249,564	253,471	3.6	3.4	-4.5	1.6	3.3
United States	108,688	181,632	192,561	213,322	238,934	3.0	3.2	10.8	12.0	5.6
Netherlands	48,197	93,091	122,565	122,271	117,855	1.6	1.6	-0.2	-3.6	4.8
France	55,907	92,750	130,365	111,636	103,674	1.5	1.4	-14.4	-7.1	2.3
Australia	47,950	57,191	72,728	76,712	78,233	1.0	1.0	5.5	2.0	6.5
Italy	28,222	38,979	50,403	51,059	52,172	0.6	0.7	1.3	2.2	6.0
Canada	21,825	28,717	35,683	38,214	41,827	0.5	0.6	7.1	9.5	7.8
China	..	19,722	33,128	45,934	41,704	0.3	0.6	38.7	-9.2	16.2
India	16,450	27,810	42,954	36,069	39,906	0.5	0.5	-16.0	10.6	7.5
Switzerland	31,018	33,938	36,203	37,319	39,591	0.6	0.5	3.1	6.1	3.1
Belgium	21,976	41,550	43,537	38,036	39,385	0.7	0.5	-12.6	3.5	-1.1
Ireland	11,616	19,753	34,806	38,437	36,799	0.3	0.5	10.4	-4.3	13.3
Sweden	16,849	21,072	30,053	32,987	36,408	0.4	0.5	9.8	10.4	11.6
Portugal	11,825	25,013	29,347	29,421	30,277	0.4	0.4	0.3	2.9	3.9
Japan	17,293	24,104	22,741	24,469	28,861	0.4	0.4	7.6	17.9	3.7
Spain	6,935	18,234	26,167	23,638	27,587	0.3	0.4	-9.7	16.7	8.6
Brazil	12,036	17,659	17,883	21,562	24,090	0.3	0.3	20.6	11.7	6.4
Denmark	9,445	15,189	19,888	20,684	21,450	0.3	0.3	4.0	3.7	7.1
Austria	17,485	22,137	21,960	20,808	20,935	0.4	0.3	-5.2	0.6	-1.1
Norway	6,631	10,839	17,982	18,959	20,636	0.2	0.3	5.4	8.8	13.7
New Zealand	12,585	13,035	16,634	16,562	18,039	0.2	0.2	-0.4	8.9	6.7
Israel	13,374	14,161	15,427	15,877	15,864	0.2	0.2	2.9	-0.1	2.3
Korea, Republic of	3,797	9,081	11,737	13,935	15,391	0.2	0.2	18.7	10.4	11.1
Taiwan (pr. of China)	35,142	15,825	13,959	16,753	13,579	0.3	0.2	20.0	-18.9	-3.0
Other interregional	124,490	152,182	163,705	155,150	159,285	2.5	2.1	-5.2	2.7	0.9
Other World/Not specified	*129,929*	*123,898*	*177,067*	*162,191*	*61,237*	*2.1*	*0.8*	*-8.4*	*-62.2*	*-13.1*

Source: World Tourism Organization (UNWTO) ©   (Data as collected by UNWTO for TMT 2006 Edition)

III.5.5 Swaziland   Southern Africa

Promotional: www.welcometoswaziland.com
Institutional/corporate: www.mintour.gov.sz ; www.gov.sz
Research and data: www.welcometoswaziland.com

Profile

Swaziland

Africa
Southern Africa

Capital		Mbabane
Year of entry in UNWTO		1999
Area (100 km²)		174
Population (2005, million)		1.1
Gross Domestic Product (GDP) (2005, US$ million)		2,546
GDP per capita (2005, US$)		2,336
GDP growth (real, %)		
'-> 2004: 2.1; 2005: 1.9; 2006*: 1.2; 2007*: 1.0		

	2003	2004	2005*	2004/2003	2005*/2004
International Arrivals					
Visitors (1000)	1,543	..	1,182		
Tourists (overnight visitors) (1000)	461	459	839	-0.4	82.8
- per 100 of inhabitants	41	40	74		
Same-day visitors (1000)	..	..	130		
Tourism accommodation					
Number of rooms	1,339	1,307	1,244	-2.4	-4.8
Nights spent in hotels and similar establishments (1000)					
by residents (domestic tourism)	136	..	39		
Outbound Tourism					
Trips abroad (1000)	..	..	1,082		
- per 100 of inhabitants	..	..	95		
Receipts and Expenditure for International Tourism					
International Tourism Receipts (US$ million)	101	54	69	-46.5	27.8
- per Tourist Arrival (US$)	219	118	82	-46.3	-30.1
- per Visitor Arrival (US$)	65	..	58		
- per capita (US$)	89	47	61		
International Fare Receipts (US$ million)	12	0	0	-99.2	200.0
International Tourism Expenditure (US$ million)	43	16	15	-62.8	-6.3
- per trip (US$)	..	..	14		
- per capita (US$)	38	14	13		
International Fare Expenditure (US$ million)	1	6	8	500.0	33.3
Δ International Tourism Balance (US$ million)	58	38	54		
Δ International Fare Balance (US$ million)	11	-6	-8		

Source: World Tourism Organization (UNWTO)   (Data as collected by UNWTO for TMT 2006 Edition)

See annex for methodological notes and reference of external sources used.

International Tourism by Origin

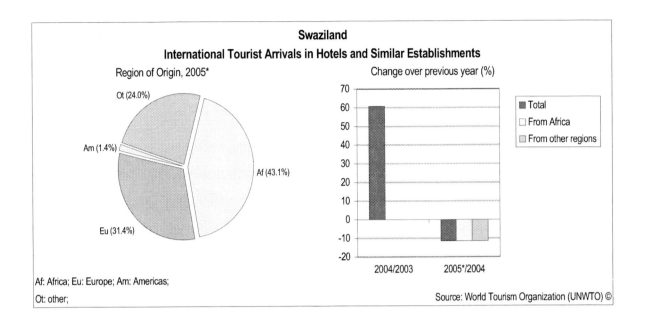

Af: Africa; Eu: Europe; Am: Americas;
Ot: other;

Source: World Tourism Organization (UNWTO) ©

Swaziland
International Tourist Arrivals in Hotels and Similar Establishments (by residence)

	1995	2000	2003	2004	2005*	Market share (%) 2000	Market share (%) 2005*	Growth rate (%) 04/03	Growth rate (%) 05*/04	Average per year (%) 2000-2005*
Total	**299,822**	**280,870**	**218,813**	**352,040**	**311,656**	**100**	**100**	**60.9**	**-11.5**	**2.1**
From Africa	*253,409*	*177,216*	*110,054*	*151,879*	*134,456*	*63.1*	*43.1*	*38.0*	*-11.5*	*-5.4*
South Africa	199,577	126,296	85,899	112,027	99,176	45.0	31.8	30.4	-11.5	-4.7
Mozambique	34,701	23,650	11,642	17,619	15,597	8.4	5.0	51.3	-11.5	-8.0
Other Africa	19,131	27,270	12,513	22,233	19,683	9.7	6.3	77.7	-11.5	-6.3
From other regions	*43,042*	*102,390*	*101,434*	*119,162*	*105,492*	*36.5*	*33.8*	*17.5*	*-11.5*	*0.6*
United Kingdom	18,195	26,562	13,702	17,776	15,737	9.5	5.0	29.7	-11.5	-9.9
All Americas	5,764	10,823	11,092	4,968	4,398	3.9	1.4	-55.2	-11.5	-16.5
Australia	3,253	6,304	701	1,725	1,527	2.2	0.5	146.1	-11.5	-24.7
Portugal	768	818	8,666	828	733	0.3	0.2	-90.4	-11.5	-2.2
Other Asia	557	749	1,642	1,760	1,558	0.3	0.5	7.2	-11.5	15.8
Other Europe	14,505	57,134	65,631	92,105	81,539	20.3	26.2	40.3	-11.5	7.4
Other World/Not specified	*3,371*	*1,264*	*7,325*	*80,999*	*71,708*	*0.5*	*23.0*	*1005.8*	*-11.5*	*124.3*

Source: World Tourism Organization (UNWTO) ©   (Data as collected by UNWTO for TMT 2006 Edition)

World Tourism Organization ©

Annex

Table of contents

1. International Tourist Arrivals

International Tourist Arrivals, 1950-2005*

	World	Africa	Americas	Asia and the Pacific	Europe	Middle East	World	Africa	Americas	Asia and the Pacific	Europe	Middle East
	International Tourist Arrivals (million)						Change over previous year (%)[1]					
1950	25.3	0.5	7.5	0.2	16.8	0.2						
1960	69.3	0.8	16.7	0.9	50.4	0.6						
1965	112.9	1.4	23.2	2.1	83.7	2.4						
1970	165.8	2.4	42.3	6.2	113.0	1.9						
1975	222.3	4.7	50.0	10.2	153.9	3.5						
1980	277.6	7.2	62.3	23.0	178.0	7.1						
1981	278.2	8.1	62.5	24.9	175.1	7.6	0.2	13.3	0.3	8.0	-1.6	7.3
1982	276.4	7.6	59.7	26.0	174.9	8.3	-0.6	-6.6	-4.5	4.5	-0.1	8.8
1983	281.2	8.2	59.9	26.6	179.0	7.5	1.7	8.4	0.4	2.3	2.4	-9.5
1984	306.2	8.8	67.4	29.5	192.8	7.7	8.9	7.5	12.5	10.8	7.7	2.3
1985	319.5	9.6	65.1	32.9	203.8	8.1	4.3	9.3	-3.4	11.6	5.7	5.6
1986	329.5	9.3	70.9	36.8	205.5	6.9	3.1	-3.1	8.9	12.1	0.9	-14.9
1987	359.0	9.8	76.6	42.1	223.3	7.2	8.9	5.1	8.0	14.3	8.6	4.0
1988	384.1	12.6	83.0	48.7	230.7	9.1	7.0	27.8	8.4	15.8	3.3	26.2
1989	409.0	13.8	86.9	49.4	249.6	9.2	6.5	10.3	4.7	1.4	8.2	1.9
1990	438.4	15.2	92.8	56.2	264.7	9.6	7.2	9.7	6.8	13.7	6.0	4.3
1991	441.3	16.3	95.3	58.0	262.8	8.9	0.6	7.1	2.7	3.3	-0.7	-7.1
1992	478.4	18.2	102.2	65.8	280.9	11.3	8.4	12.0	7.3	13.4	6.9	25.9
1993	494.2	18.8	102.2	72.3	289.5	11.4	3.3	3.2	0.0	10.0	3.0	1.4
1994	518.0	19.1	105.1	80.1	301.5	12.1	4.8	1.8	2.9	10.7	4.2	6.3
1995	538.5	20.1	109.0	82.5	313.2	13.7	3.9	4.9	3.7	3.0	3.9	12.9
1996	572.4	21.8	114.5	90.4	329.9	15.8	6.3	8.7	5.0	9.7	5.3	15.0
1997	596.0	22.8	116.2	89.7	350.6	16.7	4.1	4.5	1.5	-0.8	6.3	5.8
1998	614.3	25.2	119.2	89.4	362.5	18.0	3.1	10.6	2.5	-0.3	3.4	7.9
1999	637.4	26.7	122.0	98.8	368.4	21.5	3.8	6.0	2.4	10.5	1.6	19.5
2000	684.7	27.9	128.2	110.6	393.6	24.5	7.4	4.3	5.1	12.0	6.8	13.7
2001	684.4	28.8	122.2	115.8	393.1	24.5	0.0	3.2	-4.7	4.7	-0.1	0.3
2002	704.7	29.8	116.8	124.9	404.8	28.4	3.0	3.6	-4.4	7.8	3.0	16.0
2003	692.2	31.4	113.3	113.2	404.9	29.5	-1.8	5.3	-3.0	-9.4	0.0	3.7
2004	761.4	34.2	125.8	144.1	421.0	36.2	10.0	9.1	11.0	27.4	4.0	22.7
2005*	801.6	37.3	133.2	155.4	437.4	38.4	5.3	9.0	5.9	7.8	3.9	5.9

Average annual growth (%)	World	Africa	Americas	Asia and the Pacific	Europe	Middle East
1950-2000	6.8	8.3	5.8	13.1	6.5	10.1
1950-2005*	6.5	8.1	5.4	12.5	6.1	10.1
1950-1960	10.6	3.7	8.4	14.1	11.6	12.3
1960-1970	9.1	12.4	9.7	21.6	8.4	11.5
1970-1980	5.3	11.5	4.0	13.9	4.6	14.3
1980-1990	4.7	7.8	4.1	9.3	4.0	3.1
1980-1985	2.9	6.2	0.9	7.4	2.7	2.7
1985-1990	6.5	9.5	7.3	11.3	5.4	3.5
1990-2000	4.6	6.3	3.3	7.0	4.0	9.8
1990-1995	4.2	5.7	3.3	8.0	3.4	7.3
1995-2000	4.9	6.8	3.3	6.0	4.7	12.3
2000-2005*	3.2	6.0	0.8	7.0	2.1	9.4

Source: World Tourism Organization (UNWTO) ©   (Data as collected by UNWTO for TMT 2006 Edition)

[1] Before 1995, data are simple aggregates of country results and are not corrected for changes in series, so changes on previous year might not be in all cases correct.

International Tourist Arrivals by Country of Destination

	Series	International Tourist Arrivals (1000)						Market share in the region (%)			Change (%)		Average annual growth (%)	
		1990	1995	2000	2003	2004	2005*	1990	2000	2005*	04/03	05*/04	90-00	00-05*
Africa		*15,188*	*20,083*	*27,894*	*31,394*	*34,242*	*37,311*	*100*	*100*	*100*	*9.1*	*9.0*	*6.3*	*6.0*
North Africa		**8,398**	**7,271**	**10,240**	**11,094**	**12,769**	**13,911**	**55.3**	**36.7**	**37.3**	**15.1**	**8.9**	**2.0**	**6.3**
Algeria	VF	1,137	520	866	1,166	1,234	1,443	7.5	3.1	3.9	5.8	17.0	-2.7	10.8
Morocco	TF	4,024	2,602	4,278	4,761	5,477	5,843	26.5	15.3	15.7	15.0	6.7	0.6	6.4
Sudan	TF	33	29	38	52	61	246	0.2	0.1	0.7	15.8	305.8	1.4	45.3
Tunisia	TF	3,204	4,120	5,058	5,114	5,998	6,378	21.1	18.1	17.1	17.3	6.3	4.7	4.7
West Africa		**1,352**	**1,913**	**2,434**	**3,062**	**3,452**	**3,585**	**8.9**	**8.7**	**9.6**	**12.7**	**3.9**	**6.1**	**8.1**
Benin	TF	110	138	96	175	174	176	0.7	0.3	0.5	-0.9	1.4	-1.4	12.9
Burkina Faso	THS	74	124	126	163	222	245	0.5	0.5	0.7	36.2	10.1	5.5	14.2
Cape Verde	TF	24	28	115	150	157	198	0.2	0.4	0.5	4.7	26.0	17.0	11.5
Côte d'Ivoire	TF	196	188	..	180	..	..	1.3						
Gambia	TF	100	45	77	89	90	111	0.7	0.3	0.3	1.1	23.2	-2.5	7.5
Ghana	TF	146	286	399	531	584	429	1.0	1.4	1.1	10.0	-26.6	10.6	1.4
Guinea	TF	..	..	33	44	45	45		0.1	0.1	1.5	1.6		6.6
Mali	TF	44	42	86	110	113	143	0.3	0.3	0.4	2.1	26.8	7.0	10.6
Mauritania	TF	..	..	30	..	..	..		0.1					
Niger	TF	21	35	50	55	57	63	0.1	0.2	0.2	3.6	11.3	9.1	4.9
Nigeria	TF	190	656	813	924	962	1,010	1.3	2.9	2.7	4.1	5.0	15.6	4.4
Senegal	THS/TF	246	280	389	495	667	769	1.6	1.4	2.1	34.7	15.3	4.7	14.6
Sierra Leone	TF	98	38	16	38	44	40	0.6	0.1	0.1	14.3	-8.1	-16.6	20.1
Togo	THS	103	53	60	61	83	81	0.7	0.2	0.2	36.5	-2.3	-5.3	6.1
Central Africa		**365**	**357**	**666**	**636**	**728**	**792**	**2.4**	**2.4**	**2.1**	**14.4**	**8.9**	**6.2**	**3.5**
Angola	TF	67	9	51	107	194	210	0.4	0.2	0.6	82.3	8.0	-2.7	32.7
Cameroon	THS	89	100	277	..	190	176	0.6	1.0	0.5		-7.1	12.0	-8.6
Cent.Afr.Rep.	TF	..	26	11	6	8	12		0.0	0.0	43.4	47.1		1.4
Chad	THS	9	19	43	21	26	29	0.1	0.2	0.1	23.5	13.3	16.9	-7.3
Congo	THS	33	37	19	..	..	..	0.2	0.1				-5.4	
Dem.R.Congo	TF	55	35	103	35	30	61	0.4	0.4	0.2	-14.6	103.3	6.5	-9.9
Gabon	TF	109	125	155	222	..	..	0.7	0.6				3.6	
Sao Tome Prn	TF	3	6	7	14	11	11	0.0	0.0	0.0	-21.6	-1.9	9.0	8.1
East Africa		**2,842**	**4,752**	**6,338**	**7,206**	**7,614**	**8,059**	**18.7**	**22.7**	**21.6**	**5.7**	**5.8**	**8.4**	**4.9**
Burundi	TF	109	34	29	74	133	148	0.7	0.1	0.4	79.8	11.4	-12.4	38.6
Comoros	TF	8	23	24	14	18	20	0.1	0.1	0.1	23.7	11.1	11.6	-4.0
Djibouti	TF	33	21	20	23	26	30	0.2	0.1	0.1	13.4	14.8	-4.8	8.5
Eritrea	VF	..	315	70	80	87	83		0.3	0.2	9.1	-4.6		3.5
Ethiopia	TF	79	103	136	180	184	227	0.5	0.5	0.6	2.3	23.5	5.6	10.8
Kenya	TF	814	896	899	927	1,193	1,536	5.4	3.2	4.1	28.7	28.8	1.0	11.3
Madagascar	TF	53	75	160	139	229	277	0.3	0.6	0.7	64.6	21.3	11.7	11.6
Malawi	TF	130	192	228	424	427	438	0.9	0.8	1.2	0.8	2.4	5.8	13.9
Mauritius	TF	292	422	656	702	719	761	1.9	2.4	2.0	2.4	5.9	8.4	3.0
Mozambique	TF	..	..	..	441	470	578			1.5	6.6	23.0		
Reunion	TF	200	304	430	432	430	409	1.3	1.5	1.1	-0.5	-4.9	8.0	-1.0
Rwanda	TF	..	..	104	..	..	..		0.4					
Seychelles	TF	104	121	130	122	121	129	0.7	0.5	0.3	-1.0	6.5	2.3	-0.2
Tanzania	TF	..	285	459	552	566	590		1.6	1.6	2.5	4.2		5.1
Uganda	TF	69	160	193	305	512	468	0.5	0.7	1.3	68.2	-8.7	10.8	19.4
Zambia	TF	141	163	457	413	515	669	0.9	1.6	1.8	24.8	29.9	12.5	7.9
Zimbabwe	VF	636	1,416	1,967	2,256	1,854	1,559	4.2	7.1	4.2	-17.8	-15.9	12.0	-4.5
Southern Africa		**2,231**	**5,790**	**8,215**	**9,396**	**9,679**	**10,964**	**14.7**	**29.5**	**29.4**	**3.0**	**13.3**	**13.9**	**5.9**
Botswana	TF	543	521	1,104	1,406	1,523	1,675	3.6	4.0	4.5	8.3	10.0	7.4	8.7
Lesotho	VF	242	209	302	329	304	304	1.6	1.1	0.8	-7.8	0.0	2.2	0.1
Namibia	TF	..	272	656	695	..	778		2.4	2.1				3.5
South Africa	TF	..	4,488	5,872	6,505	6,678	7,369		21.1	19.7	2.7	10.3		4.6
Swaziland	THS	263	300	281	461	459	839	1.7	1.0	2.2	-0.4	82.8	0.7	24.5

Source: World Tourism Organization (UNWTO) ©

(Data as collected by UNWTO for TMT 2006 Edition)

International Tourist Arrivals by Country of Destination

	Series	International Tourist Arrivals (1000)						Market share in the region (%)			Change (%)		Average annual growth (%)	
		1990	1995	2000	2003	2004	2005*	1990	2000	2005*	04/03	05*/04	90-00	00-05*
Americas		*92,804*	*109,028*	*128,193*	*113,293*	*125,792*	*133,198*	*100*	*100*	*100*	*11.0*	*5.9*	*3.3*	*0.8*
North America		**71,744**	**80,664**	**91,506**	**77,418**	**85,849**	**89,891**	**77.3**	**71.4**	**67.5**	**10.9**	**4.7**	**2.5**	**-0.4**
Canada	TF	15,209	16,932	19,627	17,534	19,145	18,771	16.4	15.3	14.1	9.2	-2.0	2.6	-0.9
Mexico	TF	17,172	20,241	20,641	18,665	20,618	21,915	18.5	16.1	16.5	10.5	6.3	1.9	1.2
United States	TF	39,363	43,491	51,238	41,218	46,086	49,206	42.4	40.0	36.9	11.8	6.8	2.7	-0.8
Caribbean		**11,392**	**14,023**	**17,086**	**17,080**	**18,095**	**18,802**	**12.3**	**13.3**	**14.1**	**5.9**	**3.9**	**4.1**	**1.9**
Anguilla	TF	31	39	44	47	54	62	0.0	0.0	0.0	15.1	15.0	3.6	7.1
Antigua,Barb	TF	206	220	207	224	245	245	0.2	0.2	0.2	9.6	0.0	0.0	3.5
Aruba	TF	433	619	721	642	728	733	0.5	0.6	0.5	13.4	0.6	5.2	0.3
Bahamas	TF	1,562	1,598	1,544	1,510	1,561	1,608	1.7	1.2	1.2	3.4	3.0	-0.1	0.8
Barbados	TF	432	442	545	531	552	548	0.5	0.4	0.4	3.8	-0.7	2.4	0.1
Bermuda	TF	435	387	332	257	272	270	0.5	0.3	0.2	5.9	-0.7	-2.7	-4.1
Bonaire	TF	37	59	51	62	63	63	0.0	0.0	0.0	1.6	-0.9	3.3	4.2
Br.Virgin Is	TF	160	219	272	318	307	337	0.2	0.2	0.3	-3.2	9.7	5.4	4.4
Cayman Islands	TF	253	361	354	294	260	168	0.3	0.3	0.1	-11.4	-35.4	3.4	-13.9
Cuba	TF	327	742	1,741	1,847	2,017	2,261	0.4	1.4	1.7	9.2	12.1	18.2	5.4
Curaçao	TF	219	224	191	221	223	222	0.2	0.1	0.2	0.9	-0.6	-1.4	3.1
Dominica	TF	45	60	70	73	80	79	0.0	0.1	0.1	9.4	-1.0	4.5	2.5
Dominican Rp	TF	1,305	1,776	2,978	3,282	3,450	3,691	1.4	2.3	2.8	5.1	7.0	8.6	4.4
Grenada	TF	76	108	129	142	134	98	0.1	0.1	0.1	-6.0	-26.6	5.4	-5.3
Guadeloupe	TCE	331	640	603	439	456	372	0.4	0.5	0.3	3.9	-18.4	6.2	-9.2
Haiti	TF	144	145	140	136	96	112	0.2	0.1	0.1	-29.1	16.4	-0.3	-4.3
Jamaica	TF	989	1,147	1,323	1,350	1,415	1,479	1.1	1.0	1.1	4.8	4.5	2.9	2.3
Martinique	TF	282	457	526	453	471	484	0.3	0.4	0.4	3.9	2.8	6.4	-1.6
Montserrat	TF	13	18	10	8	10	10	0.0	0.0	0.0	13.7	1.3	-2.3	-1.3
Puerto Rico	TF	2,560	3,131	3,341	3,238	3,541	3,686	2.8	2.6	2.8	9.3	4.1	2.7	2.0
Saba	TF	..	10	9	10	11	11		0.0	0.0	7.3	4.1		4.7
Saint Lucia	TF	141	231	270	277	298	318	0.2	0.2	0.2	7.8	6.5	6.7	3.3
St.Eustatius	TF	..	9	9	10	11	10		0.0	0.0	5.8	-6.3		2.6
St.Kitts-Nev	TF	73	79	73	91	118	127	0.1	0.1	0.1	29.7	8.0	0.0	11.7
St.Maarten	TF	545	449	432	428	475	468	0.6	0.3	0.4	11.1	-1.5	-2.3	1.6
St.Vincent,Grenadines	TF	54	60	73	79	87	96	0.1	0.1	0.1	10.4	10.1	3.1	5.5
Trinidad Tbg	TF	195	260	399	409	443	463	0.2	0.3	0.3	8.2	4.7	7.4	3.0
Turks,Caicos	TF	49	79	152	164	173	200	0.1	0.1	0.2	5.8	15.6	12.0	5.6
US.Virgin Is	TF	463	454	546	538	544	582	0.5	0.4	0.4	1.1	7.0	1.7	1.3
Central America		**1,945**	**2,611**	**4,346**	**4,900**	**5,554**	**6,288**	**2.1**	**3.4**	**4.7**	**13.4**	**13.2**	**8.4**	**7.7**
Belize	TF	197	131	196	221	231	237	0.2	0.2	0.2	4.7	2.5	-0.1	3.8
Costa Rica	TF	435	785	1,088	1,239	1,453	1,679	0.5	0.8	1.3	17.3	15.6	9.6	9.1
El Salvador	TF	194	235	795	857	812	969	0.2	0.6	0.7	-5.3	19.5	15.1	4.0
Guatemala	TF	509	563	826	880	1,182	1,316	0.5	0.6	1.0	34.2	11.4	5.0	9.8
Honduras	TF	290	271	471	611	641	673	0.3	0.4	0.5	5.0	5.0	5.0	7.4
Nicaragua	TF	106	281	486	526	615	712	0.1	0.4	0.5	16.9	15.9	16.4	8.0
Panama	TF	214	345	484	566	621	702	0.2	0.4	0.5	9.8	13.0	8.5	7.7
South America		**7,722**	**11,731**	**15,255**	**13,896**	**16,295**	**18,217**	**8.3**	**11.9**	**13.7**	**17.3**	**11.8**	**7.0**	**3.6**
Argentina	TF	1,930	2,289	2,909	2,995	3,457	3,823	2.1	2.3	2.9	15.4	10.6	4.2	5.6
Bolivia	TF	254	284	319	420	478	504	0.3	0.2	0.4	13.8	5.4	2.3	9.6
Brazil	TF	1,091	1,991	5,313	4,133	4,794	5,358	1.2	4.1	4.0	16.0	11.8	17.2	0.2
Chile	TF	943	1,540	1,742	1,614	1,785	2,027	1.0	1.4	1.5	10.6	13.6	6.3	3.1
Colombia	TF	813	1,399	557	625	791	933	0.9	0.4	0.7	26.6	18.0	-3.7	10.9
Ecuador	VF	362	440	627	761	819	860	0.4	0.5	0.6	7.6	5.0	5.6	6.5
French Guiana	TF	..	..	..	..	..	95			0.1				
Guyana	TF	64	106	105	101	122	117	0.1	0.1	0.1	20.9	-4.4	5.1	2.1
Paraguay	TF	280	438	289	268	309	341	0.3	0.2	0.3	15.3	10.2	0.3	3.4
Peru	TF	317	479	828	1,070	1,277	1,486	0.3	0.6	1.1	19.4	16.4	10.1	12.4
Suriname	TF	46	43	57	82	138	160	0.0	0.0	0.1	68.1	16.1	2.2	22.9
Uruguay	TF	..	2,022	1,968	1,420	1,756	1,808		1.5	1.4	23.7	2.9		-1.7
Venezuela	TF	525	700	469	337	486	706	0.6	0.4	0.5	44.3	45.2	-1.1	8.5

Source: World Tourism Organization (UNWTO) ©

(Data as collected by UNWTO for TMT 2006 Edition)

International Tourist Arrivals by Country of Destination

	Series	International Tourist Arrivals (1000)						Market share in the region (%)			Change (%)		Average annual growth (%)	
		1990	1995	2000	2003	2004	2005*	1990	2000	2005*	04/03	05*/04	90-00	00-05*
Asia and the Pacific		*56,165*	*82,451*	*110,573*	*113,166*	*144,150*	*155,353*	*100*	*100*	*100*	*27.4*	*7.8*	*7.0*	*7.0*
North-East Asia		**26,394**	**41,313**	**58,349**	**61,732**	**79,412**	**87,576**	**47.0**	**52.8**	**56.4**	**28.6**	**10.3**	**8.3**	**8.5**
China	TF	10,484	20,034	31,229	32,970	41,761	46,809	18.7	28.2	30.1	26.7	12.1	11.5	8.4
Hong Kong (China)	TF	..	..	8,814	9,676	13,655	14,773		8.0	9.5	41.1	8.2		10.9
Japan	TF	3,236	3,345	4,757	5,212	6,138	6,728	5.8	4.3	4.3	17.8	9.6	3.9	7.2
Korea, D P Rp	*	115	..	..	..	..	..	0.2						
Korea, Republic of	VF	2,959	3,753	5,322	4,754	5,818	6,023	5.3	4.8	3.9	22.4	3.5	6.0	2.5
Macao (China)	TF	2,513	4,202	5,197	6,309	8,324	9,014	4.5	4.7	5.8	31.9	8.3	7.5	11.6
Mongolia	TF	147	108	137	201	301	338	0.3	0.1	0.2	49.4	12.4	-0.7	19.8
Taiwan (pr. of China)	VF	..	2,332	2,624	2,248	2,950	3,378		2.4	2.2	31.2	14.5		5.2
South-East Asia		**21,469**	**28,821**	**36,908**	**35,986**	**47,006**	**49,312**	**38.2**	**33.4**	**31.7**	**30.6**	**4.9**	**5.6**	**6.0**
Brunei Darussalam	VF	377	498	984	..	..	815	0.7	0.9	0.5			10.1	-3.7
Cambodia	TF	17	220	466	701	1,055	1,422	0.0	0.4	0.9	50.5	34.7	39.2	25.0
Indonesia	TF	2,178	4,324	5,064	4,467	5,321	5,002	3.9	4.6	3.2	19.1	-6.0	8.8	-0.2
Lao P.D.R.	TF	14	60	191	196	407	672	0.0	0.2	0.4	107.7	65.1	29.9	28.6
Malaysia	TF	7,446	7,469	10,222	10,577	15,703	16,431	13.3	9.2	10.6	48.5	4.6	3.2	10.0
Myanmar	TF	21	117	208	206	242	232	0.0	0.2	0.1	17.7	-4.0	25.8	2.2
Philippines	TF	1,025	1,760	1,992	1,907	2,291	2,623	1.8	1.8	1.7	20.1	14	6.9	5.7
Singapore	TF	4,842	6,070	6,062	4,703	6,553	7,080	8.6	5.5	4.6	39.3	8.0	2.3	3.2
Thailand	TF	5,299	6,952	9,579	10,082	11,737	11,567	9.4	8.7	7.4	16.4	-1.4	6.1	3.8
Vietnam	VF	250	1,351	2,140	2,429	2,928	3,468	0.4	1.9	2.2	20.6	18.4	24.0	10.1
Oceania		**5,152**	**8,084**	**9,230**	**9,023**	**10,118**	**10,488**	**9.2**	**8.3**	**6.8**	**12.1**	**3.7**	**6.0**	**2.6**
American Samoa	TF	26	34	44	..	..	25	0.0	0.0	0.0			5.4	-11.1
Australia	VF/TF	2,215	3,726	4,530	4,354	4,774	5,020	3.9	4.1	3.2	9.6	5.2	7.4	2.1
Cook Is	TF	34	48	73	78	83	88	0.1	0.1	0.1	6.4	6.1	7.9	3.9
Fiji	TF	279	318	294	431	504	550	0.5	0.3	0.4	17.0	9.1	0.5	13.3
French Polynesia	TF	132	172	252	213	212	208	0.2	0.2	0.1	-0.4	-1.8	6.7	-3.8
Guam	TF	780	1,362	1,287	910	1,160	1,228	1.4	1.2	0.8	27.5	5.8	5.1	-0.9
Kiribati	TF	3	4	5	5	4	3	0.0	0.0	0.0	-26.5	-22.4	4.8	-10.3
Marshall Is	TF	5	6	5	7	9	9	0.0	0.0	0.0	25.2	1.8	0.4	12.0
Micronesia (Fed.St.of)	TF	..	..	21	18	19	19		0.0	0.0	6.0	-1.6		-2.0
N.Mariana Is	TF	426	669	517	452	525	498	0.8	0.5	0.3	16.2	-5.1	2.0	-0.7
New Caledonia	TF	87	86	110	102	100	101	0.2	0.1	0.1	-2.4	1.1	2.4	-1.7
New Zealand	VF	976	1,409	1,787	2,104	2,334	2,366	1.7	1.6	1.5	10.9	1.3	6.2	5.8
Niue	TF	1	2	2	3	3	3	0.0	0.0	0.0	-5.8	9.5	6.6	8.0
Palau	TF	33	53	58	68	95	86	0.1	0.1	0.1	38.9	-9.2	5.8	8.2
Papua New Guinea	TF	41	42	58	56	59	69	0.1	0.1	0.0	4.9	17.3	3.5	3.6
Samoa	TF	48	68	88	92	98	102	0.1	0.1	0.1	6.1	3.7	6.2	3.0
Solomon Is	TF	9	11	5	7	..	9	0.0	0.0	0.0			-5.5	12.6
Tonga	TF	21	29	35	40	41	42	0.0	0.0	0.0	2.7	1.6	5.2	3.6
Tuvalu	TF	1	1	1	1	1	1	0.0	0.0	0.0	-6.3	-15.9	1.0	-0.3
Vanuatu	TF	35	44	58	50	61	62	0.1	0.1	0.0	21.9	1.0	5.2	1.4
South Asia		**3,150**	**4,233**	**6,086**	**6,426**	**7,613**	**7,977**	**5.6**	**5.5**	**5.1**	**18.5**	**4.8**	**6.8**	**5.6**
Bangladesh	TF	115	156	199	245	271	208	0.2	0.2	0.1	10.9	-23.4	5.6	0.9
Bhutan	TF	2	5	8	6	9	14	0.0	0.0	0.0	47.7	47.3	14.3	12.4
India	TF	1,707	2,124	2,649	2,726	3,457	3,919	3.0	2.4	2.5	26.8	13.3	4.5	8.1
Iran	TF	154	489	1,342	1,546	1,659	..	0.3	1.2		7.3		24.2	
Maldives	TF	195	315	467	564	617	395	0.3	0.4	0.3	9.4	-35.9	9.1	-3.3
Nepal	TF	255	363	464	338	385	375	0.5	0.4	0.2	13.9	-2.6	6.2	-4.1
Pakistan	TF	424	378	557	501	648	798	0.8	0.5	0.5	29.4	23.2	2.8	7.5
Sri Lanka	TF	298	403	400	501	566	549	0.5	0.4	0.4	13.1	-3.0	3.0	6.5

Source: World Tourism Organization (UNWTO) ©

(Data as collected by UNWTO for TMT 2006 Edition)

World Tourism Organization ©

International Tourist Arrivals by Country of Destination

	Series	International Tourist Arrivals (1000)						Market share in the region (%)			Change (%)		Average annual growth (%)	
		1990	1995	2000	2003	2004	2005*	1990	2000	2005*	04/03	05*/04	90-00	00-05*
Europe		*264,657*	*313,198*	*393,615*	*404,862*	*421,044*	*437,360*	*100*	*100*	*100*	*4.0*	*3.9*	*4.0*	*2.1*
Northern Europe		**30,634**	**38,259**	**43,770**	**43,886**	**47,564**	**50,902**	**11.6**	**11.1**	**11.6**	**8.4**	**7.0**	**3.6**	**3.1**
Denmark	TCE	..	..	3,535	3,474	3,663	4,562		0.9	1.0	5.4	24.5		5.2
Finland	TF	..	1,779	2,714	2,756	2,840	3,140		0.7	0.7	3.0	10.6		3.0
Iceland	TCE	142	190	634	771	836	871	0.1	0.2	0.2	8.4	4.2	16.1	6.6
Ireland	TF	3,666	4,818	6,646	6,764	6,953	7,334	1.4	1.7	1.7	2.8	5.5	6.1	2.0
Norway	TF	1,955	2,880	3,104	3,269	3,628	3,824	0.7	0.8	0.9	11.0	5.4	4.7	4.3
Sweden	TCE	..	2,309	2,746	2,952	3,003	3,133		0.7	0.7	1.7	4.3		2.7
United Kingdom	TF	17,023	21,719	23,211	22,787	25,677	28,038	6.4	5.9	6.4	12.7	9.2	3.1	3.9
Western Europe		**108,626**	**112,184**	**139,658**	**136,076**	**139,043**	**142,598**	**41.0**	**35.5**	**32.6**	**2.2**	**2.6**	**2.5**	**0.4**
Austria	TCE	19,011	17,173	17,982	19,078	19,373	19,952	7.2	4.6	4.6	1.5	3.0	-0.6	2.1
Belgium	TCE	..	5,560	6,457	6,690	6,710	6,747		1.6	1.5	0.3	0.6		0.9
France	TF	52,497	60,033	77,190	75,048	75,121	75,910	19.8	19.6	17.4	0.1	1.1	3.9	-0.3
Germany	TCE	17,045	14,838	18,992	18,399	20,137	21,500	6.4	4.8	4.9	9.4	6.8	1.1	2.5
Liechtenstein	THS	78	59	62	49	49	50	0.0	0.0	0.0	-1.0	2.6	-2.3	-4.2
Luxembourg	TCE	820	768	852	867	878	913	0.3	0.2	0.2	1.2	4.0	0.4	1.4
Monaco	THS	245	233	300	235	250	286	0.1	0.1	0.1	6.6	14.2	2.0	-1.0
Netherlands	TCE	5,795	6,574	10,003	9,181	9,646	10,012	2.2	2.5	2.3	5.1	3.8	5.6	0.0
Switzerland	TH	7,963	6,946	7,821	6,530	..	7,229	3.0	2.0				-0.2	-1.6
Central/Eastern Europe		**31,490**	**60,035**	**69,431**	**78,134**	**85,927**	**87,050**	**11.9**	**17.6**	**19.9**	**10.0**	**1.3**	**8.2**	**4.6**
Armenia	TCE	..	12	45	206	263	319		0.0	0.1	27.6	21.1		47.9
Azerbaijan	TF	..	93	681	1,014	1,349	1,177		0.2	0.3	33.0	-12.7		11.6
Belarus	TF	..	161	60	64	67	91		0.0	0.0	4.8	34.9		8.6
Bulgaria	TF	..	3,466	2,785	4,048	4,630	4,837		0.7	1.1	14.4	4.5		11.7
Czech Rep	TCE	..	3,381	4,773	5,076	6,061	6,336		1.2	1.4	19.4	4.5		5.8
Estonia	TF	..	530	1,220	1,462	1,750	1,917		0.3	0.4	19.7	9.5		9.5
Former U.S.S.R.	TF	2,286	..	..	..	..	..	0.9						
Georgia	TF	..	85	387	313	368	560		0.1	0.1	17.5	52.1		7.7
Hungary	TF	..	..	..	..	12,212	10,048			2.3		-17.7		
Kazakhstan	TF	..	..	1,471	2,410	3,073	3,143		0.4	0.7	27.5	2.3		16.4
Kyrgyzstan	TF	..	36	59	342	398	315		0.0	0.1	16.4	-20.8		39.8
Latvia	TF	..	539	509	971	1,080	1,116		0.1	0.3	11.2	3.4		17.0
Lithuania	TF	..	650	1,083	1,491	1,800	2,000		0.3	0.5	20.7	11.1		13.1
Poland	TF	..	19,215	17,400	13,720	14,290	15,200		4.4	3.5	4.2	6.4		-2.7
Rep Moldova	TF	..	32	18	21	24	23		0.0	0.0	14.3	-4.2		5.0
Romania	TCE	1,432	766	867	1,105	1,359	1,430	0.5	0.2	0.3	23.0	5.2	-4.9	10.5
Russian Federation	TF	..	..	..	20,443	19,892	19,940			4.6	-2.7	0.2		
Slovakia	TCE	822	903	1,053	1,387	1,401	1,515	0.3	0.3	0.3	1.0	8.1	2.5	7.5
Tajikistan	TF	..	..	4	..	..	..		0.0					
Turkmenistan	TF	..	218	3	8	15	12		0.0	0.0	80.2	-21.5		27.8
Ukraine	TF	..	3,716	6,431	12,514	15,629	..		1.6		24.9			
Uzbekistan	TF	..	92	302	231	262	..		0.1		13.2			
Southern/Mediter. Eu.		**93,907**	**102,720**	**140,756**	**146,766**	**148,510**	**156,809**	**35.5**	**35.8**	**35.9**	**1.2**	**5.6**	**4.1**	**2.2**
Albania	THS	30	40	32	41	42	46	0.0	0.0	0.0	2.4	9.5	0.6	7.5
Andorra	TF	..	..	2,949	3,138	2,791	2,418				-11.0	-13.4		-3.9
Bosnia & Herzg	TCE	..	..	171	165	190	217		0.0	0.0	15.0	14.2		4.9
Croatia	TCE	..	1,485	5,831	7,409	7,912	8,467		1.5	1.9	6.8	7.0		7.7
Cyprus	TF	1,561	2,100	2,686	2,303	2,349	2,470	0.6	0.7	0.6	2.0	5.2	5.6	-1.7
F.Yug.Rp.Macedonia	TCE	..	147	224	158	165	197		0.1	0.0	4.8	19.3		-2.5
Greece	TF	8,873	10,130	13,096	13,969	13,313	14,276	3.4	3.3	3.3	-4.7	7.2	4.0	1.7
Israel	TF	1,063	2,215	2,417	1,063	1,506	1,903	0.4	0.6	0.4	41.6	26.4	8.6	-4.7
Italy	TF	26,679	31,052	41,181	39,604	37,071	36,513	10.1	10.5	8.3	-6.4	-1.5	4.4	-2.4
Malta	TF	872	1,116	1,216	1,118	1,156	1,171	0.3	0.3	0.3	3.4	1.3	3.4	-0.8
Portugal	TF	8,020	9,511	12,097	11,707	10,639	10,612	3.0	3.1	2.4	-9.1	-0.3	4.2	-2.6
San Marino	THS	45	28	43	41	42	50	0.0	0.0	0.0	2.4	19.0	-0.5	3.1
Serbia & Montenegro	TCE	..	228	239	481	580	725		0.1	0.2	20.5	25.0		24.8
Slovenia	TC	..	732	1,090	1,373	1,499	1,555		0.3	0.4	9.2	3.7		7.4
Spain	TF	34,085	34,920	47,898	50,854	52,430	55,916	12.9	12.2	12.8	3.1	6.6	3.5	3.1
Turkey	TF	4,799	7,083	9,586	13,341	16,826	20,273	1.8	2.4	4.6	26.1	20.5	7.2	16.2
Yugoslav SFR	TF	7,880	..	..	..	..	..	3.0						

Source: World Tourism Organization (UNWTO) ©

(Data as collected by UNWTO for TMT 2006 Edition)

International Tourist Arrivals by Country of Destination

	Series	International Tourist Arrivals (1000)						Market share in the region (%)			Change (%)		Average annual growth (%)	
		1990	1995	2000	2003	2004	2005*	1990	2000	2005*	04/03	05*/04	90-00	00-05*
Middle East		*9,630*	*13,704*	*24,451*	*29,509*	*36,220*	*38,358*	*100*	*100*	*100*	*22.7*	*5.9*	*9.8*	*9.4*
Bahrain	TF	1,376	1,396	2,420	2,955	3,514	3,914	14.3	9.9	10.2	18.9	11.4	5.8	10.1
Egypt	TF	2,411	2,871	5,116	5,746	7,795	8,244	25.0	20.9	21.5	35.7	5.8	7.8	10.0
Iraq	VF	748	61	78	..	..	..	7.8	0.3				-20.2	
Jordan	TF	572	1,075	1,580	2,353	2,853	2,987	5.9	6.5	7.8	21.2	4.7	10.7	13.6
Kuwait	THS	15	72	78	94	91	..	0.2	0.3		-3.2		17.9	
Lebanon	TF	..	450	742	1,016	1,278	1,140		3.0	3.0	25.9	-10.9		9.0
Libyan Arab Jamahiriya	TF	96	56	174	142	149	..	1.0	0.7		4.9		6.1	
Oman	THS/TF	149	279	571	1,039	1,195	..	1.5	2.3		15.0		14.4	
Palestine	THS	..	..	310	37	56	88		1.3	0.2	51.4	57.1		-22.3
Qatar	TF	136	309	378	557	732	913	1.4	1.5	2.4	31.5	24.6	10.8	19.3
Saudi Arabia	TF	2,209	3,325	6,585	7,332	8,599	8,037	22.9	26.9	21.0	17.3	-6.5	11.5	4.1
Syrian Arab Republic	TCE/TF	562	815	1,685	2,085	3,033	3,368	5.8	6.9	8.8	45.5	11.0	11.6	14.9
Untd Arab Emirates	THS	973	2,315	3,907	5,871	..	..	10.1	16.0				14.9	
Yemen	THS	52	61	73	155	274	336	0.5	0.3	0.9	77.0	22.8	3.5	35.7

Source: World Tourism Organization (UNWTO) ©

(Data as collected by UNWTO for TMT 2006 Edition)

| : change of series.

2. International Tourism Receipts

International Tourism Receipts, World

	International Tourism Receipts (billion)							Change current prices (%)				Change constant prices (%)			
	1990	1995	2000	2002	2003	2004	2005*	02/01	03/02	04/03	05*/04	02/01	03/02	04/03	05*/04
Local currencies								1.8	1.0	12.9	6.3	-0.5	-1.4	9.8	3.1
US$	263.9	404.7	474.1	480.1	527.2	629.0	675.7	3.9	9.8	19.3	7.4	2.2	7.3	16.2	3.9
Euro	207.2	309.4	513.3	507.7	466.0	505.7	543.1	-1.6	-8.2	8.5	7.4	-3.8	-10.1	6.3	5.1

Source: World Tourism Organization (UNWTO) ©   (Data as collected in UNWTO database November 2006)

International Tourism Receipts by (Sub)region

	Change Local currencies, constant prices (%)					US$ Receipts (billion)		US$ Receipts per arrival 2005*	euro Receipts (billion)		euro Receipts per arrival 2005*	Market share (%) 2005*
	01/00	02/01	03/02	04/03	05*/04	2004	2005*	2005*	2004	2005*	2005*	2005*
World	-1.9	-0.5	-1.4	9.8	3.1	629.0	675.7	845	505.7	543.1	680	100
Africa	17.1	5.3	23.9	5.9	10.4	18.9	21.6	580	15.2	17.4	465	3.2
North Africa	21.3	-5.6	-2.3	13.4	15.0	6.1	7.0	505	4.9	5.6	405	1.0
West Africa	12.5	1.3	5.4	0.0	20.8	1.4	1.9	530	1.2	1.5	425	0.3
Central Africa	27.2	-2.2	14.1	-3.0	13.9	0.3	0.3	410	0.2	0.3	330	0.0
East Africa	14.5	0.7	8.0	18.2	2.2	3.8	4.1	505	3.1	3.3	405	0.6
Southern Africa	15.0	26.9	75.0	-4.0	8.8	7.3	8.3	760	5.9	6.7	610	1.2
Americas	-10.3	-6.3	-2.1	11.6	3.8	132.0	144.5	1,085	106.1	116.2	870	21.4
North America	-12.8	-6.7	-4.7	12.9	4.2	98.2	107.1	1,190	79.0	86.1	955	15.8
Caribbean	-3.7	-2.6	5.5	5.0	1.6	19.3	20.4	1,085	15.5	16.4	875	3.0
Central America	-7.4	3.4	13.2	12.1	10.9	4.0	4.6	740	3.2	3.7	595	0.7
South America	3.6	-12.0	5.2	12.9	1.7	10.6	12.4	680	8.5	10.0	545	1.8
Asia and the Pacific	7.3	6.6	-8.7	25.1	4.0	123.9	134.5	865	99.6	108.1	695	19.9
North-East Asia	8.7	12.3	-10.7	33.4	7.9	58.6	65.4	745	47.1	52.5	600	9.7
South-East Asia	8.4	-1.0	-16.8	26.1	-0.7	32.8	33.8	685	26.4	27.2	550	5.0
Oceania	3.1	3.7	2.9	7.6	0.9	23.8	25.6	2,445	19.1	20.6	1,965	3.8
South Asia	2.0	9.0	17.8	20.1	4.3	8.6	9.6	1,210	6.9	7.7	970	1.4
Europe	-1.9	-0.9	-1.5	3.1	2.5	328.9	348.8	795	264.4	280.3	640	51.6
Northern Europe	-3.5	2.3	-1.9	6.0	7.7	49.3	53.9	1,060	39.6	43.3	850	8.0
Western Europe	-1.0	-0.5	-3.3	2.0	1.7	117.9	122.5	860	94.8	98.4	690	18.1
Central/Eastern Europe	-4.5	-4.4	-2.6	5.3	0.9	28.9	32.4	375	23.3	26.1	300	4.8
Southern/Mediter. Eu.	-1.5	-1.6	0.6	2.7	1.5	132.8	140.0	895	106.8	112.5	715	20.7
Middle East	4.8	6.0	27.5	25.3	-1.8	25.2	26.3	685	20.3	21.1	550	3.9

Source: World Tourism Organization (UNWTO) ©   (Data as collected in UNWTO database November 2006)

International Tourism Receipts, 1950-2005

	World	Africa	Americas	Asia and the Pacific	Europe	Middle East	World	Africa	Americas	Asia and the Pacific	Europe	Middle East
	International Tourism Receipts (US$, billion)						International Tourism Receipts (euro/ECU, billion)					
1950	2.1	0.1	1.1	0.04	0.9	0.03						
1960	6.9	0.2	2.5	0.2	3.9	0.1						
1965	11.6	0.3	3.4	0.5	7.2	0.3						
1970	17.9	0.5	4.8	1.2	11.0	0.4						
1975	40.7	1.3	10.2	2.5	25.9	0.9	34.1	1.1	8.6	2.1	21.7	0.7
1980	103.4	3.4	24.7	10.3	61.6	3.5	75.4	2.5	18.0	7.5	44.9	2.6
1981	105.0	3.7	27.8	12.1	57.1	4.4	75.4	2.6	19.9	8.7	41.0	3.1
1982	99.0	3.4	25.7	12.2	55.5	2.2	88.7	3.1	23.0	10.9	49.7	2.0
1983	102.2	3.5	26.3	12.8	55.2	4.4	104.3	3.6	26.9	13.0	56.3	4.5
1984	110.7	3.2	32.0	13.7	57.2	4.7	124.4	3.6	35.9	15.3	64.2	5.3
1985	117.4	3.1	33.3	14.5	62.2	4.2	148.8	3.9	42.2	18.4	78.9	5.3
1986	142.8	3.6	38.4	18.8	78.5	3.5	187.2	4.7	50.4	24.6	102.9	4.6
1987	176.0	4.6	43.1	24.8	99.0	4.5	178.8	4.7	43.7	25.2	100.5	4.6
1988	203.5	5.5	51.3	32.4	109.9	4.3	176.3	4.8	44.5	28.0	95.2	3.8
1989	260.9	5.7	60.2	36.1	153.8	5.2	220.7	4.8	51.0	30.5	130.0	4.4
1990	263.9	6.4	69.2	41.1	142.9	4.3	239.5	5.8	62.8	37.3	129.7	3.9
1991	277.5	6.0	76.3	42.9	147.8	4.5	217.9	4.7	59.9	33.7	116.1	3.5
1992	320.4	6.8	83.7	51.0	172.4	6.6	258.6	5.5	67.5	41.1	139.1	5.3
1993	327.0	6.9	89.1	57.0	167.1	6.9	251.9	5.3	68.7	43.9	128.8	5.3
1994	356.2	7.6	92.4	67.3	180.9	8.1	304.2	6.5	78.9	57.4	154.5	6.9
1995	404.7	8.5	98.4	75.9	212.1	9.7	340.2	7.1	82.8	63.8	178.3	8.2
1996	438.3	9.7	108.2	84.8	224.6	11.0	335.1	7.4	82.8	64.9	171.7	8.4
1997	441.8	9.5	114.4	82.2	223.5	12.1	347.9	7.5	90.1	64.7	176.0	9.6
1998	444.1	10.2	115.2	72.1	234.6	12.0	391.6	9.0	101.6	63.6	206.9	10.5
1999	457.3	10.8	119.9	79.0	233.6	14.0	407.9	9.7	106.9	70.4	208.4	12.5
2000	474.1	10.4	130.8	85.2	232.4	15.2	444.9	9.8	122.7	80.0	218.1	14.3
2001	462.2	11.5	119.8	88.0	227.4	15.6	500.4	12.4	129.7	95.3	246.2	16.9
2002	480.1	11.9	113.4	96.3	242.2	16.2	536.0	13.3	126.7	107.5	270.4	18.1
2003	527.2	16.0	114.1	93.5	283.8	19.7	557.5	17.0	120.7	98.9	300.1	20.9
2004	629.0	18.9	132.0	123.9	328.9	25.2	556.0	16.7	116.7	109.5	290.7	22.3
2005	675.7	21.6	144.5	134.5	348.8	26.3	543.2	17.4	116.2	108.1	280.4	21.1

Source: World Tourism Organization (UNWTO) ©　　　　　　　　　　　(Data as collected by UNWTO for TMT 2006 Edition)

[1] Receipts data are in current US$ and euro (based on the average annual exchange rate for euro or ECU to US$) and can be strongly influenced by exchange rate fluctuations.

See for tables in euro values pages Annex - 16 to Annex - 20

International Tourism Receipts by Country of Destination

	International Tourism Receipts (US$, million)						Market share in the region (%)			Change (%)		Receipts per arrival[1]	Receipts per capita[1]
	1990	1995	2000	2003	2004	2005*	1990	2000	2005*	04/03	05*/04		US$
Africa	*6,402*	*8,504*	*10,404*	*16,032*	*18,934*	*21,642*	*100*	*100*	*100*	*18.1*	*14.3*	*580*	*27*
North Africa	**2,333**	**2,867**	**3,822**	**4,938**	**6,093**	**7,018**	**36.4**	**36.7**	**32.4**	**23.4**	**15.2**	**505**	**61**
Algeria	105	33	96	112	179	184	1.6	0.9	0.9	59.4	3.1	130	6
Morocco	1,259	1,296	2,039	3,225	3,924	4,621	19.7	19.6	21.4	21.6	17.8	790	141
Sudan	21	8	5	18	21	89	0.3	0.0	0.4	16.7	324.4	365	2
Tunisia	948	1,530	1,682	1,582	1,970	2,124	14.8	16.2	9.8	24.5	7.8	335	211
West Africa	**605**	**541**	**944**	**1,329**	**1,442**	**1,891**	**9.5**	**9.1**	**8.7**	**8.5**	**31.1**	**530**	**7**
Benin	55	85	77	106	119	..	0.9	0.7		12.3		685	16
Burkina Faso	11	..	19	29	45	..	0.2	0.2		55.3		205	3
Cape Verde	6	10	41	87	99	127	0.1	0.4	0.6	13.9	28.5	645	305
Côte d'Ivoire	51	89	49	69	82	83	0.8	0.5	0.4	18.8	1.2	385	5
Gambia	26	28	48	51	58	62	0.4	0.5	0.3	12.5	8.2	560	39
Ghana	81	11	335	414	466	796	1.3	3.2	3.7	12.6	70.8	1,855	36
Guinea	30	1	12	31	30	..	0.5	0.1		-3.2		670	3
Guinea-Bissau	..	..	..	2	1	..				-50.0			1
Mali	47	25	40	128	140	148	0.7	0.4	0.7	9.4	5.7	1,035	13
Mauritania	9	11	..	..	..	..	0.1						
Niger	17	7	23	28	31	34	0.3	0.2	0.2	10.7	9.7	535	3
Nigeria	25	17	101	49	21	18	0.4	1.0	0.1	-57.6	-14.2	20	0
Senegal	167	168	144	209	212	..	2.6	1.4		1.4		320	19
Sierra Leone	19	57	11	60	58	64	0.3	0.1	0.3	-3.3	10.3	1,600	11
Togo	58	13	8	15	19	..	0.9	0.1		26.7		230	4
Central Africa	**98**	**133**	**143**	**261**	**274**	**323**	**1.5**	**1.4**	**1.5**	**5.0**	**18.0**	**410**	**3**
Angola	13	10	18	49	66	88	0.2	0.2	0.4	34.3	34.0	420	7
Cameroon	53	36	57	114	..	..	0.8	0.5					7
Cent.Afr.Rep.	3	4	5	4	4	..	0.0	0.0		0.0		490	1
Chad	8	43	14	..	..	..	0.1	0.1					
Congo	8	14	12	29	22	34	0.1	0.1	0.2	-24.1	54.5		9
Dem.R.Congo	7	..	..	1	1	..	0.1			2.3		30	0
Equatorial Guinea	1	1	5	..	..	..	0.0	0.0					
Gabon	3	18	20	15	10	..	0.0	0.2		-33.3		70	7
Sao Tome Prn	2	..	10	11	13	14	0.0	0.1	0.1	20.8	6.3	1,295	73
East Africa	**1,285**	**2,323**	**2,377**	**3,065**	**3,802**	**4,074**	**20.1**	**22.8**	**18.8**	**24.0**	**7.2**	**505**	**15**
Burundi	4	1	1	1	1	2	0.1	0.0	0.0	71.4	25.0	10	0
Comoros	2	22	15	11	13	14	0.0	0.1	0.1	16.8	12.8	720	21
Djibouti	..	4	..	7	7	7			0.0	-1.8	4.3	235	15
Eritrea	..	58	36	74	73	66		0.3	0.3	-1.4	-9.6	790	14
Ethiopia	25	16	57	114	174	168	0.4	0.5	0.8	52.6	-3.3	740	2
Kenya	443	486	283	347	486	579	6.9	2.7	2.7	39.8	19.2	375	17
Madagascar	40	58	121	44	56	62	0.6	1.2	0.3	27.3	10.7	225	3
Malawi	16	17	25	23	24	24	0.2	0.2	0.1	2.9	-0.1	55	2
Mauritius	244	430	542	696	853	871	3.8	5.2	4.0	22.5	2.2	1,145	708
Mozambique	..	..	74	98	95	130		0.7	0.6	-2.4	36.0	225	7
Reunion	..	283	296	413	448	442		2.8	2.0	8.5	-1.3	1,080	569
Rwanda	10	2	4	26	44	49	0.2	0.0	0.2	69.1	11.4		6
Seychelles	126	129	139	171	172	192	2.0	1.3	0.9	0.3	11.9	1,495	2,366
Tanzania	65	502	377	647	746	824	1.0	3.6	3.8	15.4	10.4	1,395	22
Uganda	10	78	165	184	256	381	0.2	1.6	1.8	39.1	48.8	815	14
Zambia	41	47	111	149	161	164	0.6	1.1	0.8	8.1	1.9	245	15
Zimbabwe	60	145	125	61	194	99	0.9	1.2	0.5	217.5	-48.9	65	8
Southern Africa	**2,081**	**2,640**	**3,118**	**6,439**	**7,323**	**8,336**	**32.5**	**30.0**	**38.5**	**13.7**	**13.8**	**760**	**163**
Botswana	117	162	222	457	549	562	1.8	2.1	2.6	20.2	2.3	335	343
Lesotho	17	27	24	28	34	30	0.3	0.2	0.1	21.4	-11.8	100	15
Namibia	85	278	160	330	403	348	1.3	1.5	1.6	22.1	-13.8	445	171
South Africa	1,832	2,125	2,675	5,523	6,282	7,327	28.6	25.7	33.9	13.7	16.6	995	165
Swaziland	30	48	37	101	54	69	0.5	0.4	0.3	-46.5	27.8	80	61

International Tourism Receipts by Country of Destination

	International Tourism Receipts (US$, million)						Market share in the region (%)			Change (%)		Receipts per arrival[1]	Receipts per capita[1]
	1990	1995	2000	2003	2004	2005*	1990	2000	2005*	04/03	05*/04		US$
Americas	*69,191*	*98,438*	*130,800*	*114,116*	*132,023*	*144,523*	*100*	*100*	*100*	*15.7*	*9.5*	*1,085*	*164*
North America	**54,872**	**77,491**	**101,472**	**84,256**	**98,213**	**107,067**	**79.3**	**77.6**	**74.1**	**16.6**	**9.0**	**1,190**	**246**
Canada	6,339	7,917	10,778	10,546	12,871	13,584	9.2	8.2	9.4	22.0	5.5	725	414
Mexico	5,526	6,179	8,294	9,362	10,796	11,803	8.0	6.3	8.2	15.3	9.3	540	111
United States	43,007	63,395	82,400	64,348	74,547	81,680	62.2	63.0	56.5	15.8	9.6	1,660	276
Caribbean	**8,639**	**12,236**	**17,154**	**17,842**	**19,292**	**20,415**	**12.5**	**13.1**	**14.1**	**8.1**	**5.8**	**1,085**	**526**
Anguilla	35	50	56	60	69	86	0.1	0.0	0.1	15.3	24.7	1,390	6,512
Antigua,Barb	298	247	291	300	338	327	0.4	0.2	0.2	12.7	-3.3	1,330	4,758
Aruba	350	521	814	859	1,056	1,091	0.5	0.6	0.8	22.9	3.4	1,490	15,245
Bahamas	1,333	1,346	1,734	1,757	1,884	2,072	1.9	1.3	1.4	7.2	9.9	1,290	6,865
Barbados	494	622	723	758	776	776	0.7	0.6	0.5	2.3	0.1	1,420	2,784
Bermuda	490	488	431	348	426	430	0.7	0.3	0.3	22.4	0.9	1,595	6,578
Bonaire	18	37	59	84	84	85	0.0	0.0	0.1	-0.7	1.7	1,360	
Br.Virgin Is	132	211	345	342	393	437	0.2	0.3	0.3	14.9	11.2	1,295	19,302
Cayman Islands	236	394	559	518	519	353	0.3	0.4	0.2	0.2	-32.0	2,105	7,974
Cuba	243	963	1,737	1,846	1,915	1,920	0.4	1.3	1.3	3.7	0.3	850	169
Curaçao	120	175	189	223	222	239	0.2	0.1	0.2	-0.4	7.5	1,075	
Dominica	25	42	48	54	61	56	0.0	0.0	0.0	12.3	-7.2	710	815
Dominican Rp	818	1,571	2,860	3,128	3,152	3,518	1.2	2.2	2.4	0.8	11.6	955	389
Grenada	38	76	93	104	83	71	0.1	0.1	0.0	-19.5	-14.4	725	798
Guadeloupe	197	458	418	..	..	246	0.3	0.3	0.2			660	548
Haiti	46	90	128	93	87	110	0.1	0.1	0.1	-6.5	26.4	980	14
Jamaica	740	1,069	1,333	1,355	1,438	1,545	1.1	1.0	1.1	6.1	7.4	1,045	565
Martinique	240	384	302	247	291	280	0.3	0.2	0.2	17.8	-3.8	580	647
Montserrat	7	17	9	7	9	9	0.0	0.0	0.0	17.1	4.7	925	962
Puerto Rico	1,366	1,828	2,388	2,677	3,024	3,239	2.0	1.8	2.2	13.0	7.1	880	828
Saint Lucia	154	230	281	282	326	356	0.2	0.2	0.2	15.5	9.3	1,120	2,140
St.Kitts-Nev	58	63	58	75	103	107	0.1	0.0	0.1	37.3	4.1	845	2,753
St.Maarten	316	349	511	538	613	619	0.5	0.4	0.4	13.9	1.1	1,325	
St.Vincent,Grenadines	56	53	82	91	96	105	0.1	0.1	0.1	5.5	9.4	1,100	893
Trinidad Tbg	95	77	213	249	341	453	0.1	0.2	0.3	36.9	32.8	980	421
Turks,Caicos	37	53	285	..	..	..	0.1	0.2					
US.Virgin Is	697	822	1,206	1,257	1,356	1,491	1.0	0.9	1.0	7.9	10.0	2,560	13,715
Central America	**735**	**1,523**	**2,958**	**3,421**	**3,965**	**4,645**	**1.1**	**2.3**	**3.2**	**15.9**	**17.2**	**740**	**120**
Belize	44	78	111	117	133	214	0.1	0.1	0.1	13.5	60.7	905	760
Costa Rica	275	681	1,302	1,199	1,359	1,570	0.4	1.0	1.1	13.3	15.6	935	391
El Salvador	18	85	217	383	441	543	0.0	0.2	0.4	15.1	23.2	560	81
Guatemala	185	213	482	621	776	869	0.3	0.4	0.6	25.0	12.0	660	72
Honduras	29	107	260	356	414	464	0.0	0.2	0.3	16.3	12.1	690	65
Nicaragua	12	50	129	160	192	206	0.0	0.1	0.1	19.9	7.4	290	38
Panama	172	309	458	585	651	780	0.2	0.4	0.5	11.3	19.8	1,110	248
South America	**4,946**	**7,189**	**9,216**	**8,597**	**10,553**	**12,397**	**7.1**	**7.0**	**8.6**	**22.8**	**17.5**	**680**	**33**
Argentina	1,131	2,222	2,904	2,006	2,235	2,729	1.6	2.2	1.9	11.4	22.1	715	69
Bolivia	55	55	68	167	192	239	0.1	0.1	0.2	15.1	24.5	475	27
Brazil	1,492	972	1,810	2,479	3,222	3,861	2.2	1.4	2.7	30.0	19.8	720	21
Chile	540	911	819	883	1,095	1,109	0.8	0.6	0.8	24.0	1.3	545	69
Colombia	406	657	1,030	893	1,058	1,218	0.6	0.8	0.8	18.5	15.1	1,305	28
Ecuador	188	255	402	406	462	486	0.3	0.3	0.3	13.8	5.0	565	36
French Guiana	..	..	..	..	..	45			0.0			475	230
Guyana	27	33	75	26	27	35	0.0	0.1	0.0	3.8	29.6	300	46
Paraguay	128	137	73	64	70	78	0.2	0.1	0.1	9.5	11.5	230	12
Peru	217	428	837	963	1,142	1,308	0.3	0.6	0.9	18.6	14.6	880	47
Suriname	1	21	16	4	17	45	0.0	0.0	0.0	325.0	164.7	280	103
Uruguay	238	611	713	345	494	594	0.3	0.5	0.4	43.3	20.3	330	174
Venezuela	496	849	423	331	502	650	0.7	0.3	0.4	51.7	29.5	920	26

Source: World Tourism Organization (UNWTO) ©

(Data as collected by UNWTO for TMT 2006 Edition)

World Tourism Organization ©

International Tourism Receipts by Country of Destination

	International Tourism Receipts (US$, million)						Market share in the region (%)			Change (%)		Receipts per arrival[1]	Receipts per capita[1]
	1990	1995	2000	2003	2004	2005*	1990	2000	2005*	04/03	05*/04		US$
Asia and the Pacific	*41,138*	*75,928*	*85,224*	*93,536*	*123,900*	*134,475*	*100*	*100*	*100*	*32.5*	*8.5*	*865*	*37*
North-East Asia	**17,284**	**31,339**	**39,428**	**42,336**	**58,627**	**65,368**	**42.0**	**46.3**	**48.6**	**38.5**	**11.5**	**745**	**42**
China	2,218	8,730	16,231	17,406	25,739	29,296	5.4	19.0	21.8	47.9	13.8	625	22
Hong Kong (China)	4,682	7,760	5,907	7,137	8,999	10,292	11.4	6.9	7.7	26.1	14.4	695	1,492
Japan	3,578	3,224	3,373	8,817	11,269	6,630	8.7	4.0	4.9	27.8	-41.2	985	52
Korea, D P Rp	29	..	..	..	..	..	0.1						
Korea, Republic of	3,559	5,150	6,834	5,358	6,069	5,806	8.7	8.0	4.3	13.3	-4.3	965	119
Macao (China)	1,473	3,102	3,208	5,155	7,479	7,980	3.6	3.8	5.9	45.1	6.7	885	17,765
Mongolia	5	21	36	143	185	177	0.0	0.0	0.1	29.4	-4.4	525	63
Taiwan (pr. of China)	1,740	3,286	3,738	2,977	4,054	4,977	4.2	4.4	3.7	36.2	22.8	1,475	217
South-East Asia	**14,479**	**27,354**	**26,710**	**25,084**	**32,843**	**33,847**	**35.2**	**31.3**	**25.2**	**30.9**	**3.1**	**685**	**59**
Cambodia	..	53	304	389	604	840		0.4	0.6	55.1	39.2	590	62
Indonesia	2,105	5,229	4,975	4,037	4,798	4,521	5.1	5.8	3.4	18.8	-5.8	905	19
Lao P.D.R.	3	51	114	87	119	147	0.0	0.1	0.1	36.7	23.4	220	24
Malaysia	1,667	3,969	5,011	5,898	8,198	8,543	4.1	5.9	6.4	39.0	4.2	520	357
Myanmar	9	151	162	56	84	..	0.0	0.2		50.0		345	2
Philippines	1,306	1,136	2,156	1,544	2,017	2,265	3.2	2.5	1.7	30.6	12.3	865	26
Singapore	4,937	7,611	5,142	3,781	5,221	5,908	12.0	6.0	4.4	38.1	13.2	835	1,335
Thailand	4,326	8,039	7,468	7,828	10,034	9,591	10.5	8.8	7.1	28.2	-4.4	830	149
Vietnam	85	..	..	1,400	1,700	1,880	0.2			21.4	10.6	540	23
Oceania	**7,321**	**13,831**	**14,289**	**19,386**	**23,802**	**25,622**	**17.8**	**16.8**	**19.1**	**22.8**	**7.6**	**2,445**	**783**
American Samoa	10	..	..	..	..	..	0.0						
Australia	4,246	8,125	9,274	12,349	15,191	16,866	10.3	10.9	12.5	23.0	11.0	3,360	840
Cook Is	16	28	36	69	72	92	0.0	0.0	0.1	4.3	27.8	1,040	4,301
Fiji	202	291	182	340	420	434	0.5	0.2	0.3	23.3	3.3	790	485
French Polynesia	171	326	..	480	523	522	0.4		0.4	8.9	-0.3	2,505	1,928
Guam	936	..	..	..	..	..	2.3						
Kiribati	1	2	3	..	..	..	0.0	0.0					
Marshall Is	..	3	4	..	..	..		0.0					
Micronesia (Fed.St.of)	..	..	15	17	17	17		0.0	0.0	-1.2	3.6	900	158
N.Mariana Is	455	655	..	..	..	..	1.1						
New Caledonia	94	108	111	196	241	253	0.2	0.1	0.2	22.7	5.1	2,515	1,170
New Zealand	1,030	2,318	2,267	3,981	4,790	4,865	2.5	2.7	3.6	20.3	1.6	2,055	1,206
Niue	..	2	..	..	..	1			0.0			430	
Palau	..	..	53	76	97	97		0.1	0.1	28.2	0.3	1,130	4,789
Papua New Guinea	41	25	21	16	18	4	0.1	0.0	0.0	16 1	-80.3	50	1
Samoa	20	35	41	54	70	77	0.0	0.0	0.1	29.6	10.0	755	434
Solomon Is	7	16	4	2	4	2	0.0	0.0	0.0	127.4	-56.2	165	3
Tonga	9	10	7	14	15	11	0.0	0.0	0.0	7.1	-26.7	265	98
Vanuatu	39	45	56	52	64	74	0.1	0.1	0.1	23.1	15.6	1,190	360
South Asia	**2,055**	**3,404**	**4,797**	**6,729**	**8,628**	**9,638**	**5.0**	**5.6**	**7.2**	**28.2**	**11.7**	**1,210**	**6**
Bangladesh	11	25	50	57	67	70	0.0	0.1	0.1	17.2	4.8	335	0
Bhutan	2	5	10	8	12	19	0.0	0.0	0.0	50.0	48.6	1,360	8
India	1,539	2,581	3,460	4,463	6,170	7,524	3.7	4.1	5.6	38.2	21.9	1,920	7
Iran	61	67	467	1,033	1,044	992	0.1	0.5	0.7	1.1	-5.0	630	15
Maldives	89	211	321	402	408	287	0.2	0.4	0.2	1.6	-29.7	725	821
Nepal	64	177	158	200	230	132	0.2	0.2	0.1	15.0	-42.7	350	5
Pakistan	156	110	81	122	179	181	0.4	0.1	0.1	46.7	1.1	225	1
Sri Lanka	132	226	248	441	513	429	0.3	0.3	0.3	16.3	-16.4	780	21

Source: World Tourism Organization (UNWTO) © (Data as collected by UNWTO for TMT 2006 Edition)

International Tourism Receipts by Country of Destination

	International Tourism Receipts (US$, million)						Market share in the region (%)			Change (%)		Receipts per arrival[1]	Receipts per capita[1]
	1990	1995	2000	2003	2004	2005*	1990	2000	2005*	04/03	05*/04		US$
Europe	*142,885*	*212,105*	*232,446*	*283,753*	*328,888*	*348,765*	*100*	*100*	*100*	*15.9*	*6.0*	*795*	*396*
Northern Europe	**26,267**	**33,916**	**35,938**	**41,399**	**49,275**	**53,891**	**18.4**	**15.5**	**15.5**	**19.0**	**9.4**	**1,060**	**605**
Denmark	3,645	3,673	3,694	5,265	5,670	4,956	2.6	1.6	1.4	7.7	-12.6	1,085	912
Finland	1,167	1,641	1,411	1,873	2,076	2,186	0.8	0.6	0.6	10.8	5.3	695	419
Iceland	151	186	229	320	372	409	0.1	0.1	0.1	16.2	10.1	470	1,378
Ireland	1,453	2,208	2,633	3,856	4,398	4,744	1.0	1.1	1.4	14.1	7.9	645	1,181
Norway	1,570	2,238	2,050	2,659	3,136	3,495	1.1	0.9	1.0	18.0	11.5	915	761
Sweden	2,906	3,471	4,064	5,297	6,196	7,427	2.0	1.7	2.1	17.0	19.9	2,370	825
United Kingdom	15,375	20,500	21,857	22,656	28,221	30,675	10.8	9.4	8.8	24.6	8.7	1,095	508
Western Europe	**63,114**	**80,776**	**82,774**	**103,183**	**117,870**	**122,459**	**44.2**	**35.6**	**35.1**	**14.2**	**3.9**	**860**	**658**
Austria	13,417	12,927	9,931	13,954	15,582	16,012	9.4	4.3	4.6	11.7	2.8	800	1,956
Belgium	..	4,548	6,592	8,191	9,233	9,868		2.8	2.8	12.7	6.9	1,465	952
Belgium/Luxembourg	3,702	..	..	..	..	..							
France	20,184	27,541	30,757	36,593	40,841	42,276	14.1	13.2	12.1	11.6	3.5	555	697
Germany	14,245	18,001	18,693	23,106	27,668	29,173	10.0	8.0	8.4	19.7	5.4	1,355	354
Luxembourg	..	1,721	1,806	2,994	3,657	3,616		0.8	1.0	22.2	-1.1	3,960	7,716
Netherlands	4,155	6,578	7,217	9,159	10,333	10,475	2.9	3.1	3.0	12.8	1.4	1,045	638
Switzerland	7,411	9,459	7,777	9,186	10,556	11,040	5.2	3.3	3.2	14.9	4.6	1,525	1,474
Central/Eastern Europe	**2,097**	**19,633**	**20,350**	**24,047**	**28,930**	**32,445**	**1.5**	**8.8**	**9.3**	**20.3**	**12.2**	**375**	**85**
Armenia	..	1	38	73	85	141		0.0	0.0	16.4	65.9	445	47
Azerbaijan	228	70	63	58	65	77	0.2	0.0	0.0	12.1	18.5	65	10
Belarus	..	23	93	267	270	253		0.0	0.1	1.1	-6.3	2,785	25
Bulgaria	320	473	1,076	1,693	2,221	2,430	0.2	0.5	0.7	31.2	9.4	500	326
Czech Rep	419	2,880	2,973	3,556	4,172	4,668	0.3	1.3	14.4	17.3	11.9	735	456
Estonia	..	357	508	669	891	951		0.2	0.3	33.2	6.8	495	714
Georgia	..	..	97	147	177	241		0.0	0.1	20.1	36.7	430	52
Hungary	824	2,953	3,757	4,046	4,061	4,271	0.6	1.6	1.2	0.4	5.2	425	427
Kazakhstan	..	122	356	564	718	701		0.2	0.2	27.3	-2.4	225	46
Kyrgyzstan	..	5	15	48	76	73		0.0	0.0	58.3	-3.9	230	14
Latvia	..	20	131	222	267	341		0.1	0.1	20.1	27.8	305	149
Lithuania	..	77	391	638	776	921		0.2	0.3	21.7	18.7	460	256
Poland	358	6,614	5,677	4,069	5,833	6,274	0.3	2.4	1.8	43.4	7.6	415	163
Rep Moldova	..	57	39	58	96	107		0.0	0.0	65.5	11.1	4,635	24
Romania	106	590	359	448	505	1,060	0.1	0.2	0.3	12.7	109.9	740	47
Russian Federation	..	4,312	3,429	4,502	5,225	5,564		1.5	1.6	16.1	6.5	280	39
Slovakia	70	623	433	865	901	1,210	0.0	0.2	0.3	4.2	34.3	800	223
Tajikistan	..	..	..	2	1	2			0.0	-50.0	100.0		0
Ukraine	..	191	394	935	2,560	3,125		0.2	0.9		22.1	165	66
Uzbekistan	..	..	27	24	28	..		0.0		16.7		105	1
Southern/Mediter. Eu.	**51,408**	**77,781**	**93,385**	**115,124**	**132,812**	**139,970**	**36.0**	**40.2**	**40.1**	**15.4**	**5.4**	**895**	**624**
Albania	4	65	389	522	727	860	0.0	0.2	0.2	39.3	18.3	18,705	241
Bosnia & Herzg	..	..	233	376	483	514		0.1	0.1	28.5	6.5	2,365	116
Croatia	..	1,349	2,782	6,304	6,848	7,463		1.2	2.1	8.6	9.0	880	1,660
Cyprus	1,258	1,798	1,941	2,091	2,252	2,331	0.9	0.8	0.7	7.7	3.5	945	2,988
F.Yug.Rp.Macedonia	..	19	38	57	72	84		0.0	0.0	26.6	16.9	425	41
Greece	2,587	4,135	9,219	10,741	12,872	13,731	1.8	4.0	3.9	19.8	6.7	960	1,287
Israel	1,396	2,993	4,088	2,060	2,380	2,853	1.0	1.8	0.8	15.6	19.9	1,500	455
Italy	16,458	28,731	27,493	31,247	35,656	35,398	11.5	11.8	10.1	14.1	-0.7	970	609
Malta	496	654	590	721	773	759	0.3	0.3	0.2	7.2	-1.9	650	1,903
Portugal	3,555	4,831	5,243	6,616	7,707	7,712	2.5	2.3	2.2	16.5	0.1	725	730
Serbia & Montenegro	..	42	30	201	..	..		0.0				420	19
Slovenia	..	1,082	965	1,340	1,630	1,801		0.4	0.5	21.6	10.5	1,160	895
Spain	18,484	25,252	29,968	39,645	45,248	47,970	12.9	12.9	13.8	14.1	6.0	860	1,189
Turkey	3,225	4,957	7,636	13,203	15,888	18,152	2.3	3.3	5.2	20.3	14.2	895	261
Yugoslav SFR	2,774	..	..	..	..	..	1.9						

Source: World Tourism Organization (UNWTO) ©

(Data as collected by UNWTO for TMT 2006 Edition)

World Tourism Organization ©

International Tourism Receipts by Country of Destination

	International Tourism Receipts (US$, million)						Market share in the region (%)			Change (%)		Receipts per arrival[1]	Receipts per capita[1]
	1990	1995	2000	2003	2004	2005*	1990	2000	2005*	04/03	05*/04		US$
Middle East	*4,279*	*9,744*	*15,242*	*19,740*	*25,239*	*26,254*	*100*	*100*	*100*	*27.9*	*4.0*	*685*	*133*
Bahrain	135	247	573	720	864	920	3.2	3.8	3.5	20.0	6.5	235	1,337
Egypt	1,100	2,684	4,345	4,584	6,125	6,851	25.7	28.5	26.1	33.6	11.8	830	88
Iraq	173	18	2	..	..	..	4.1	0.0					
Jordan	512	660	723	1,062	1,330	1,441	12.0	4.7	5.5	25.2	8.3	480	250
Kuwait	132	121	98	117	176	164	3.1	0.6	0.6	50.2	-6.8	1,940	70
Lebanon	..	..	..	6,374	5,411	5,432			20.7	-15.1	0.4	4,765	1,420
Libyan Arab Jamahiriya	6	2	75	205	218	250	0.1	0.5	1.0	6.3	14.7	1,465	43
Oman	69	..	221	385	414	481	1.6	1.5	1.8	7.4	16.4	345	160
Palestine	..	255	283	107	56	..		1.9		-47.7		1,000	15
Qatar	..	..	128	369	498	760		0.8	2.9	35.0	52.8	835	881
Saudi Arabia	..	..	..	3,413	6,486	5,177			19.7	90.0	-20.2	645	196
Syrian Arab Republic	320	1,258	1,082	773	1,800	2,175	7.5	7.1	8.3	132.9	20.8	645	118
Untd Arab Emirates	315	632	1,063	1,439	1,594	2,200	7.4	7.0	8.4	10.8	38.0	245	858
Yemen	20	50	73	139	213	262	0.5	0.5	1.0	53.2	23.0	780	13

Source: World Tourism Organization (UNWTO) ©

(Data as collected by UNWTO for TMT 2006 Edition)

[1] Last year with data available

| : change of series.

See for tables in US$ values pages Annex - 11 to Annex – 15

International Tourism Receipts by Country of Destination

	International Tourism Receipts (euro, million)						Market share in the region (%)			Change (%)		Receipts per arrival[1]	Receipts per capita[1]
	1990	1995	2000	2003	2004	2005*	1990	2000	2005*	04/03	05*/04		euro
Africa	*5,027*	*6,502*	*11,264*	*14,173*	*15,221*	*17,396*	*100*	*100*	*100*	*7.4*	*14.3*	*465*	*22*
North Africa	**1,832**	**2,192**	**4,138**	**4,365**	**4,899**	**5,641**	**36.4**	**36.7**	**32.4**	**12.2**	**15.2**	**405**	**49**
Algeria	82	25	104	99	144	148	1.6	0.9	0.9	44.9	3.1	100	5
Morocco	989	991	2,208	2,851	3,154	3,714	19.7	19.6	21.4	10.6	17.8	635	114
Sudan	16	6	5	16	17	72	0.3	0.0	0.4	6.1	324.3	290	2
Tunisia	744	1,170	1,821	1,399	1,584	1,707	14.8	16.2	9.8	13.2	7.8	270	169
West Africa	**475**	**414**	**1,022**	**1,175**	**1,159**	**1,520**	**9.5**	**9.1**	**8.7**	**-1.3**	**31.1**	**425**	**6**
Benin	43	65	83	94	96	..	0.9	0.7		2.1		550	13
Burkina Faso	9	..	21	26	37	..	0.2	0.2		41.2		165	3
Cape Verde	5	8	44	77	80	102	0.1	0.4	0.6	3.6	28.5	520	245
Côte d'Ivoire	40	68	53	61	66	67	0.8	0.5	0.4	8.1	1.2	340	4
Gambia	20	21	52	45	46	50	0.4	0.5	0.3	2.3	8.2	450	31
Ghana	64	8	363	366	375	640	1.3	3.2	3.7	2.4	70.8	1,495	29
Guinea	24	1	13	27	24	..	0.5	0.1		-12.0		540	3
Guinea-Bissau	..	..	..	2	1	..				-54.5			1
Mali	37	19	43	113	113	119	0.7	0.4	0.7	-0.5	5.7	835	10
Mauritania	7	8	..	..	..	..	0.1						
Niger	13	5	25	25	25	27	0.3	0.2	0.2	0.7	9.7	430	2
Nigeria	20	13	109	44	17	14	0.4	1.0	0.1	-61.4	-14.2	15	0
Senegal	131	128	156	185	170	..	2.6	1.4		-7.8		255	15
Sierra Leone	15	44	12	53	47	51	0.3	0.1	0.3	-12.1	10.3	1,285	9
Togo	46	10	9	13	15	..	0.9	0.1		15.2		185	3
Central Africa	**77**	**102**	**155**	**230**	**220**	**260**	**1.5**	**1.4**	**1.5**	**-4.5**	**18.0**	**330**	**2**
Angola	10	8	19	43	53	71	0.2	0.2	0.4	22.1	34.0	340	6
Cameroon	42	28	62	101	..	..	0.8	0.5					6
Cent.Afr.Rep.	2	3	5	4	3	..	0.0	0.0		-9.1		395	1
Chad	6	33	15	..	..	..	0.1	0.1					
Congo	6	11	13	26	18	27	0.1	0.1	0.2	-31.0	54.5		8
Dem.R.Congo	5	..	..	1	1	..	0.1			-6.9		25	0
Equatorial Guinea	1	1	5	..	..	..	0.0	0.0					
Gabon	2	14	22	13	8	..	0.0	0.2		-39.4		60	6
Sao Tome Prn	2	..	11	9	10	11	0.0	0.1	0.1	9.8	6.2	1,040	58
East Africa	**1,009**	**1,776**	**2,573**	**2,710**	**3,056**	**3,275**	**20.1**	**22.8**	**18.8**	**12.8**	**7.1**	**405**	**12**
Burundi	3	1	1	1	1	1	0.1	0.0	0.0	55.9	25.0	10	0
Comoros	2	17	16	9	10	11	0.0	0.1	0.1	6.2	12.8	580	17
Djibouti	..	3	..	6	5	6			0.0	-10.7	4.3	190	12
Eritrea	..	44	39	65	59	53		0.3	0.3	-10.3	-9.6	635	11
Ethiopia	20	12	62	101	140	135	0.4	0.5	0.8	38.8	-3.3	595	2
Kenya	348	372	306	307	390	465	6.9	2.7	2.7	27.1	19.2	305	14
Madagascar	31	44	131	39	45	50	0.6	1.2	0.3	15.7	10.7	180	3
Malawi	13	13	28	21	19	19	0.2	0.2	0.1	-6.4	-0.1	45	2
Mauritius	192	329	587	615	686	700	3.8	5.2	4.0	11.4	2.2	920	569
Mozambique	..	..	80	86	77	104		0.7	0.6	-11.2	36.0	180	5
Reunion	..	216	320	365	360	355		2.8	2.0	-1.4	-1.3	870	457
Rwanda	8	2	5	23	35	39	0.2	0.0	0.2	53.8	11.3		5
Seychelles	99	99	151	151	138	154	2.0	1.3	0.9	-8.8	11.9	1,200	1,902
Tanzania	51	384	408	572	600	662	1.0	3.6	3.8	4.9	10.4	1,120	18
Uganda	8	60	179	163	206	306	0.2	1.6	1.8	26.5	48.8	655	11
Zambia	32	36	120	132	129	132	0.6	1.1	0.8	-1.7	1.8	195	12
Zimbabwe	47	111	135	54	156	80	0.9	1.2	0.5	188.8	-48.9	50	7
Southern Africa	**1,634**	**2,019**	**3,376**	**5,692**	**5,887**	**6,700**	**32.5**	**30.0**	**38.5**	**3.4**	**13.8**	**610**	**131**
Botswana	92	124	241	404	442	452	1.8	2.1	2.6	9.3	2.3	270	275
Lesotho	13	21	26	25	27	24	0.3	0.2	0.1	10.4	-11.8	80	12
Namibia	67	213	173	292	324	279	1.3	1.5	1.6	11.1	-13.8	360	138
South Africa	1,438	1,625	2,896	4,883	5,050	5,890	28.6	25.7	33.9	3.4	16.6	800	133
Swaziland	24	37	40	89	43	55	0.5	0.4	0.3	-51.4	27.8	65	49

Source: World Tourism Organization (UNWTO) ©

(Data as collected by UNWTO for TMT 2006 Edition)

World Tourism Organization ©

International Tourism Receipts by Country of Destination

	International Tourism Receipts (euro, million)						Market share in the region (%)			Change (%)		Receipts per arrival[1]	Receipts per capita[1]
	1990	1995	2000	2003	2004	2005*	1990	2000	2005*	04/03	05*/04		euro
Americas	*54,335*	*75,258*	*141,618*	*100,880*	*106,136*	*116,167*	*100*	*100*	*100*	*5.2*	*9.5*	*870*	*131*
North America	**43,090**	**59,243**	**109,864**	**74,484**	**78,956**	**86,060**	**79.3**	**77.6**	**74.1**	**6.0**	**9.0**	**955**	**198**
Canada	4,978	6,053	11,669	9,323	10,347	10,918	9.2	8.2	9.4	11.0	5.5	580	333
Mexico	4,339	4,724	8,980	8,276	8,679	9,488	8.0	6.3	8.2	4.9	9.3	435	89
United States	33,773	48,467	89,215	56,885	59,930	65,654	62.2	63.0	56.5	5.4	9.6	1,335	222
Caribbean	**6,784**	**9,354**	**18,573**	**15,773**	**15,509**	**16,409**	**12.5**	**13.1**	**14.1**	**-1.7**	**5.8**	**875**	**423**
Anguilla	27	38	61	53	56	69	0.1	0.0	0.1	4.9	24.7	1,115	5,234
Antigua,Barb	234	189	315	265	272	263	0.4	0.2	0.2	2.5	-3.3	1,070	3,825
Aruba	275	398	881	759	849	877	0.5	0.6	0.8	11.8	3.4	1,195	12,254
Bahamas	1,047	1,029	1,878	1,554	1,515	1,665	1.9	1.3	1.4	-2.5	9.9	1,035	5,518
Barbados	388	476	783	670	623	624	0.7	0.6	0.5	-6.9	0.1	1,140	2,237
Bermuda	385	373	467	308	342	346	0.7	0.3	0.3	11.3	0.9	1,280	5,287
Bonaire	14	28	64	75	67	68	0.0	0.0	0.1	-9.7	1.7	1,095	
Br.Virgin Is	104	161	374	302	316	351	0.2	0.3	0.3	4.5	11.2	1,040	15,515
Cayman Islands	185	301	605	458	417	284	0.3	0.4	0.2	-8.9	-32.0	1,690	6,409
Cuba	191	736	1,881	1,632	1,540	1,543	0.4	1.3	1.3	-5.7	0.2	680	136
Curaçao	94	134	205	197	179	192	0.2	0.1	0.2	-9.4	7.5	865	
Dominica	20	32	52	48	49	45	0.0	0.0	0.0	2.1	-7.2	570	655
Dominican Rp	642	1,201	3,097	2,765	2,534	2,828	1.2	2.2	2.4	-8.4	11.6	765	312
Grenada	30	58	101	92	67	57	0.1	0.1	0.0	-26.8	-14.4	585	642
Guadeloupe	155	350	453	..	..	198	0.3	0.3	0.2			530	441
Haiti	36	69	139	82	70	88	0.1	0.1	0.1	-14.9	26.4	790	11
Jamaica	581	817	1,443	1,198	1,156	1,242	1.1	1.0	1.1	-3.5	7.4	840	454
Martinique	188	294	327	218	234	225	0.3	0.2	0.2	7.1	-3.8	465	520
Montserrat	5	13	10	6	7	7	0.0	0.0	0.0	6.5	4.7	745	773
Puerto Rico	1,073	1,397	2,585	2,366	2,431	2,603	2.0	1.8	2.2	2.7	7.1	705	666
Saint Lucia	121	176	304	249	262	286	0.2	0.2	0.2	5.0	9.3	900	1,720
St.Kitts-Nev	46	48	63	66	83	86	0.1	0.0	0.1	24.9	4.1	680	2,213
St.Maarten	248	267	553	476	493	498	0.5	0.4	0.4	3.6	1.0	1,065	
St.Vincent,Grenadines	44	41	89	80	77	84	0.1	0.1	0.1	-4.1	9.4	885	718
Trinidad Tbg	75	59	231	220	274	364	0.1	0.2	0.3	24.5	32.8	785	339
Turks,Caicos	29	41	309	..	..	..	0.1	0.2					
US.Virgin Is	547	628	1,306	1,111	1,090	1,198	1.0	0.9	1.0	-1.9	9.9	2,060	11,024
Central America	**577**	**1,164**	**3,203**	**3,025**	**3,187**	**3,734**	**1.1**	**2.3**	**3.2**	**5.4**	**17.1**	**595**	**96**
Belize	35	60	120	104	107	172	0.1	0.1	0.1	3.2	60.7	725	611
Costa Rica	216	521	1,410	1,060	1,092	1,262	0.4	1.0	1.1	3.0	15.5	750	314
El Salvador	14	65	235	339	354	436	0.0	0.2	0.4	4.6	23.1	450	65
Guatemala	145	163	522	549	624	698	0.3	0.4	0.6	13.6	12.0	530	58
Honduras	23	82	281	314	332	373	0.0	0.2	0.3	5.7	12.1	555	52
Nicaragua	9	38	139	142	154	166	0.0	0.1	0.1	9.0	7.4	235	30
Panama	135	236	496	517	523	627	0.2	0.4	0.5	1.2	19.8	895	200
South America	**3,884**	**5,496**	**9,978**	**7,599**	**8,484**	**9,964**	**7.1**	**7.0**	**8.6**	**11.6**	**17.5**	**545**	**27**
Argentina	888	1,699	3,144	1,773	1,797	2,193	1.6	2.2	1.9	1.3	22.1	575	55
Bolivia	43	42	74	147	154	192	0.1	0.1	0.2	4.7	24.4	380	22
Brazil	1,172	743	1,960	2,191	2,590	3,104	2.2	1.4	2.7	18.2	19.8	580	17
Chile	424	696	887	781	880	891	0.8	0.6	0.8	12.7	1.3	440	56
Colombia	319	502	1,116	790	851	979	0.6	0.8	0.8	7.7	15.1	1,050	23
Ecuador	148	195	435	359	372	390	0.3	0.3	0.3	3.5	5.0	455	29
French Guiana	..	..	..	..	..	36			0.0			380	185
Guyana	21	25	81	23	22	28	0.0	0.1	0.0	-5.6	29.6	240	37
Paraguay	101	105	79	56	56	62	0.2	0.1	0.1	-0.4	11.5	185	10
Peru	170	327	906	851	918	1,052	0.3	0.6	0.9	7.8	14.5	710	38
Suriname	1	16	17	4	14	36	0.0	0.0	0.0	286.5	164.7	225	83
Uruguay	187	467	772	305	397	478	0.3	0.5	0.4	30.3	20.3	265	140
Venezuela	389	649	458	293	404	522	0.7	0.3	0.4	37.9	29.5	740	21

Source: World Tourism Organization (UNWTO) ©

(Data as collected by UNWTO for TMT 2006 Edition)

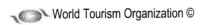

International Tourism Receipts by Country of Destination

	International Tourism Receipts (euro, million)						Market share in the region (%)			Change (%)		Receipts per arrival[1]	Receipts per capita[1]
	1990	1995	2000	2003	2004	2005*	1990	2000	2005*	04/03	05*/04		euro
Asia and the Pacific	*32,305*	*58,048*	*92,272*	*82,687*	*99,606*	*108,090*	*100*	*100*	*100*	*20.5*	*8.5*	*695*	*29*
North-East Asia	**13,573**	**23,959**	**42,688**	**37,426**	**47,132**	**52,543**	**42.0**	**46.3**	**48.6**	**25.9**	**11.5**	**600**	**34**
China	1,742	6,674	17,573	15,387	20,692	23,548	5.4	19.0	21.8	34.5	13.8	505	18
Hong Kong (China)	3,677	5,932	6,395	6,309	7,234	8,273	11.4	6.9	7.7	14.7	14.4	560	1,199
Japan	2,810	2,465	3,652	7,794	9,059	5,329	8.7	4.0	4.9	16.2	-41.2	790	42
Korea, D P Rp	23	..	..	..	..	..	0.1						
Korea, Republic of	2,795	3,937	7,400	4,737	4,879	4,667	8.7	8.0	4.3	3.0	-4.4	775	96
Macao (China)	1,157	2,372	3,474	4,557	6,013	6,414	3.6	3.8	5.9	32.0	6.7	710	14,280
Mongolia	4	16	39	126	149	142	0.0	0.0	0.1	17.6	-4.4	420	51
Taiwan (pr. of China)	1,366	2,512	4,047	2,632	3,259	4,000	4.2	4.4	3.7	23.8	22.7	1,185	175
South-East Asia	**11,370**	**20,912**	**28,919**	**22,175**	**26,403**	**27,206**	**35.2**	**31.3**	**25.2**	**19.1**	**3.0**	**550**	**47**
Cambodia	..	41	329	344	485	675		0.4	0.6	41.1	39.2	475	50
Indonesia	1,653	3,998	5,386	3,569	3,857	3,634	5.1	5.8	3.4	8.1	-5.8	725	15
Lao P.D.R.	2	39	123	77	96	118	0.0	0.1	0.1	24.3	23.4	175	19
Malaysia	1,309	3,034	5,425	5,214	6,590	6,867	4.1	5.9	6.4	26.4	4.2	420	287
Myanmar	7	115	175	50	68	..	0.0	0.2		36.4		280	1
Philippines	1,026	868	2,334	1,365	1,622	1,821	3.2	2.5	1.7	18.8	12.3	695	21
Singapore	3,877	5,819	5,567	3,342	4,197	4,749	12.0	6.0	4.4	25.6	13.2	670	1,073
Thailand	3,397	6,146	8,085	6,920	8,066	7,709	10.5	8.8	7.1	16.6	-4.4	665	120
Vietnam	67	..	..	1,238	1,367	1,511	0.2		1.4	10.4	10.6	435	18
Oceania	**5,749**	**10,574**	**15,471**	**17,137**	**19,135**	**20,595**	**17.8**	**16.8**	**19.1**	**11.7**	**7.6**	**1,965**	**630**
American Samoa	8	..	..	..	..	..	0.0						
Australia	3,334	6,212	10,041	10,917	12,212	13,557	10.3	10.9	12.5	11.9	11.0	2,700	675
Cook Is	13	21	39	61	58	74	0.0	0.0	0.1	-5.1	27.8	835	3,457
Fiji	159	222	197	301	337	349	0.5	0.2	0.3	12.1	3.3	635	390
French Polynesia	134	249	..	424	420	419	0.4		0.4	-0.9	-0.3	2,015	1,550
Guam	735	..	..	..	..	..	2.3						
Kiribati	1	2	3	..	..	..	0.0	0.0					
Marshall Is	..	2	4	..	..	..		0.0					
Micronesia (Fed.St.of)	..	..	16	15	13	14		0.0	0.0	-10.1	3.6	725	127
N.Mariana Is	357	501	..	..	..	..	1.1						
New Caledonia	74	83	120	174	194	204	0.2	0.1	0.2	11.5	5.1	2,020	940
New Zealand	809	1,772	2,454	3,519	3,851	3,911	2.5	2.7	3.6	9.4	1.5	1,655	969
Niue	..	2	..	..	..	1			0.0			345	
Palau	..	..	57	67	78	78		0.1	0.1	16.6	0.3	905	3,849
Papua New Guinea	32	19	23	14	15	3	0.1	0.0	0.0	5.6	-80.3	40	1
Samoa	16	27	44	48	56	62	0.0	0.0	0.1	17.9	10.0	610	349
Solomon Is	5	12	4	1	3	1	0.0	0.0	0.0	106.8	-56.2	130	2
Tonga	7	8	8	12	12	9	0.0	0.0	0.0	-2.6	-26.7	210	79
Vanuatu	31	34	61	46	51	59	0.1	0.1	0.1	11.9	15.6	960	289
South Asia	**1,614**	**2,602**	**5,194**	**5,949**	**6,936**	**7,747**	**5.0**	**5.6**	**7.2**	**16.6**	**11.7**	**970**	**5**
Bangladesh	9	19	54	50	54	56	0.0	0.1	0.1	6.6	4.8	270	0
Bhutan	2	4	11	7	10	15	0.0	0.0	0.0	36.4	48.5	1,095	7
India	1,208	1,973	3,746	3,945	4,960	6,048	3.7	4.1	5.6	25.7	21.9	1,545	6
Iran	48	51	506	913	839	797	0.1	0.5	0.7	-8.1	-5.0	505	12
Maldives	70	161	347	355	328	230	0.2	0.4	0.2	-7.6	-29.7	585	660
Nepal	50	135	171	177	185	106	0.2	0.2	0.1	4.6	-42.7	280	4
Pakistan	123	84	88	108	144	145	0.4	0.1	0.1	33.4	1.1	180	1
Sri Lanka	104	173	269	390	412	345	0.3	0.3	0.3	5.8	-16.4	630	17

Source: World Tourism Organization (UNWTO) ©

(Data as collected by UNWTO for TMT 2006 Edition)

World Tourism Organization ©

International Tourism Receipts by Country of Destination

	International Tourism Receipts (euro, million)						Market share in the region (%)			Change (%)		Receipts per arrival[1]	Receipts per capita[1]
	1990	1995	2000	2003	2004	2005*	1990	2000	2005*	04/03	05*/04		euro
Europe	*112,205*	*162,159*	*251,670*	*250,843*	*264,400*	*280,335*	*100*	*100*	*100*	*5.4*	*6.0*	*640*	*318*
Northern Europe	**20,627**	**25,930**	**38,910**	**36,597**	**39,614**	**43,317**	**18.4**	**15.5**	**15.5**	**8.2**	**9.3**	**850**	**487**
Denmark	2,862	2,808	3,999	4,655	4,559	3,984	2.6	1.6	1.4	-2.1	-12.6	875	733
Finland	916	1,255	1,528	1,656	1,669	1,757	0.8	0.6	0.6	0.8	5.3	560	336
Iceland	119	142	247	283	299	329	0.1	0.1	0.1	5.7	10.0	375	1,108
Ireland	1,141	1,688	2,851	3,409	3,536	3,813	1.0	1.1	1.4	3.7	7.8	520	950
Norway	1,233	1,711	2,220	2,350	2,521	2,809	1.1	0.9	1.0	7.3	11.4	735	612
Sweden	2,282	2,654	4,400	4,682	4,981	5,969	2.0	1.7	2.1	6.4	19.9	1,905	663
United Kingdom	12,074	15,672	23,665	20,028	22,688	24,656	10.8	9.4	8.8	13.3	8.7	880	408
Western Europe	**49,562**	**61,755**	**89,620**	**91,216**	**94,759**	**98,432**	**44.2**	**35.6**	**35.1**	**3.9**	**3.9**	**690**	**529**
Austria	10,536	9,883	10,752	12,336	12,527	12,870	9.4	4.3	4.6	1.5	2.7	645	1,572
Belgium	..	3,477	7,137	7,241	7,423	7,932		2.8	2.8	2.5	6.9	1,175	765
Belgium/Luxembourg	2,907	..	..	..	..	..							
France	15,850	21,056	33,301	32,349	32,833	33,981	14.1	13.2	12.1	1.5	3.5	450	560
Germany	11,187	13,762	20,239	20,426	22,243	23,449	10.0	8.0	8.4	8.9	5.4	1,090	284
Luxembourg	..	1,316	1,956	2,646	2,940	2,906		0.8	1.0	11.1	-1.2	3,185	6,202
Netherlands	3,263	5,029	7,814	8,097	8,307	8,420	2.9	3.1	3.0	2.6	1.4	840	513
Switzerland	5,820	7,232	8,420	8,121	8,486	8,874	5.2	3.3	3.2	4.5	4.6	1,230	1,185
Central/Eastern Europe	**1,647**	**15,010**	**22,032**	**21,258**	**23,257**	**26,079**	**1.5**	**8.8**	**9.3**	**9.4**	**12.1**	**300**	**68**
Armenia	..	1	41	65	68	113		0.0	0.0	5.9	65.9	355	38
Azerbaijan	179	54	68	51	52	62	0.2	0.0	0.0	1.9	18.4	55	8
Belarus	..	18	101	236	217	203		0.0	0.1	-8.0	-6.3	2,240	20
Bulgaria	251	362	1,165	1,496	1,785	1,953	0.2	0.5	0.7	19.3	9.4	405	262
Czech Rep	329	2,202	3,219	3,144	3,354	3,752	0.3	1.3	1.3	6.7	11.9	590	366
Estonia	..	273	550	591	716	764		0.2	0.3	21.1	6.7	400	574
Georgia	..	..	105	130	142	194		0.0	0.1	9.2	36.7	345	41
Hungary	647	2,258	4,067	3,577	3,265	3,433	0.6	1.6	1.2	-8.7	5.1	340	343
Kazakhstan	..	93	386	499	577	563		0.2	0.2	15.7	-2.4	180	37
Kyrgyzstan	..	4	16	42	61	59		0.0	0.0	44.0	-4.0	185	11
Latvia	..	15	142	197	215	274		0.1	0.1	9.2	27.8	245	120
Lithuania	..	59	424	564	624	740		0.2	0.3	10.6	18.6	370	206
Poland	281	5,057	6,147	3,597	4,689	5,043	0.3	2.4	1.8	30.4	7.5	330	131
Rep Moldova	..	44	43	51	77	86		0.0	0.0	50.5	11.0	3,725	19
Romania	83	451	389	396	406	852	0.1	0.2	0.3	2.5	109.9	595	38
Russian Federation	..	3,297	3,713	3,980	4,200	4,472		1.5	1.6	5.6	6.5	225	31
Slovakia	55	476	469	765	724	972	0.0	0.2	0.3	-5.3	34.2	640	179
Tajikistan	..	..	..	2	1	2			0.0	-54.5	100.0		0
Ukraine	..	146	427	827	2,058	2,512		0.2	0.9		22.1	130	53
Uzbekistan	..	..	29	21	23	..		0.0		6.1		85	1
Southern/Mediter. Eu.	**40,369**	**59,465**	**101,108**	**101,771**	**106,771**	**112,507**	**36.0**	**40.2**	**40.1**	**4.9**	**5.4**	**715**	**502**
Albania	3	50	421	461	585	692	0.0	0.2	0.2	26.7	18.3	15,035	194
Bosnia & Herzg	..	..	252	332	388	413		0.1	0.1	16.8	6.4	1,900	93
Croatia	..	1,031	3,012	5,573	5,506	5,999		1.2	2.1	-1.2	9.0	710	1,334
Cyprus	988	1,375	2,102	1,848	1,811	1,874	0.9	0.8	0.7	-2.0	3.5	760	2,402
F.Yug.Rp.Macedonia	..	15	41	50	58	67		0.0	0.0	15.2	16.8	340	33
Greece	2,032	3,161	9,981	9,495	10,348	11,037	1.8	4.0	3.9	9.0	6.7	775	1,035
Israel	1,097	2,288	4,426	1,821	1,914	2,293	1.0	1.8	0.8	5.1	19.8	1,205	365
Italy	12,924	21,965	29,767	27,623	28,665	28,453	11.5	11.8	10.1	3.8	-0.7	780	490
Malta	389	500	639	638	622	610	0.3	0.3	0.2	-2.5	-1.9	520	1,530
Portugal	2,792	3,693	5,677	5,849	6,195	6,199	2.5	2.3	2.2	5.9	0.1	585	587
Serbia & Montenegro	..	32	32	178	..	..		0.0				370	16
Slovenia	..	827	1,045	1,184	1,310	1,447		0.4	0.5	10.6	10.5	930	720
Spain	14,515	19,306	32,446	35,047	36,376	38,558	12.9	12.9	13.8	3.8	6.0	690	956
Turkey	2,533	3,790	8,268	11,672	12,773	14,590	2.3	3.3	5.2	9.4	14.2	720	209
Yugoslav SFR	2,178	..	..	..	..	..	1.9						

Source: World Tourism Organization (UNWTO) ©

(Data as collected by UNWTO for TMT 2006 Edition)

International Tourism Receipts by Country of Destination

	International Tourism Receipts (euro, million)						Market share in the region (%)			Change (%)		Receipts per arrival[1]	Receipts per capita[1]
	1990	1995	2000	2003	2004	2005*	1990	2000	2005*	04/03	05*/04		euro
Middle East	*3,360*	*7,449*	*16,502*	*17,450*	*20,290*	*21,103*	*100*	*100*	*100*	*16.3*	*4.0*	*550*	*107*
Bahrain	106	189	620	636	695	739	3.2	3.8	3.5	9.1	6.5	190	1,074
Egypt	864	2,052	4,704	4,052	4,924	5,506	25.7	28.5	26.1	21.5	11.8	670	71
Iraq	136	14	2	..	..	..	4.1	0.0					
Jordan	402	505	783	939	1,069	1,158	12.0	4.7	5.5	13.9	8.3	390	201
Kuwait	104	93	106	104	142	132	3.1	0.6	0.6	36.6	-6.9	1,560	57
Lebanon	..	..	..	5,635	4,350	4,366			20.7	-22.8	0.4	3,830	1,141
Libyan Arab Jamahiriya	5	2	81	181	175	201	0.1	0.5	1.0	-3.3	14.7	1,175	35
Oman	54	..	239	340	332	387	1.6	1.5	1.8	-2.3	16.3	280	129
Palestine	..	195	306	95	45	..		1.9		-52.4		805	12
Qatar	..	..	138	326	400	611		0.8	2.9	22.8	52.7	670	708
Saudi Arabia	..	..	..	3,017	5,214	4,162			19.7	72.8	-20.2	520	158
Syrian Arab Republic	251	962	1,171	683	1,447	1,748	7.5	7.1	8.3	111.8	20.8	520	95
Untd Arab Emirates	247	483	1,151	1,272	1,281	1,768	7.4	7.0	8.4	0.7	38.0	215	690
Yemen	16	38	79	123	171	211	0.5	0.5	1.0	39.4	23.0	625	10

Source: World Tourism Organization (UNWTO) ©

(Data as collected by UNWTO for TMT 2006 Edition)

[1] Last year with data available

| : change of series.

3. Methodological Notes

3.1 Concepts and Definitions

According to the UNWTO/United Nations *Recommendations on Tourism Statistics*, Tourism comprises *the activities of persons travelling to and staying in places outside their usual environment for not more than one consecutive year for leisure, business and other purposes.*

This concept can be applied to different forms of tourism. Depending upon whether a person is travelling to, from or within a certain country the following forms can be distinguished:

- **Inbound Tourism**, involving the non-residents received by a destination country from the point of view of that destination;
- **Outbound Tourism**, involving residents travelling to another country from the point of view of the country of origin;
- **Domestic tourism**, involving residents of a given country travelling within that country.

All types of travellers engaged in tourism are described as visitors. Visitors can be distinguished as same-day visitors or tourists (overnight visitors).

There are various units of measure to quantify the volume of tourism. An overview is set out below:

Unit of measurement			Comment
Visitors	*Arrivals*	*- at frontiers (VF)*	or at a specific place in case of domestic tourism
Tourists (overnight visitors)	*Arrivals*	*- at frontiers (TF)*	
		- at collective tourism establishments (e.g. hotels and other, such as campings, etc.) (TCE) *- at hotels and similar establishments (THS)*	- excludes tourism in private accommodation; - arrivals are counted in every new accommodation visited
	Nights	*- at collective tourism establishments (e.g. hotels and other) (NCE)* *- at hotels and similar establishments (NHS)*	

Inbound Tourism

Unless otherwise stated, this report concentrates on **International Tourism** as measured from an **Inbound Tourism** perspective, i.e. the tourism received by any given destination country (and in a few cases territories) from non-residents travelling to that destination.

The most common unit of measure used to quantify the volume of International Tourism for statistical purposes is the number of International Tourist Arrivals. For a proper understanding of this unit, two considerations should be taken into account:

- Data refer exclusively to tourists (overnight visitors): 'a visitor who stays at least one night in a collective or private accommodation in the country visited'. Same-day visitors are not included.
- Data refer to the number of arrivals and not to the number of persons. The same person who makes several trips to a given country during a given period will be counted as a

new arrival each time, as well as a person who travels through several countries on one trip is counted as a new arrival each time.

Figures on the volume of international tourism presented in the regional and subregional tables, preferably relate to the concept of *international tourist arrivals at frontiers*. However, as not all countries are collecting data according to this concept, another series may be used instead. In the tables, the series are indicated as follows:

TF: International tourist arrivals at frontiers (excluding same-day visitors);
VF: International visitor arrivals at frontiers (including tourists and same-day visitors);
TCE: International tourist arrivals at collective tourism establishments;
THS: International tourist arrivals at hotels and similar establishments.

With respect to the inbound tourism volume, if available, in the profile tables for individual countries in Chapter III, except for data on International Tourist Arrivals, furthermore, data is included on International Visitor Arrivals, Same-day Visitor Arrivals, Cruise passengers (considered as a special category of same-day visitors) and Nights spent in collective establishments and / or in hotels and similar establishments.

Outbound Tourism

Data on outbound tourism volume in this series of reports originate from two different sources and likewise relate to two dissimilar concepts:

- On one hand, many countries are reporting the number of outbound trips of their residents. Data availability and comparability, however, is still limited and it is often not clear whether the reported figures refer only to tourists or to visitors in general.

- On the other hand, data are synthesised from the data on inbound tourism to destination countries (an arrival received in a destination can also be taken as an arrival generated by the generating country). Data on arrivals to destinations broken down by region of origin are taken to estimate and aggregate the number of arrivals originating from each region. The unit of measurement is the number of international tourist arrivals generated by the region of origin concerned. For a proper understanding, it should be borne in mind that these figures do not correspond to the number of trips, as one trip taken might result in various arrivals in destinations.

Domestic Tourism

International comparable data on domestic tourism is unfortunately still rather scarce. If available for a certain country, this series is represented in the profile tables for countries in Chapter III of the regional volumes in the form of the number of nights spent by residents at hotels and similar establishments and / or at all collective tourism establishments.

Accommodation

As a measure for the capacity of accommodation, data is included on the number of rooms or the number of bed places in the country. When expressed in bed places, the number of rooms roughly will be half, as rooms on average count two bed places. The actual capacity of a country might eventually be larger, as some countries exclude hotels below a certain category or less than a certain size.

International Tourism Receipts and Expenditure

International Tourism Receipts are the receipts earned by a destination country from inbound tourism and cover all tourism receipts resulting from expenditure made by visitors from abroad, on for instance lodging, food and drinks, fuel, transport in the country, entertainment, shopping, etc. This concept includes receipts generated by overnight as well as by same-day trips, which can be substantial, as will be the case with countries where a lot of shopping for goods and services takes place by visitors from neighbouring countries. It excludes, however, the receipts related to international transport contracted by residents of other countries (for instance ticket receipts from foreigners travelling with a national company). These receipts are covered in the separate category **International Fare Receipts**, which for most recent years is estimated at about 15-20% of total tourism and fare receipts.

International Tourism Expenditure is the expenditure on tourism outside their country of residence made by visitors (same-day visitors and tourists) from a given country of origin.

Data on receipts and expenditure related to international tourism are generally gathered in the framework of the Balance of Payments under the items 'Services, Travel, Credit and Debit' (International Tourism Receipts and Expenditure) and 'Transportation, Passenger Services, Credit and Debit' (International Fare Receipts and Expenditure). See the *Balance of Payments Statistics Yearbook, Part 2 and Part 3* of the International Monetary Fund (IMF) for details on methodologies, compilation practices and data sources.

The International Tourism Balance and International Fare Balance as included in the profile tables in Chapter III of the regional volumes correspond to the net receipts or expenditure of a given country on respectively international tourism or international fares, i.e. receipts less expenditure.

Further information
More detailed information on concepts, definitions, classifications, indicators, methods of compiling and units of measure can be obtained from:
- the *Basic References on Tourism Statistics* on the UNWTO website under the link <http://www.unwto.org/statistics/index.htm> setting out the main components that make up the System of Tourism Statistics (STS);

or from the following UNWTO publications:
- *Recommendations on tourism statistics* (1994),
- *Technical Manual No. 1: Concepts Definitions, and Classifications for Tourism Statistics* (1995);
- *Technical Manual No. 2: Collection for Tourism Expenditure Statistics* (1995);
- *Technical Manual No. 3: Collection of Domestic Tourism Statistics* (1995);
- *Technical Manual No. 4: Collection and Compilation of Tourism Statistics* (1995);
- *Data Collection & Analysis for Tourism Management, Marketing & Planning* (2000).

3.2   Sources, Data Treatment and Acknowledgement

General
Quantitative tourism-related data in this report is based on a selection of data included in the UNWTO database on World Tourism Statistics. This database contains a variety of series for over 200 countries and territories covering data for most countries from the 1980's on. The database is maintained by the UNWTO Secretariat and is updated on a continuous base.

Except where otherwise indicated, statistical data has been collected by the UNWTO Secretariat from the official institutions of the countries and territories (UNWTO member as well as non-member countries) or from other international bodies, e.g. the Caribbean Tourism Organization (CTO), the International Monetary Fund (IMF), etc.

The data for individual countries corresponding to 2005 are based on full year results, or projections, as communicated to the UNWTO Secretariat by the authorities of the countries and territories or disseminated through news releases, publications or on the Internet. For many countries, 2005 figures are still preliminary and subject to revision.

In the world and (sub)regional aggregates, estimates are included for countries and territories with data still missing based upon data available for a part of the year or the general trend for the region. In particular for the Middle East and Africa, the regional and subregional aggregates should be treated with caution as estimations are based on a relatively small number of countries and territories that supplied data for the entire year. In the tables, provisional figures are marked with an asterisk (*).

UNWTO tourism statistics generally refer to figures for a country as a whole. In the collection of statistics, however, except for independent states, there are also a number of dependencies or territories of special sovereignty included (for instance Hong Kong (China) or French Polynesia). These territories report tourism figures independently and are for the sake of tourism statistics considered as an entity in itself. Because of this, where reference is made to "countries" the term generally should be taken to mean "countries and territories". In a few other cases, dependencies are not separately listed but included in the total for the country they depend upon (for instance Guernsey, Jersey and the Isle of Man in United Kingdom).

In general, UNWTO does not collect data on the level of regions, states, provinces or specific destinations within a country (Hawaii is one of the few exceptions made because of its relevance for Asian outbound travel; in the overview tables, however, Hawaii is included in the United States figure). Most countries will have a further regional breakdown available as well as other series not included in the UNWTO database on World Tourism Statistics. Please refer to national sources for this data.

The regional country groupings are according to the UNWTO regional commissions. See the tables by country in the annex for the countries and territories included in the various regions and subregions.

The World Tourism Organization is aware of the limitations of the available statistical information on tourism. Despite the considerable progress made in recent decades, international tourism statistics are often not uniform, because definitions and methods of data collection tend to differ. Every user of this information should bear in mind that the international comparability of statistical data is still not optimal.

Tourism series in this report

The tourism data series in Chapter II and in the profile tables of countries in Chapter III correspond to the basic indicators included in the UNWTO *Compendium of Tourism Statistics*. Please refer to the latest publication for additional series, methodological references and notes on the series for specific countries.

A number of derived series are included relating tourism volume to the size of the population or tourism receipts and expenditure to tourism volume. In the profile tables in Chapter III, those series are marked with '-'. Ratios are based on simple divisions of the concept in question by the population or of the receipts or expenditure by the corresponding concepts:

$$\text{International Tourist Arrivals per 100 of inhabitants} = \frac{\text{International Tourist Arrivals}}{\text{Population}} * 100$$

$$\text{Trips abroad per 100 of inhabitants} = \frac{\text{Trips abroad}}{\text{Population}} * 100$$

$$\text{International Tourism Receipts per International Tourist Arrival} = \frac{\text{International Tourism Receipts}}{\text{International Tourist Arrivals}}$$

$$\text{International Tourism Receipts per International Visitor Arrival} = \frac{\text{International Tourism Receipts}}{\text{International Visitor Arrivals}}$$

$$\text{International Tourism Receipts per capita} = \frac{\text{International Tourism Receipts}}{\text{Population}}$$

$$\text{International Tourism Expenditure per trip abroad} = \frac{\text{International Tourism Expenditure}}{\text{Trips Abroad}}$$

$$\text{International Tourism Expenditure per capita} = \frac{\text{International Tourism Expenditure}}{\text{Population}}$$

Financial data is generally collected and kept in the UNWTO database in US dollars. In the cases where countries report in local currency, values are transferred by UNWTO into US dollars applying the average exchange rate for the corresponding year. However, part of the tables are also published in euros. These euro values are in general derived from the US dollar values using the corresponding average annual exchange rates for the two currencies. The following exchange rates have been applied:

Exchange rates US$ versus euro (ECU for the years before 1999) annual averages

	€/ECU per US$	Change (%)	US$ per €/ECU	Change (%)
1995	0.76452		1.30801	
1996	0.78756	3.0	1.26975	-2.9
1997	0.88180	12.0	1.13404	-10.7
1998	0.89199	1.2	1.12109	-1.1
1999	0.93828	5.2	1.06578	-4.9
2000	1.08270	15.4	0.92361	-13.3
2001	1.11653	3.1	0.89563	-3.0
2002	1.05756	-5.3	0.94557	5.6
2003	0.88402	-16.4	1.13120	19.6
2004	0.80392	-9.1	1.24390	10.0
2005	0.80379	0.0	1.24410	0.0

Source: Eurostat, European Central Bank (ECB)

As exchange rates fluctuate substantially over time, the evolution of International Tourism Receipts is estimated in (weighted) local currencies. For this, receipts in US dollars are recomputed in local currencies using an exchange rate table provided by IMF. In order to take care of inflation, receipts are calculated in constant prices using country data on inflation from IMF as deflator.

The data in the tables on international tourist or visitor arrivals and nights of international tourists by country of origin included in Chapter III correspond to the series as included in the UNWTO *Yearbook of Tourism Statistics*. Please refer to the latter publication for additional series, metrological references and notes on the series for specific countries.

Series from external sources

Information included, but not referring to tourism indicators, are in general taken from specialised international organizations and not collected by the UNWTO Secretariat from the individual countries and territories. Data are meant as indicators, providing a context for tourism performance and do not necessarily coincide fully with national data. The following series are included:

Population

Data refer to total midyear population as included in the International Database (IDB) of the International Programs Center (IPC) of the Population Division of the U.S. Bureau of the Census, <www.census.gov/ipc/www>. The IDB combines data from country sources (especially censuses and surveys) with IPC's estimates and projections to provide information dating back as far as 1950 and as far ahead as 2050. The IDB can be considered as a practically complete and consistent set of population data covering 227 countries and areas with 1998 populations of 5,000 or more.

Area

Data on the dimension of the area of countries and territories are taken from the Statistical database of the Food and Agriculture Organization of the United Nations (FAO) <www.fao.org> and refer to the total area of the country, including area under inland water bodies for the year 2000. In the case of Belgium and Luxembourg data is taken from national sources.

Economic Indicators

The series on Gross Domestic Product (GDP), Gross Domestic Product per capita and economic growth (annual per cent change of Real Gross Domestic Product) are based on the World Economic Outlook (WEO) of the International Monetary Fund (IMF). See <www.imf.org/external/pubs/ft/weo/weorepts.htm>.

4. Sources of Information

A. *UNWTO website <www.unwto.org>*

The UNWTO has a comprehensive website available with news and information on its programme activities, members, regional activities, publications, special projects, etc. in English, French and Spanish with a growing section in Russian, including:.

- A qualitative and quantitative overview of world tourism and selected statistical country data, available under the *Facts & Figures* link (see Tourism Indicators), including the most updated tourism trends and data in the *UNWTO World Tourism Barometer;*

- An overview of available publications and electronic products with detailed information on each item including contents and sample chapters can be found in the UNWTO Infoshop at <http://pub.unwto.org> or the WTOelibrary at <www.WTOelibrary.org>.

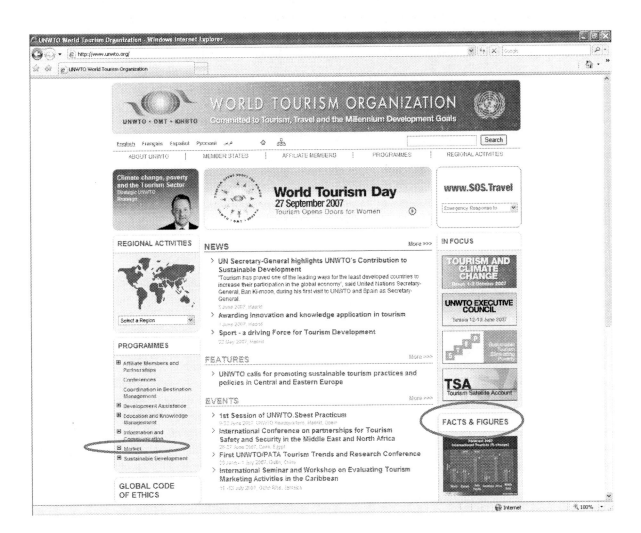

B. Related Publications of the World Tourism Organization

Inbound Tourism

This report is part of the *Tourism Market Trends, 2006 Edition* series consisting of 6 volumes:
- World Overview and Tourism Topics (in English, French and Spanish);
- Africa (in English and French);
- Americas (in English and Spanish);
- Asia and the Pacific (in English);
- Europe (in English and French);
- Middle East (in English).

Excerpts of this series are included in:
- *Tourism Highlights, 2006 Edition* (in English, French, Spanish and Russian). The electronic version can be downloaded free of charge from the Facts & Figures section of the UNWTO website at <http://www.unwto.org/facts/menu.html>.

- *Special report No 23:* Inbound Tourism to the Middle East and North Africa (2003; in English).

Outbound Tourism

- *Tourism Generating Markets: Overview and Country Profiles* (1999; in English, French and Spanish).
- Special Reports on specific markets:
  - No. 4: *Outbound Tourism of Korea* (2001; in English).
  - No. 5: *Outbound Tourism of Australia* (2001; in English).
  - No. 6: *Outbound Tourism of Japan* (2001; in English).
  - No. 7: *Outbound Tourism of Belgium* (2001; in English).
  - No. 8: *Outbound Tourism of Spain* (2001; in English and Spanish).
  - No. 9: *Outbound Tourism of Japan & Korea, Results 2000* (2001; in English).
  - No. 21: *Outbound Tourism of Scandinavia, Market Profile* (2002; in English).
- *Youth Outbound Travel of the Germans, the British & the French* (2002, in English, French and Spanish).
- *Chinese Outbound Tourism* (2003; in English).
- *Outbound Tourism from Saudi Arabia* (2003; in English).

Short-term Indicators

- *UNWTO World Tourism Barometer* (3 times a year since June 2003; in electronic format (PDF) and print, in English, French and Spanish).

The *UNWTO World Tourism Barometer* monitors the short-term evolution of tourism and aims at providing adequate and timely information on the state of the sector. The Barometer is published three times a year (January, June, and October). It contains an overview of short-term tourism data from destination countries and tourism sectors such as air transport, a retrospective and prospective evaluation of tourism performance by the UNWTO Panel of Tourism Experts and selected economic data relevant for tourism.

For more information see the "Facts & Figures" section of the UNWTO website www.unwto.org.

Forecasting

UNWTO's long-term forecast *Tourism 2020 Vision* has been published in a series of 7 reports consisting of one summary volume and six regional volumes (2000, 2001):

– Global Forecasts and Profiles of Market Segments (in English, French and Spanish).
– Africa (in English and French).
– Americas (in English and Spanish).
– East Asia and the Pacific (in English).
– Europe (in English and French).
– Middle East (in English).
– South Asia (in English).

Tourism Products

– Tourism and Sport:
  - *Sport and Tourism. 1ˢᵗ World Conference* (in English, French and Spanish; forthcoming). Excerpts of the presentations and of the results of the World Conference on Sport and Tourism held February 2001 in Barcelona, Spain.
  - *Introductory Report on Sport & Tourism* (2001).
  - *Sport Activities during the outbound holidays of the Germans, the Dutch and the French* (2001, in English, French and Spanish).
  - *Deporte Y Turismo: Destino América Latina* (2003; in Spanish only).
– Ecotourism:
  - *Special report No. 10: The German Ecotourism Market* (2001).
  - *Special report No. 11: The British Ecotourism Market* (2001).
  - *Special report No. 12: The U.S. Ecotourism Market* (2002).
  - *Special report No. 13: The Italian Ecotourism Market* (2002).
  - *Special report No. 14: The Spanish Ecotourism Market* (2002).
  - *Special report No. 15: The Canadian Ecotourism Market* (2002).
  - *Special report No. 16: The French Ecotourism Market* (2002).
– MICE:
  - *MICE Outbound Tourism 2000* (2003; in English).
– Cruises:
  - *Worldwide Cruise Ship Activity* (2003; in English, French and Spanish).
– Cultural Tourism:
  - *City Tourism and Culture: The European Experience (*2005; in English, French and Spanish).

UNWTO Tourism Recovery Committee

– Special report No. 17: *The impact of the attacks in the United States on international tourism: An initial analysis* (included in the Annex of Special report No. 18, not available separately).
– Special report No. 18: *Tourism after 11 September 2001: Analysis, remedial actions and prospects* (2001; in English, French and Spanish).
– Special report No. 19: *Tourism Recovery Committee for the Mediterranean Region* (2002; in English, French and Spanish).
– Special report No. 20: *The impact of the September 11th attacks on tourism: The light at the end of the tunnel* (2002; in English, French and Spanish).
– Special report No. 21: *2002: Climbing Towards Recovery?* (2002; in English).
– Special report No. 22: *Fourth Meeting of the Tourism Recovery Committee - ITB Berlin 2003* (2003; in English).

Basic Statistical Reference

- *Compendium of Tourism Statistics* (2005; tri-lingual edition in English, French and Spanish and table descriptions in Arabic and Russian).
- *Yearbook of Tourism Statistics* (2005; tri-lingual edition in English, French and Spanish).

Statistical Methodology

- *Recommendations on Tourism Statistics* (1994; in English, French, Spanish, Russian, Arabic and Chinese).
- *Technical Manuals* (1995; in English, French, Spanish and Russian):
  - *No. 1: Concepts, Definitions and Classifications for Tourism Statistics.*
  - *No. 2: Collection of Tourism Expenditure Statistics.*
  - *No. 3: Collection of Domestic Tourism Statistics.*
  - *No. 4: Collection and Compilation of Tourism Statistics.*
- *Data Collection and Analysis for Tourism Management, Marketing and Planning* (2000; in English).

See for detailed information on concepts, definitions, classifications, indicators, methods of compiling and units of measure also the *Basic References on Tourism Statistics*, setting out the main components that make up the System of Tourism Statistics (STS), on the UNWTO website at: <http://www.unwto.org/statistics/index.htm>.

See for documentation on the Tourism Satellite Account methodology the UNWTO website at: <http://www.unwto.org/statistics/index.htm>.

Other

- *Tourism in the Age of Alliances, Mergers and Acquisitions* (2002, in English, French and Spanish).
- *Apuntes de la Metodología de la Investigación en Turismo* (2001, in Spanish only).
- *Marketing Papers No.1* (2002).
- *Evaluating NTO Marketing Activities* (2003; in English, French and Spanish).
- Special report No 26 - *The impact of rising oil prices on International Tourism* (2006; in English, French and Spanish).
- Structures and Budgets of National Tourism Organizations, 2004-2005 (2006; in English and Spanish)
- Handbook on Tourism Market Segmentation – Maximizing Marketing Effectiveness (2007, in English)

C.   References

International Organizations

- United Nations; <www.un.org>.
- United Nations Development Programme; <www.undp.org>.
- International Monetary Fund (IMF); <www.imf.org>.
- World Bank; <www.worldbank.org>.
- Organisation for Economic Cooperation and Development (OECD); <www.oecd.org>.
- World Trade Organization (WTO); <www.wto.org>.

Country Sources

References for information on the Internet of National Tourism Administrations (NTA), National Tourism Organisations (NTO) and / or web directions for research and data are included in the country contributions of Chapter III of the regional volumes of the *Tourism Market Trends, 2006* series.